Donald E. Carr
THE SEXES

HEINEMANN : LONDON

William Heinemann Ltd
15 Queen Street, Mayfair, London W1X 8BE
LONDON MELBOURNE TORONTO
JOHANNESBURG AUCKLAND

First published in Great Britain 1971
Copyright © 1970 by Donald E. Carr
434 10910 x

Printed Offset Litho and bound in Great Britain
by Cox & Wyman Ltd,
London, Fakenham and Reading

To Nancy and Michael

Contents

Preface

It can hardly be denied that man as an animal is, in the language of the conservationists, an "endangered species." It is true that danger does not come from a pathetic thinning away of individual families because of the pre-emption of their homeland, as in the case of the whooping crane, or from the effect of insidious biological world poisons which cause egg fragility in falcons and bald eagles or fish misbirths, as in the case of DDT. Man is an endangered species because he has outgrown the normal instincts which in other mammals (and in fact in all the rest of the animal kingdom) automatically limit the population to a tolerable equilibrium. Man is an endangered species precisely because of his unbridled sexuality.

The human sperm and the human egg in conjunction have become more sinister than the plutonium or the hydrogen bombs and their triggers.

It has seemed worthwhile to consider this sexuality in some depth and in a comparative way. How and why did sex come about in the first place? We shall examine sex from the standpoint of biological history in the first part of this book. As we become acquainted with the details of sexual behavior at various levels of evolution, we shall be impressed with at least two things. One is that modern human "swingers" who imagine they have invented devilishly chic or terrifyingly new perversions have been anticipated by some millions of years in a huge variety of creatures. Sadism, masochism, fetishism, homosexuality, weird forms of masturbation, group sex (in the "French party" sense), child molestation and rape, incest, sex with cannibalism—all these and more have been practiced and continue to be practiced as eon-old patterns of established behavior. In some species a Myra Breckinridge is not a best-selling pervert but a respectable, normal individual. The periodic change of sex is mandatory as frequently as is hermaphroditism.

The second salient point we shall constantly meet up with is the frequent (perhaps *increasingly* frequent) superfluity of the male. Since parthenogenesis (birth of female young without impregnation of the mother by a male) has been accomplished in animals as close to us in nature as rabbits, there seems to be absolutely no doubt that future man could do away with the troublesome male and the complex antics of physical love. This might be a way to a gentler world but it is probably not the best way to a really superior universe.*

In the second part of this book I describe animal societies (including those of man) and show that the formation of such societies is itself originally an instrumentation to avoid overpopulation in a single species. In fact even sex itself—the mutual seeking and pairing process—may be regarded in a fundamental sense as a means of population control, since it is a much more difficult way of reproduction than simply to divide oneself in half or to form buds or spores without getting on intimate terms with another creature.

Unfortunately for man, the society-forming habit (because *biological* evolution has long since been superseded in our species by *cultural* evolution) now leads not to population control but to the exact opposite—unlimited and catastrophic proliferation. We

---

* I have described better ways in an as yet unpublished work, *An Ark of Wiser Animals,* and have also alluded to the nature of such universes in a published book, *The Eternal Return.*

can anticipate the great Asian and South American populaces growing up as badly nourished swarms of unmanageable morons. In our country we shall probably see first a crisis in the numbers of automobiles, piles of trash and of the pollutions that accompany enormous hordes. Visitors to the Yosemite will not only be faced with Los Angeles-type traffic problems as at present, but the Yosemite and all other lovely spots will be developed into realty subdivisions where one pays $50,000 a square yard for scenic lots.

One word of apology: throughout this and other books I have used the word "evolution" in a rather playful sense as representing a brilliant but fallible character—a kind of researching Santa Claus with likes and dislikes and even unreasonable prejudices. It is perhaps inherent in our Aryan languages to anthropomorphize vast subtle processes—to pretend that they are manlike creatures with intentions rather than mathematical functions. Certainly it is much too late in the twentieth century to be required to define evolution again scientifically. If the reader has got this far along in this century without understanding in a general way what evolution is as a process, this book is not for him. (And in that case, what book other than the endlessly marketable infantile graffiti of sex play *is* for him?)

PART I
The Rise of Sex

For chemists, the recent developments in molecular biology and immunology are immensely exciting. A few years ago one of my friends, an aerodynamicist at Cal Tech, gave up his precious research shock-wave tube and took to the study of nucleic acids, the "threads of life," and he represents but one of a vast pilgrimage of scientists who as converts have been drawn to the brilliant mecca of modern biochemistry. As a writer, however, I realized that to the average educated reader chemistry of any kind is a total bore. But sex is not. In this book the only chemistry will be in the following short paragraph:

In any living system (whether a yeast spore, a worm's gut or the human brain) certain complicated chemical compounds are invariably present. The nucleic acids, deoxyribonucleic (DNA) and ribonucleic (RNA), are necessary to reproduce the protoplasm, or more accurately, the proteins, which are the main "stuff" of living tissue. Yet to make the nucleic acids, certain special proteins known as enzymes are required. Also there must be a source of energy, which may be oxygen plus sugar and fat or the bundles of chemical power known as adenosine phosphates. It is a good and baffling question as to which came first, in the beginning of life, the nucleic acids or the enzymes. Probably it took evolution more

*time to make a single living cell than to evolve from this decep-
tively simple-looking creature such advanced animals as dogs and
gorillas and men. The simple single-celled creature, in the first
place, had to have a membrane or skin to protect its very complex
private chemical business. The next step was to find a way of
reproducing—of forming two intact membranes containing the
same quota of chemical machinery as the parent. Chemically this
was made possible by the structure of the DNA molecule, which
is usually a double ribbon in helical form which can serve as an
exact pattern for enzymes to guide the duplication of another
precisely similar chemical ribbon.*

*Sex, as we shall see, was a kind of afterthought. Biochemically
speaking, sex is a luxury. It is a matter of chance—luck or mis-
fortune, however one views it—that the present ruling animals of
the planet are sexual animals. Yet certainly for writers and poets
and marriage counselors it was a very fruitful happening indeed.*

1. Sex Begins

In a sexless world, evolution had a good thing going as long as it stuck to single-celled animals. For reproduction it had invented an effective though far from simple process. Since in the beautiful double helix of deoxyribonucleic acid (DNA) molecules it had a foolproof method for biochemical duplicating (a kind of biological Xerox process), all that was needed was a mechanism for assuring that when a mother cell silently sacrifices its personality to two daughter cells, all the factors that have made the mother cell work as a successful animal are fairly shared with the progeny in binary fission (dividing into two). For this, evolution invented the microscopically eerie process of mitosis. What is this?

When the urge to divide is upon the mother cell, genes consisting of DNA, grouped in tiny clumps called chromosomes, begin a ritual of exquisite precision. Each chromosome divides and half of it drifts to one end of a spindle-shaped form which takes up a large part of the cell space. The partners face each other across threads of protoplasm, like celebrants of some grave fiesta. The threads disappear, the membrane of the mother cell, now in its last moments as an individual, gulps in from opposite sides, joins and forms two blobs with the new chromosomes now set adrift in their separate tiny tents. Hastily the newly isolated chromosomes clump together in the new nuclei to take over the housekeeping duties of two identical cells. Division has occurred. Two new individuals have been formed.*

But evolution detected something wrong in this—exactly what, we don't know. It was a smooth business but it lacked variety. *Or perhaps it was the exact opposite.* On paper it is a magnificent way to create a living universe composed of identical twins, but in very small one-celled creatures the center of living processes is not far removed from the dangerous world of lifeless matter; the microscopic membranes may not be able to protect the DNA from the invasion of radioactivity or of semi-living things such as viruses. Such invasions might do worse than kill the cells: they might make them aberrant monsters who would produce further monsters of a type that would be displeasing to evolution. Furthermore, the DNA molecules can make mistakes and produce unacceptable genes, thus infecting the whole future population of cells with a disease which we call "old age." The simplest way to get around these unpleasant possibilities would be to see to it that the genes are scrambled up and reorganized every once in a while, so that no bad chemical habits become established and weak genes are invigorated by shuffling with strong ones.

Evolution found some cunning ways to accomplish these shufflings and reorganizations. Superficially the simplest and yet the most mystifying is the process called *endomixis.* This is reshuffling within a single cell. If you keep a microscopic eye on some strains of the protozoan (single-celled) *Paramecium,* you may see a strange happening. The macronucleus and the micronucleus, ap-

---

* Every binary fission comes up with some mechanical problems. In single-celled animals, such as diatoms, that have limestone shells, the protoplasm within the shell shoves the two halves of the shell apart and each division takes one shell with it. Both creatures then grow new half shells to compensate for the one lost. But the diatom that has inherited the smaller shell will, in dividing again, produce one daughter with a still smaller shell and this process of reduction goes on until further division is not feasible. At this point the diatom protoplasm has the ingenuity to ooze out of its inadequate tent and to seek a full-sized, well-shelled diatom and to merge with its protoplasmic contents.

parently going steadily about their business, all of a sudden virtually *disappear*. It is as if at an alarm bell the cytoplasm of the cell had been trained to swallow up its captains. From a tiny residual part of the micronucleus gradually emerge a new macronucleus and a new micronucleus, freshly synthesized, full of young vigor and resolve. What has happened is a complete breakdown and reconstitution of the nuclear material—chromosomes, genes, DNA and all. This does not result in a new kind of animal. Quite the opposite: in the super-conservative world of the protozoan, the new directors are there precisely to see that the business of the paramecium goes on even more strictly and briskly than before. Old genes that have been falling asleep at the executive desk find themselves replaced with new genes that are dedicated to the more efficient performance of the job for which the infirm genes had originally been hired. *Plus ça change, plus c'est la même chose.*

Although some kinds of paramecium can continue in this pattern of simple fission, varied with periods of endomixis, indefinitely (and may have been doing it for a billion years) other similar one-celled animals have learned another form of reorganization and renewal, which begins to look suspiciously sexy. Two protozoans get together and fuse with each other in the region of their buccal grooves (mouths). Although this is a temporary marriage, it is a profoundly intimate one. The union involves the exchange of nuclear material. After the two cells separate, each "ex-conjugant" now has a nucleus of double origin. This is an extremely smart invention, since the result is the appearance of *two* cells with reorganized chromosomes, whereas in endomixis only one cell has been reorganized. It is true that the directors are simply exchanged rather than representing new young officers, but one must assume that in the mere act of reciprocity some degree of revivification has occurred. It would be no use to have that same sleepy old gene simply in a new office building. In the ciliates, where such behavior is common, some species practice conjugation after 200 generations of fission. On the other hand, otherwise closely related species have shown no tendency to take up conjugation after thousands of generations. It is not known whether these insistently independent strains indulge in endomixis, when we're not looking, or whether they have discovered some other secret of eternal youth. It would be basically important for us to find out what the secret is, if we are to make fundamental advances in the science of geriatrics.

Conjugation in many kinds of protozoans has gone one step further and has resulted in the permanent union of two cells and their nuclei. This is called *syngamy** and is nearly equivalent to the sexual union of a sperm and an egg, except that the animals themselves act as a combination sperm-egg. New individuals which result from this mutual fertilization share the DNA of both original animals. The result is only qualitatively different from that achieved in conjugation. No unusual effects have been added, even in comparison with endomixis, since the marriage is not only totally incestuous but is the apex of inbreeding, because it involves identical twins. However, it should be noted that it is basically a far more intimate and profound merging than is the case of the germ and egg cells of multiple-celled animals. The corresponding chromosomes of the two nuclei merge also, so that in the renewed single cell there are the same number of chromosomes that existed in each cell before syngamy. If this were not so, each act of syngamy would result in a monster with twice the normal number of chromosomes.

With syngamy we are still in the stage of true reproduction, since the union of identical twins is hardly likely to change the pattern, even though it may tend to correct errors in the pattern and was probably evolved for this conservative purpose. It is only when a more sexy kind of sex enters the picture, that we actually tend to get away from reproduction (in the Xerox sense). Sex is one of evolution's attempts to make evolution possible. As we shall see, this means that variations from the identical-twin principle must be encouraged by increasing the number of ways that genes can be combined on a chromosomal string; in short, by abolishing the certainty of identical twins.

*From the Greek root meaning "marriage."

Sex presumably originated in colonies of protozoans. If one simply has a lot of single-celled animals grouping together (in itself a revolutionary change of habit from the adventurous swarm of single identical twins and probably resulting from the tendency to indulge in the plantlike luxury of being sessile and letting the food drift to one's mouth rather than chasing after it), there is still a biological abyss between the colonial single-celled organism and the true multicelled animal (metazoan). The essence of this abyss is that in the metazoan there are two kinds of cells, the somatic cell (which must die) and the germ cell (which is conditionally immortal if it can find a mate). In a few colonial protozoans specialized germ cells, or gametes, developed, and it was only these that could unite with each other in syngamy.

Evolution is not quite sure of itself in this bold adventure, as shown by the behavior of the pioneer colony-forming protozoan, *Volvox*. Although this animalcule evidently was the first to set up a difference between immortal sex cells and somatic cells, which only eat and die (they no longer divide), there are three kinds of sex cells in it. One, the agamete, merely propagates by dividing rapidly inside the colonial ball. It is essentially a high-powered version of the old-style protozoan. The macrogametes are like eggs and the microgametes are like sperm cells. The latter two unite in essentially sexual fusion. At a somewhat more elaborate stage we have *Vorticella,* a bell animalcule, which consists of ciliate infusorians living in colonies. Each member of the colony is attached to a common base by a thin stem and virtually all are technically female, at least as far as behavior is concerned. Now and then, however, in most *Vorticella* colonies a male is allowed to be born. It is a smaller, stemless vorticel who can free himself. As a "swarmer" he swims boldly around to visit other colonies (the first exogamic, or anti-incestuous, pattern in the history of life). When he perceives a colony not entirely consisting of his own sisters, he climbs up the stems of one of these females, slips into her body and donates his nucleus to her, then he separates again, shrinks and dies. Although sophisticated and pretty, note that this

is not really as close to true sex as the union of *Volvox's* micro-
and macrogametes, since it is only the male animal that exists as
a separate germ cell.

When we have male and female gametes pairing to add their
chromosomes together, there is a profound distinction between
animals in which the chromosomes fuse and those in which they
remain separate in the cell fusion product or the fertilized egg. In
nearly all the multicellular sexual animals that we are familiar with,
the chromosomes from the male and from the female exist in the
tissues of the progeny as separate, not fused, and in fact seem to
pay no attention to each other. Thus the fertilized egg has twice
the number of chromosomes as the unfertilized egg or the sperm
cell. That works out fine except when the fertilized egg grows up
and decides as an adult to have its own children. Obviously something quite drastic must be done, since we cannot go on doubling
the chromosome number from generation to generation. Evolution
saw this dilemma coming and invented the incredibly delicate and
subtle process of *meiosis* ("to diminish"). This is the reverse of
mitosis in that the chromosomes destined for the germ cells
(gametes) of the animal are reduced to half the number of the
cells in the common tissue. The number of chromosomes in the
set of a germ cell is called the haploid number, and a sex cell containing only one set is called haploid. A body cell with two sets
of chromosomes is called diploid. While in mitosis, or ordinary
cell division in growth or regeneration, the two sets of chromosomes, one from the male and one from the female parent, pay
each other little heed, in the process of meiosis they suddenly become passionately conscious of each other. They seek each other
out and come to lie side by side, closely aligned at every point
from one end to the other. This pairing of corresponding chromosomes is called synapsis,* and obviously its purpose is to insure
that the germ cells (either egg or sperm) which are to be passed
on to another generation possess a statistical likelihood of getting

* From a Greek root meaning "joining" or "fastening."

hereditary representation from both mother and father of the individual who is storing the germ cell.

The meiotic process involves two different divisions and it is the second one that winds up with half the number of chromosomes. In the first meiotic division, the chromosomes of paternal and maternal origin are separated into separate cells, hence into separate gametes. This is the physical basis for Mendel's law of segregation of hereditary factors in the formation of sperms or eggs. If, for example, a paternal chromosome carried a factor (allele) for red hair and the corresponding maternal chromosome carried a factor for black hair, one half the gametes would receive chromosomes containing the gene for red, and the other half, the chromosomes carrying the gene for black. The way one pair of paternal and maternal chromosomes separates after lying together in the synaptic embrace is independent of the way any other pair separates. This means that almost no two eggs or two sperms will have exactly the same assortment of maternal and paternal chromosomes.

The probability that any given sperm (or egg) will carry only paternal (or maternal) chromosomes is an incredibly small number. Fertilization then compounds the amount of variation in meiosis, so that the total possible kinds of zygotes (or fertilized eggs) any human couple can produce is about sixty-four trillion.* It will be realized that evolution rightly picked upon sexual union as a means of getting away from Xerox reproduction.

Yet the march to complete bisexual reproduction is by no means an irresistible cavalcade. Natural parthenogenesis (in which the germ cells develop without fertilization) is another way to appear in the universe and is seen in certain kinds of crustaceans, rotifers, aphids** and a few other groups. This style of being born

---

* Actually it is much more than this, because of the phenomenon known as "crossing over." During synapsis the tightly paired chromosomes often become twisted and when separation occurs the chromosomes are seen to have changed parts.

** When the parthenogenetic reproduction of green aphids was discovered by Leeuwenhoek, the Catholic Church hastened to point out that this proved the possibility of virgin birth.

has the disadvantage of holding the mixing of gene pools to a minimum and may be a form of emergency degeneration (perhaps due to occasional wholesale failures of males or of spermatozoa). The reason this seems likely is that everything appears to be prepared for fertilization: meiosis, or the halving of the body-cell chromosome count in the gametes, has taken place but, since the male did not show up, the egg decided to grow anyway. In certain very small crustaceans (phyllopods and ostracods) no males have ever been discovered, but perhaps a more common course of events is for generation after generation of complacent females to be born, then when hard times come (a bad winter or drought), suddenly both females and males appear. In this case, the production of males seems to be a sort of defense reaction to the environment—or possibly semi-starvation yields males because they are usually smaller and eat less. Actually there is recent evidence that it comes down to a matter of vitamin E (specifically the tocopherol constituent of vitamin E) in the diet. Food rich in vitamin E will cause a parthenogenetic race of rotifers to change to sexual reproduction. The eggs of these particular, sexually produced females, in the case of rotifers, demand fertilization and when fertilized ("winter eggs") they develop protective cysts and remain dormant for a long time until happy days are here again. Then they grow up to be females and the debonair reign of all-female generations continues.

The existence of natural parthenogenesis provoked the question in Jacques Loeb's mind at the turn of the century: in truly sexual animals, what does the sperm do to save the life of the egg? What happens in fertilization to remove the block that prevents cell division and the growth of an egg into an adult animal? Although an enormous amount of research has gone into satisfying this query, we still don't know the answer. Nor do we know what stimulates an ordinary somatic cell to subdivide. The entrance of a sperm first of all causes the construction of a fertilization membrane, within which the egg is free to rotate. This membrane has the laudable purpose of preventing other sperms from entering the egg. It is the egg's way of saying, "I am married."* There is no evidence that in metazoan animals the sperm is like an arrow with a message it is bound to deliver. The innumerable spermatozoa appear to swim blindly about at random and occasionally one of them hits the target, simply because the ovum is relatively so big. It has been variously thought that the entrance of the sperm removes some inhibiting substance that has glued the egg in its non-dividing state or that the sperm triggers the activity of some essential enzyme. The permeability of the egg changes, not only becoming impermeable to other sperms but much more permeable than before to certain ions. Potassium and calcium exchange between the egg cytoplasm and the surrounding water increases by a factor of fifteen. Phosphorus is taken up by the fertilized egg one hundred times as readily as by the virgin egg. From the marked acceleration of protein synthesis following fertilization, it might be supposed that immediately after the sperm nucleus arrives, the zygote (combined sperm and egg) nucleus begins to pour out messenger RNA** into the cytoplasm. However, it has been found that an enucleated egg (simply a mass of cytoplasm) can be induced to begin dividing into a shapeless and grotesque blob of cells—certainly not the beginning of a meaningful animal, but a lot of protein being synthesized. What is more, messenger RNA can be extracted from the unfertilized eggs. Perhaps it is the ribosomes (center of protein synthesis) that are masked or gagged. This is made probable by the results of the ingenious experiments of Alberto Monroys (University of Palermo), who measured the degree of protein synthesis from amino acids with (1) mixtures of ribosomes from unfertilized eggs and messenger RNA from beef liver (in which nothing happened) and (2) mixtures of ribosomes from

---

* As we shall see later in the case of the extraordinary infertility of unmarried but licentious Polynesian and Melanesian girls, it is possible that an environment of mixed sperms from a variety of potential fathers may not only defeat this selective membrane but prevent fertilization almost entirely.

** Ribonucleic acid (RNA) is the molecule that, so to speak, executes the orders of the central DNA molecules. It assures that the correct proteins are manufactured, the seat of this manufacture being the ribosomes, located outside of the nucleus.

liver and messenger RNA from unfertilized eggs (in which protein synthesis began immediately).

Loeb found an embarrassing number of answers to his question with his discovery of artificial parthenogenesis. He found that the unfertilized eggs of sea urchins can be stimulated to divide and to produce healthy adult sea urchins. Such eggs could be fathered by weak acids, temperature shock, treatment with fat solvents (such as ether, alcohol and benzene), osmotic changes produced by sugar or urea solutions, ultraviolet light and even the educated prick of a needle. John Shaver later showed that if unfertilized eggs are injected with a centrifuged fraction of adult tissue containing ribosomes, parthenogenesis is inevitable. These techniques work not only with the coelenterates but with annelid worms, with frogs and even with rabbits. There seems to be no theoretical reason why some version of the technique could not be made to work with human beings, in which case theoretically the existence of human males would be an unwarranted luxury, considering especially that they cause most of the trouble in the world and are an annoyance to evolution.

Before evolution produced a species capable of containing biologists as genial as Jacques Loeb, it did a lot of playing around with various versions of the sex theme. Even before losing interest in the protozoans, evolution showed how many tunes can be played with sexuality. For example, *Paramecium amelia* has eight different "sexes." *Chlamydomonas* has ten sexes, five "male" and five "female"—all reacting with varying degrees of intensity to their opposite sexes.* On the other hand, many forms of asexual reproduction continued to reflect in multicelled animals nostalgia for the "good old days" of binary fission. The habit of internal budding developed in certain plantlike animals; it consisted of the fragment-

---

* By some unfettered imaginations, such as that of Olaf Stapledon, it has seemed inevitable that "group sex" would in the future become a rewarding social function for man. Stapledon did not have in mind the ancient wild party of Sodom or what has been called in modern times "having a ball" but the participation of people of different shades of sex in psychical exchanges or confrontations—an intellectual love-in.

ing of a mass of specialized germinal tissue, followed by the organization into individuals of the next generation. In the phylum of Mesozoa the simplicity of form and function may be degeneration, since all the species are parasitic during most of the life cycle (some savants believe they regressed from flatworms). From a single one of their axial cells (and it is not critical *which* one it is) many agametes are formed. They are not exactly eggs and they develop without fertilization into a new generation. This is close to the casual reproductive habits of some coelenterates, such as the hydra, in which totipotent (all-powerful) cells, cells that lurk around interstitially between working body cells, are capable at certain seasons of becoming germ cells and producing a new individual without any messing around with sex. (This would be analogous to the white corpuscles of our own bodies deciding to become little men or women.) It may be that totipotency of this sort is at the root of cancer. If so, it is a regression to the earliest structures of life. Hydras frequently produce their young by asexual budding. The process differs from the simple fission of protozoans in that the mass of new cells produced is organized by some integrating influence into multicellular individuals with the characteristics of the parent. In some coelenterates the gonozooids constitute a separate rank, called "persons," who are not released but produce gametes which undergo spontaneous development. Incidentally, whenever asexual reproduction occurs among metazoans, it is connected with an extraordinary capacity for regeneration.

2. Wormy Sex

For some worms which would be unlikely to find mates before their life span is completed, evolution invented the package of two sexes in the same body, precisely equivalent to monoecious plants, which fertilize themselves.* Thus in the pork tapeworm, a system of male and female organs develops in every proglottid, or segment. The penis may be inserted into the vagina of the same proglottid (perhaps the *ne plus ultra* of incestuousness) or of a different proglottid if the worm is in the habit of folding in upon itself. When several of these worms are present in the same host (the abdominal tissues of a pig), the self-fertilization may change to cross-fertilization, but the results are the same. Eventually the greater part of the proglottid containing the vagina is occupied by a branching uterus containing tens of thousands of eggs. The ripe proglottids become detached, pass out of the host with the pig's feces and disintegrate, leaving the embryos to survive and to be spread like encysted protozoans. It might be assumed that a tape-

* One cannot imagine today the prudishness of the eighteenth-century Lutheran Church. In 1787 Sprengel wrote an essay on the fertilization of flowers, disposing of the illusion that flowers had no sex. At the insistence of the church authorities, he was dismissed from his teaching post and his book was withdrawn from circulation.

worm's segments consist essentially of sexual organs which the head of the worm repeatedly forms by budding. The tapeworm is impelled by instinct to mutilate itself by constantly breaking off its ripe sexual segments and regenerates itself by substituting new segments for those it has thrown down the drain.

In planarian worms, although complete male and female systems are present in each individual, some conditions which we don't understand prevent self-fertilization. Only a few species of freshwater planarians produce fertile eggs without copulation. Some are parthenogenetic but others may be self-fertilized.

The advantage of being hermaphroditic is for an animal like a worm or a snail quite obvious and that is why evolution looked upon it with favor. Consider the arithmetic of chance. Usually, for a reason that will be made clear shortly, a bisexual population consists of males and females in equal numbers. This means that only half of the random encounters of one animal with another will be fruitful. Having no wings and not being able to get around quickly in some other way, a worm or a snail must make every random meeting count or life will slide away before the animal has had a chance for sexual parenthood. Evolution's quick, if indecent, answer is to be a hermaphrodite. Every encounter is a reproductive success because in every encounter insemination is mutual. Being a hermaphrodite may be the ambition of most primitive male animals, because in a bisexual society they are sorely put upon. On the other hand, there are some luxuries. The male is often eaten by the female, not in the frenzied sense of devouring what is left of him after copulation, but in that the method of fertilization is frequently to be swallowed by the female and then to find one's way to her egg cells. In some species the males, while still in the womb, copulate with their sisters and die before they themselves are born. (This must be the secret life of the libido to which Freudians claim we all unconsciously aspire.) In the star worm *Bonella viridis* the female looks like a microscopic pickle. The males are born and live as parasites inside the bodies of the females. Numbers of them lodge in a female's sexual organs, feeding on her body juices and fertilizing all eggs which slide down the oviduct. (This utopian

existence recalls W. C. Fields' classic remark "If they'd air-
condition them, I'd *live* in one.")* Among the free-swarming larvae of some star worm species, sex is not yet determined. Once a
larva attaches itself to the proboscis of a mature female, under the
influences of nose-hormone, it is transformed into a dwarf male.
Eventually it moves down the gullet and into the female's sexual
parts. Larvae that *don't* find females convert themselves into females. Those that hold on for too short a time to the proboscis
are transformed into hermaphrodites. (In such species the overwhelming effect of hormones on sex determination first becomes
apparent. There are some barriers to this mode of sex control,
especially when we come to more advanced phyla.) The parasite
worms that live on the gills of carplike fishes are hermaphrodites
of a rather special and fatalistic kind. Although they are theoretically capable of self-fertilization, the preference is for two worms
to grow together in the middle of their bodies and then to become
siamese twins for life. The vagina of each half becomes permanently attached to the sperm duct of the other half in a lifelong,
double-barreled marriage.

In mating, two earthworms (both hermaphrodites) lie side by
side, so that the head of one touches the tail of the other. Unlike
the parasite worms, however, they merely exchange sperm by way
of the seminal receptacles. The female halves of each are still in-
active and only later will receive the stored sperm accumulated as
the result of this purely homosexual act. When the eggs of the
earthworm are ready to be fertilized, the "he-she" performs a most
intricate gynecological operation. The mid-segments of the worm
have by now swollen up into a kind of muff-like girdle, which secretes nutritive fluid. By muscular contractions, the earthworm
pushes this food ring up to the fourteenth segment, where the
mature eggs are located. The eggs are discharged into the food muff
and the "he-she" then pushes the egg-filled girdle up to the ninth
and tenth segments, where the seminal receptacles have been storing the sperm obtained in the homosexual love affair. The sperm
flows into the girdle but still does not fertilize the eggs. By a final

* He was not referring to worms.

supreme contortion the worm pushes the girdle up over its head and simultaneously wraps it into a cocoon, which slowly hardens in the ground. There the sperms fertilize the eggs and the cycle of producing busy queers is started all over again. (As we shall see throughout this essay, the *storing* of sperm obtained from another individual is a common process throughout the animal world, even in some mammals, but, perhaps unfortunately, not in primates.)

The mature liver flukes are also hermaphroditic and spend their double-barreled honeymoons cross-copulating in the bile duct of their final hosts. There is a fantastic sequence of instincts that enables certain flukes at one stage of their life cycle to take over the brain of an ant and compel it to climb to the top of pasture grass so that the fluke may manage to wind up in the liver of a grazing animal. During such stages in their lives flukes are not interested in reproduction but only in working out incredibly elaborate plans to assure their arrival in an eventual palace of food and love. These plans involve the unwilling co-operation of intermediate hosts, who, like the ants, are ruthlessly sacrificed in the interests of promising the survival of a thoroughly pestilent and unlovely creature. Thus the fluke *Leucochoridium paradoxum* in larval form lives in the tissues of the aquatic amber snail, but as a mature sexual animal it has a gnawing compulsion to inhabit the intestines of songbirds. How to get from one to another? Such transferals are easy for a fluke, blindly relying on instincts that have been operative ever since there were songbirds and snails and flukes. It first forms a sporocyst and sends branches cautiously through the tissues of the snail without killing it, until the malefic protoplasm has reached the tips of the snail's antennae, or feelers. Here the sporocyst branches swell so thickly that the snail is unable to use his natural defense tactics: he can no longer withdraw into his shell when a bird approaches. But the fluke spores are not content with this paralyzing stratagem; the bird must be attracted to the snail. Thus the sporocyst branches are green and white and are plainly visible since the skin of the snail's feelers is so stretched as to be transparent. The bird imagines it has seen a caterpillar, so it picks up the snail by its swollen, twitching feeler and carries it back to the baby birds in the nests, who grow up worm-infested, since it is in these tiny avian intestines that the flukes grow to fully sexed worms and have a ball.

In various worms, evolution is not too fussy about whether reproduction is accomplished by hermaphroditism or by individuals of distinct sex. It depends on the way the worm makes a living and on the degree of social contact between worms. Species that are likely to flock together in immense swarms or periodic colonial mobs are usually bisexual, since in such crowds it is easy for boy to meet girl. Related species that do not have the wild-party habit are usually hermaphroditic. And because sex is a sometimes thing and depends so much on easily unbalanced hormones, one sex may readily transform into the other. Some of the sea-swarming worms put on quite a show. In the fall along the coasts of Samoa and the Fiji Islands, the islanders feast on what they call the *palolo* worm. At breeding time the water may be so viscous with the forms of the annelid *Eunice viridis* that an oar thrown into this seething mass of procreation will stand upright for a time. What the natives banquet upon are not whole worms but only the detached sexual parts. Since the palolo is bisexual, there are female ends and male ends. The different segments discharge their cells into the water and, after eggs and sperms have united, the fertilized eggs sink to the bottom. This dense sexual rite is apparently regulated by the phases of the moon, as Rachel Carson has so poetically described in *The Sea Around Us.* In one variety of *Syllis,* also an annelid worm, the females of the sexual generation burn their candle at both ends, giving off a gentle light, to which males respond by blinking like fireflies. When the couple mates, both lights are instantly turned out. In another species of *Syllis* the female changes to a male once she has laid eggs, then goes on the prowl for females to mate with. Such females can be artificially converted into males by cutting off the hind ring of the body. External hormones play a crucial chemical role in the love life of the clamworm. The males perform a sort of group masturbation ritual—apparently stimulated by the new moon—and ejaculate their sperm into the water. Females swimming by are stimulated by chemicals released from the sperm cloud and immediately lay eggs.

Although there are many animals, as previously described, in which the male is swallowed in order to fertilize the female from within, the rather highly evolved bristle worm *Platynereis megalops* has invented a selective form of this cannibalistic intercourse, in which only the sexual apparatus of the male is swallowed. The male organs of the platynereids are attached to the body proper, much as a trailer is attached to a truck. The males seduce the females by snaking past them with the trailer appendage dangling. When the females eat this package, the sperm travels within the abdominal cavity and fertilizes the eggs, and the male truck continues to go about its brief business of renewed bachelorhood.

The females of the bumblebee eelworm after fertilization undergo a revolting transformation which seems like the dream of a sex-crazed maniac. Each eelworm becomes a gigantic vagina from which the rest of the body hangs like a desiccated ghost. Before this Freudian horror occurs, the bisexual worms have copulated in damp earth and the male, as is so often the case, has died of erotic exhaustion. The impregnated females seek out queen bumblebees (which spend the winter in the ground) and penetrate their hibernating bodies. It is soon afterward that the vagina of the eelworm undergoes its fearful apotheosis. The vagina absorbs the uterus and the ovary and continues to grow until the young worms have hatched out of the eggs and have left their monstrous home.

Leeches have a habit similar to that of earthworms. In the homosexual phase, they exchange stores of sperm. But, to emphasize evolution's caprices in such animals, some leeches, including the leech of historical medicine, *Hirudo medicinalis,* are bisexual. The male has a penis which introduces cartridges of sperm into the female's sexual orifice. Others, such as the so-called proboscis leech, have a more sadistic habit. They use their vicious tube-shaped penis to penetrate the female's skin at any point, leaving the sperms to find their own way to the eggs.*

* So polymorphically perverse is man that, in off-color stories, he has duplicated all the peculiar features of animal sex, invertebrate as well as mammalian. One recalls, in this particular context, the yarn about the wild man that had to be ejected from the house of prostitution because he insisted on making his own holes.

3. The Voluptuous Mollusks

Of all the phyla alien to man and the vertebrates, perhaps the most complete encyclopedia of sex practices is found among the mollusks. The changes in tune that mollusks have been able to ring in sex vary from the passionate, superheated Anthony-and-Cleopatra marriages of squids and octopuses to the quite modern Hollywood "dirty-book" combinations of hermaphroditism with deliberate and cunning sadism-cum-masochism in the garden snail. The snail's "love darts" are as specific in brutal purpose as the whips of the Marquis de Sade and must discourage people who are trying to invent new perversions. Everything has been done that can be done, not only six thousand years ago in ancient Sodom and Gomorrah but two hundred million years ago among the gastropods.

Before we consider the mollusks, however, let us say a few words about the barnacles, or *Cirripedia*. Here we see a rather wild divergence in sexual identity, showing a hesitancy on evolution's part on just how the sexes should be dealt out. Most barnacles are hermaphroditic but in some species there is the popular theme of having a dwarf male, who is scarcely more than an elaborate sperm. The tiny males are commonly without much structure and have little life expectancy. In some cases they seem to have no clear function at all. Thus some are attached to hermaphrodites. They are "complemental males," not necessary to the perpetuation of the species, and hang around briefly, probably the most useless individuals on the face of the earth. Yet evolution must have seen some point in their lives, since evidently they have persisted in being born, often without digestive systems, for a billion or more generations of *Cirripedia*. (One is somehow reminded of the small, meek, faceless men who run errands for prostitutes or for prize-fighters.)

Bivalves are not particularly interesting from the standpoint of sexual behavior. Some of the species are bisexual; some are hermaphroditic, but the female and male organs become ripe at different times in the same individual (the European oyster, for instance), thus avoiding the scandal of self-fertilization. (As we ascend the scale of life forms, evolution seems to want to make it more certain that the mother and father are not the same person.) An individual oyster can be female one day and suck sperm into its gills. A week later it becomes a male and concentrates on ejecting sperm.

It is within the somewhat more advanced type of mollusk, such as the gastropod, that we begin to see new dimensions of sexuality. Some gilled and pulmonary snails have developed gang or tandem hermaphroditic habits. They form copulatory chains of five or six mates. Sexually the American slipper snail is a sly and protean creature. It may be a male or a female depending on its age and position in a wild party. When grown, this snail is sedentary, female and stays on the same spot. In youth, *all* the slipper snails are male and get around. When once they decide to attach themselves to something, they turn into females. This "something" may be a female, in which case the male copulates before he loses his masculinity. A third male comes around and in turn copulates with the top female; he in turn changes sex, and this process may continue until a sexual tower of ten to fourteen snails is built up. The lowest level consists of females; the middle, of males changing into females; and the topmost is still a male, and he can be seen using his penis.*

In the edible hermaphroditic Roman snail and the garden snail the sex glands are not located in the lower regions of the body but high up in the shell. A rather complex system of ducts leads from these glands to the sexual orifices and to various subsidiary glands which furnish lubricant for the sex act. Spermatozoa make their way down these ducts when the partner is to be fertilized and upwardly when the snail itself is to be fertilized. Each individual has a vagina and an astonishingly huge erectile penis. Since the act of mutual copulation involves in this otherwise phlegmatic animal four separate sex organs (a vagina and penis on each lover), it is apparent that evolution decided on a rather extreme method of stimulation to be sure that all organs were prepared. This method was sadism. Each snail carries a sac, or quiver, of darts made of calcium carbonate. After a sort of slow-motion love dance in which the partners rear up, foot to foot, and rock back and forth, exchanging kisses, one of them starts the rough business by driving a dart into the body of the mate. (Although both are evidently driven to the extremes of sexual excitement by this act, it is a serious wound and sometimes fatal.) The pained and ecstatic snail strikes back. The masochist becomes a sadist. Both now protrude their enormous penises and, after frenzied writhing, each inserts his member in the vagina of the other. The consummating embrace lasts for several minutes, since the male organ must penetrate as deeply as possible into the female genital in order to deposit the semen in a bladder-shaped nest, where sometime later it will be used to fertilize the eggs. Both partners seem to ejaculate sperm at the same time. As recorded by neurological tests, the curve of excitement and final release of tension indicates that both partners have experienced orgasm. We cannot ask a snail, "Did you have

* Again we are reminded of some human analogies. When the doughboys of World War I came home, properly impressed by certain French homosexual habits, they started the famous unprintable story whose punch line was "Ah, zee lucky Alphonse!" There is another story that is probably as old as human navies, in which the captain impatiently orders the men to form a circle.

an orgasm?" But the electrical record and the behavior are the same as those observed in the copulation of primates, including human beings. The chances are that the orgasms are, however, purely male and in fact there is little clear evidence of female orgasm until we get to *Homo sapiens*. It is perhaps the combination of sadistic-masochistic practice with true mutual male orgasm that evolution has found worthwhile to introduce in order to assure the survival of an animal so otherwise dispassionate and level-headed as a snail. The mystifying degree of enervation of the snail's foot may be connected with the masochistic act, since the target of the love darts is usually the foot. If, however, the darts pierce the lungs or the abdomen, instead of a hermaphroditic union, we have a sex murder. In Africa there are naked (shell-less) snails which carry a dozen love darts an inch to an inch and a half in length.

In spite of the perversity of the snail's act of fertilization, it is very efficient and, although usually delayed, the eggs are carefully deposited or stored in broad pouches. Actually the development of the young in land snails is syncopated. The offspring are hatched in a stage far in advance of the larval form of marine species.

The passion of true bisexual love sweeps the cephalopod (squids, octopuses, nautiloids, etc.) like a wild feverish disease. When a squid is separated from his lady fair at mating time and imprisoned in an aquarium he becomes so melancholy that he finally ends up in madness. He kills himself by eating his own arms. When male and female embrace, it is a wholehearted, sixteen-tentacle affair which at first involves dances of the most unashamed and pulsing character. One can almost hear the big beat and the "Yeah, yeah!" The dance and the copulatory posture were known to the ancient Greeks and pictured on vases.

The males of all the dibranches (octopuses, squids, etc.) have a "hectocotylized" structure; that is, they have one or more tentacles or arms which serve as tools of procreation. In most of the higher cephalopods (such as squid and octopus) only one arm is hectocotylized; in some species, two arms; and in the pearly nautilus, which is still close to the ancient mollusks of the Mesozoic, sexual arms may merge into a penislike organ.

After the octopus dance, there occurs a period of what can only be described by the human term of the 1920's as "petting." The male strokes and excites his sweetheart in close embrace. Then, when he has decided she is quite ready, he reaches his special arm into his own breathing funnel, brings out several cartridges of semen from his mantle cavity and thrusts them gently but firmly into the female's mantle cavity. Thus is love consummated. Although to a human female this might seem something like reaching a climax by being fed a piece of chocolate candy out of the man's pocket, the female octopus feels it is adequate, and that is what counts. And in truth it seems a much more civilized procedure than all the sweat and exudations involving excited organs and mucous membranes that are notable for their ugliness and proximity to the body's channels of elimination. Sex is a much prettier and more delicate, yet none the less ardent, thing among the higher mollusks. (Maybe it would have been a sweeter planet if they *had* managed to take it over.)

In some species of dibranches the sexual arm or part of it becomes detached in the act of mating and is left in the mantle cavity of the female as a token of affection. She most likely eats it, but the loss of the arm of love does not embarrass the male, since he quickly regenerates a new one. (Occasionally one may see such love-soaked arms floating alone in the ocean until they are snapped up by barracuda.) There is a good deal of fragrant variety in this method of copulation. We have described the first method: the hectocotylized arm, charged with spermatophores (sperm capsules) is liberated in the mantle cavity of the female. In a variation, the arm never severs itself but is so organized nervously that it can transfer spermatophores precisely to the region of the oviduct in the female's mantle cavity. In a third method, a slight modification, one arm enables the male to grasp spermatophores as they appear at the mouth of the funnel leading from his mantle cavity and to transfer them with great speed either to the mantle cavity of the female or, in certain squids, to the membrane surrounding her mouth, known as the buccal membrane. Fertilization may take place either in the mantle cavity or in the membrane. In many cases, however, the sperm is saved for later. When the female squid deposits her eggs they are usually embedded in strings of a jellylike substance which glue to a surface. Before attaching them she holds the eggs between her arms, molding them into a cone-shaped receptacle at the same time, much as a baker manipulates dough. A mother octopus or squid will deposit about thirty of these racemes of some 800 eggs during laying. Unlike most marine invertebrates, the young cephalopod does not pass through a larval stage but hatches from its large, heavily yoked egg as a small adult. When the young begin to scramble single-mindedly from the egg capsules, the mother becomes very agitated and will dash at a man's hand in the tank of an aquarium.

The most endearing feature of sex among the cephalopods is that in all cases the act of sexual union involves only the arms and the specialized parts of the mouth. It is as if in our species fertilization could be accomplished by passionate kissing.* Most refined people would agree that this would be preferable to our present process, but evolution is not known for its universal tact.

---

* As a young boy, reading books more advanced than the *Rover Boys,* I was led to the conclusion that kissing was indeed the final procreative act. This was because in the novels of the Edwardian era a passionate embrace was followed (as in H. G. Wells) by triple dots . . . and in the next chapter the young woman was pregnant.

4. Spider Love

The graceful and pleasing technique of sexual intercourse by the male delivering by hand, so to speak, a package of spermatozoa as a postman inserts a Christmas package in the mailbox is by no means confined to the cephalopods. It is seen also in the great arthropod phylum, notably in the crustaceans (crabs, etc.) and among the spiders and their relatives. But before we go into further details, we must inquire as to the methods by which evolution determines whether a given individual is going to be a male or a female. In many of the animals we have reviewed so far in this book, sex seems to be a peculiarly temporary matter. One sees males changing into females and females into males, while among the hermaphrodites one or the other sex may predominate, depending on the mood of the hormones. Sex seemed to us largely a whim of chemical secretions. Yet in the early part of this century the study of insects showed that the chromosomes could determine sex. In females all the chromosome pairs of any cell in the body were found to match perfectly. In the males, however, there is one chromosomal pair in which the two chromosomes do not match, even though they pair together in the process of synapsis. They approach each other end to end rather than lengthwise, as the other chromosomes do. These are called the X and Y chromosomes. During meiosis (in preparation for starting another generation) the females always have two X chromosomes, the males an X and a Y. After meiosis each egg will carry an X chromosome, but half the sperms will carry an X and half a Y chromosome. Since sex is determined by the nature of the sperm, the sex of the offspring is decided at the instant of fertilization.*

The X and Y chromosomes of course contain other genes than those solely concerned with sex. Thus there are a number of sex-linked genes. However, in view of the vast importance of hormones in the phenomena of sex, it is important to distinguish between sex-linked genes and genes whose action is especially influenced by sex hormones. To skip ahead for a moment to the mammals, there are genes in certain breeds of sheep which will produce horns in the normal ram. In a castrated ram or a female, where the male hormones are lacking, these genes do not produce horns. Such genes are not necessarily located on the sex chromosomes—in fact, they usually are not. In some vertebrates and invertebrates, notably insects and crustaceans, many sexual differences are controlled by local gene action within the tissues rather than by a hormone circulating in the blood. The classical case is that of gynandromorphism in the fruit fly (*Drosophila*), where because of a chromosomal accident one half of the body is male and the other half female. The female side of the fly has an XX chromosome composition, while the male side has lost one of the X's and is XO, which in this animal gives a male. Sometimes the front half may be male or female and the hind half (containing the sex organs) may be the opposite. In this case the fruit fly behaves according to the sex of its brain.

One further question needs to be asked. In most animals which come in two sexes the ratio of the number of male to the number

* This so-called heterogametic property of males is by no means universal. In some animals, including frogs and butterflies, it is the female which is heterogametic. There are two kinds of eggs produced and only one kind of sperm.

of female individuals is close to one. Why should that be? The answer to this is a matter of evolutionary arithmetic first proposed by R. A. Fisher, and it involves an exercise in the logic of natural selection, as follows:

(1) Suppose that male births for some reason are exceeded by female births.

(2) The male now has a better mating prospect and will have more offspring than the female.

(3) Thus parents genetically disposed to produce males tend to have more grandchildren. (This is the key stage of the syllogism.)

(4) Thus the genes for male-producing tendencies spread and male births become more common.

(5) As the one-to-one ratio of male to female is approached, the advantage of being a male (more mating prospects) dies away.

(6) The same reasoning holds if female births at one time or another are exceeded by male births. Therefore one to one is the equilibrium ratio.

Among the crustaceans, a typically delightful and interesting sex life is indulged in by the fiddler crab. As most lovers of shore life know, the male of this species has developed one claw into an enormous chela that is useless as an eating utensil but is fine for signaling his masculinity and occasionally for tussles with other males. In a colony of fiddler crabs feeding on the tidal mud, a wave of nervous excitement will suddenly seize upon all the males. About every two seconds each of them raises his impressive snow-white claw to attract a female. (It has been polished with his little eating claw until it shines like a Texan's boot.) If a male is lucky and impresses a female, he dances her along within the curve of his great claw-arm, never touching her, trying to tease her over to his hole. Sometimes a conquest is not so easy and he has to perform a dance. In a rhythmic way, with his long, thin legs, he goes through definite and age-old figures, which vary with each of the many subspecies. The nearer the female approaches, the more furious his capers become. If the lady crab is at last obviously impressed, he bows low, drums on the ground with his giant claw and vanishes into his hole, which is generally a yard deep, hoping she will follow. She may or may not and considerable tension will arise if she pauses instead at a rival male's hole. Because of the sacred law of territorialism, no male may invade another's burrow, but the two owners may confront each other on the property line and indian-wrestle with their claws. The object is with a sudden wrench to break the other one's claw off, but this is humiliation rather than manslaughter, since after a few days of sulking in his hole the loser will grow another one.

As the tide turns, signaling and flirting cease. Everybody has to get back to a hole. In an emergency an uncourted female will enter the nearest male hole, where she is received without question (although the entrance of another male would start a violent fight). No advantage is taken of her under the circumstances, since mating without the preliminary ceremonial is inconceivable to the mind of the crab. Such animals live on a rhythm based on the tides and all their activities are tuned to methodical sequence. Periods of courtship battles, hole building—all come at the time appointed by the gravitational pulls of the sun and the moon upon the waters of the earth. Give a crab a tide and he is as comforted as a songbird at seeing the sun come up in the morning.

Another crustacean whose love habits are of practical interest to us is the lobster. Unfortunately the people who set the lobster laws of the state of Maine evidently do not understand the lobster's love life, since they protect large lobsters by statute and thereby contribute to the population implosion. The Maine lobster is dying out, to a great degree on account of this senseless law. It is senseless because the older, larger male lobsters cannot mate with smaller females. Yet the law favors the catching of the smaller males, who can. The result is that the female, who can only mate for a forty-eight-hour period every two years, loses her big chance and the population of baby lobsters falls to a statistically dismal level.

All decapods (crabs, lobsters, etc.)* reproduce by union of the two sexes, and since the means of fertilization is quite similar to that in spiders, we now direct our attention to this fascinating but rather old-fashioned class of animals. Like the octopus and squid, crustaceans, millipedes and spiders use the *gonopod* system, in which one appendage is modified in the male to perform an agile act of delivering sperm to the appropriate female receptable. The male spider in general has transformed the claws on the end of the *pedipalpi* (leglike appendages on each side of the head in both sexes) into an intromittent organ like a syringe, or hypodermic needle. These male organs, or *palpi,* have no connection with the gonads of the abdomen (any more than a man's hands are connected with his scrotum), so the spider must first perform a sort of masturbatory act, but one of great elegance. He spins out a little web, deposits a globule of semen on it, then sucks it into the syringe of each palpus. In front of her genital pore the female has paired pouches for the storage of the semen, each shaped precisely to receive the palpus of the male. Differences between the genitals of spiders of allied groups are sufficient to make hybrid pairing impossible. The key must fit the lock. The female's ability to store semen has in the past confused many observers into believing that spiders could reproduce parthenogenetically. The semen may be stored for weeks or months, so that one cannot predict, after seeing spiders copulate, that eggs will be hatched in such and such a time. The eggs are fertilized and hatched whenever the female spider makes up her mind to it. Probably this depends on how many eggs she can lay. Curiously the number seems to depend on the size of the mother. *Argiope* and *Theraphosa,* giant spiders, lay as many as 3,000. In *Argiope*'s case, the eggs are covered with a tough cocoon, yet the average survival is only two. On the other hand, *Peckhamia picata,* a tiny spider that looks like an ant, lays only three eggs. The evolutionary assumption here is

* The large river crayfish must grip the female with his claws and throw her on her back. Otherwise his copulatory appendages cannot place the sperm in the right spot. When the female is not willing, this constitutes one of the only apparent cases of violent rape in the non-human animal world.

that, since ants have few enemies and these spiders resemble them, it is not necessary to produce great amounts of eggs.

The egg case of a spider is fundamentally different from the insect cocoon, which the larval insect spins around itself. Most female spiders have a set of glands designed especially for spinning egg sacs. The silk is different in color from web silk and is never viscous. The great flabby egg purses of tarantulas are prepared in the burrow and guarded until long after the young emerge. The delicate bags of the trap-door spider often hang from the side of the burrow. Some of the most elaborate sacs are spun by the sedentary (orb-spinner) spiders and may even be left hanging among the threads. Some especially wise mothers divide the risk by putting their eggs in several baskets. The wolf spiders (hunting types) drop to the ground a sac attached to their spinnerets and later carry the young around on their backs.

It is believed probable that at one time in evolution there was little difference in the size of the male and female. In modern spiders of nearly equal sex-size, an outstanding feature of the male is his longer legs (as in the trap-door spiders), which give him a greater range of sensory perception—for evading and overpowering the female. Since the ancient, halcyon days of more or less equality of the sexes, the trend has been in the direction of larger females and smaller males. Generally the male must be cautious, patient and nimble in achieving his sexual purpose, for he is very likely to be eaten before or after the act. Spiders are entirely carnivorous and the appetite for the male's body as food often overcomes the desire for motherhood. Difference in size has proceeded to the positively ridiculous in the case of massive females, such as *Mastophora* and *Nephilena,* but the male is then relatively safe because he is too small to be regarded as serious prey. He inhabits the female externally on her abdomen as a parasite and she tolerates him as she tolerates very small insects running over her body and as she refuses to eat an insect caught in her web that is below a certain acceptable size. The typical fate of a slightly larger male is that of the wheel-web *Argiope.* Here the puny male exhausts himself in his copulatory act and the female consumes his dead body. This is only appropriate, since fertilized carnivores are always hungry for protein.

The male hunting spider catches a fly, wraps it in silk from his spinneret and hands the package to the female as a bridal gift. She is occupied in munching this, while he goes about the business of impregnating her. This type of propitiation is common not only through various kinds of spiders where sexual dimorphism (difference in size) is the rule, but among the carnivorous insects.

The courtship techniques may vary. Among aerial spiders and other web spinners, wooing is started by the male pulling the threads of the female's web ("Can I come in?") and later by his stroking the body of the female. Among the spiders with better developed eyes, there is more posturing and visible ritual. The males tend to produce more pigment, so those able to develop colored spots in front are able to survive more often, because the female scowlingly recognizes a lover rather than a prey. The male of *Xysticus* spins a web over the female, or a bridal veil. Many crab spiders use this pretty and prudent technique. Among short-sighted hunters, who are entirely nocturnal, the male's approach is quite bold, since he is approximately the female's equal in size. Mutual recognition is by taste or smell. The male strokes and tickles her body while maintaining a firm grasp on her with his legs or claws. Among the long-sighted hunters, the love dance (as in crabs) is practical. This is true of the wolf spider, the lynx spider and the jumping spider. The postures and rhythmic dances are distinct for all species and the female responds only to the dance that she was born to recognize. The "purring" spider (*Lycosa gulosa*) on contacting the female begins to drum his palpi rapidly against anything solid. This is love incitement in the same sense as the male tweaks on the web among web-building species.

It is pleasant to be able to report that in not all cases does the female represent a hideous risk of life on the part of the male for the privilege of placing his semen-moistened palpus in her hairy belly. In the species *Theridon tepidariorum* the first steps of courtship are, in fact, often made by the female, who even goes so far as to leave undevoured food to approach the male. She is the one that opens the telephone conversation by signaling on the web line. This unusually amiable lady may in fact mate with many males (a totally untypical act among spiders) and, except when actually groaning with heavy eggs, rarely rejects the advances of any suitor. Whereas male spiders, if they are able to leave on their own legs at all, usually make a hurried departure after mating, in some species of the *Theridon* group, the male moves to one side of the web, refills his palpi with semen and returns to the nuptial couch. In general there are two standard positions of copulation. In the so-called *Dysdora* embrace, the male holds his cephalothorax beneath the female's sternum and applies the palpi directly. In web spiders the female hangs inverted below the male as he applies his semen-soaked palpi. It has been shown recently that palpless male spiders rather pathetically will go through the whole rigmarole of intercourse; hence the urge to copulate is not, as formerly believed, triggered by a "feeling of emptiness" in the palpi, which stimulates the sperm-dipping preparatory act. Although most female spiders, once impregnated, will not copulate again, the females who go through the profitless act with the males whose palpi have been cut off are still ready for another suitor. The female knows at least when the sperm have gotten into her pouches and does not take seriously the mock mating with the sexual cripple.

Among those with cordial and durable marriages are the European water spiders. The male is never threatened or even spoken harshly to by the female. After mating, the two co-operate in spinning underwater an airtight nest consisting of two linked diving bells. The eggs are suspended from the roof of this lovely apartment and the young spiders, when they hatch, are tended affectionately by both parents.

Scorpions show no such marital bliss (although in courting, the male scorpion goes so far as to stand on his head) but the scorpion mother is a very busy and fussy one. The young hatch out immediately after the eggs are laid and scamper at once onto their mother's back. They live there until their first molt. (This behavior, which is also common with the European tarantula, always delighted Fabre.) If the little scorpions are brushed off her back, the

mother hunts for them and urges them back on. The offspring of
other scorpions are just as welcome and she generously adopts
them.

The more phylogenetically ancient the spider the longer its life,
the modern trend being for spiders to spin complex webs and to
die in the fall. The American tarantulas, representing the spirit of
the past, do not even mature sexually until they are about ten years
old. The final molting at this time gives the males a new outlook
on life. They desert the burrow and wander about looking for
mates. From July into November they may be seen crossing the
highways of the Southwest, being squashed by the thousands under
auto wheels.

There are degraded relatives of the proud spiders, the arachnids
known as ticks and mites, and, since most of them are parasites
and most unlikable creatures, their sex habits are mainly rude or
bizarre. However, since the mites alone number some 10,000 species, one could expect a wide variation of copulatory techniques
and that is what we see. Some male water mites hold their partners
with hooks and in addition glue themselves to their tiny females.
Some male mites have a penis; others resemble their spider superiors in transferring sperm by means of diminutive palpi. Others
give the female all the responsibility: they leave a cartridge of
semen near her and leave the rest to her. Among those revolting
creatures the ordinary ticks, sexual union becomes a crude and
nasty obstetric operation. When the female has dug well into a
warm-blooded animal and is busily bloating herself with blood,
the male crawls under her body and introduces his nose into her
vagina. By snouting around he widens the vagina, then deposits a
packet of sperm nearby. Lacking a penis, he must use his proboscis
and antennae to push the packet up into the female orifice, while
blindly and complacently she continues to suck blood. One of
the most savage of all mating habits is that of the moth mite
Pyemotes herpi. The females are parasites upon certain caterpillars.
Like many parasitic arachnids and insects, they give birth to fairly
well developed young who have already passed their larval stages
within the mother's body. If males are born, they linger around

the mother's vagina, bore into her body, feeding on her juices, while they await the birth of their sisters. When the head of a young female appears in the orifice, the male grips his sister fiercely, jerks her out like a drunken obstetrician and copulates with her. Thus we have a combination of juvenile molestation and incestuous rape. Nevertheless this appears to be a successful way of continuing this species.

The true spiders would not dream of such intercourse. Although the solitary nature of spiders and their quick scattering after hatching makes inbreeding improbable, certain species are still further discouraged from incest by biological timing. The average male black widow matures in seventy days and lives about 180 days; the female matures in ninety days and lives 270 days. Thus mating between brothers and sisters is made highly unlikely.

5. The Queen Concept and Mandatory Incest

Among the highly evolved social insects, such as the bees, incest, on the other hand, is made certain. A hive consists of a mother, a working colony of sisters and a few brothers kept for stud purposes. There is a basic question of biological mechanics involved here. Curious as it may seem at first glance, the quickest way to achieve quick evolutionary changes is to form a relatively tight colony of animals and to practice strict inbreeding. The reason is that any viable and useful mutants are preserved rather than being erased in a large, diverse pool of genes. The human race, with a universal prejudice against incest among primitive as well as advanced peoples, represents now a biological entity that is completely non-evolutionary. The trend toward exogamy progressed so far, so early that it no longer was possible to isolate colonies of *Homo sapiens* sufficiently long to hope for the formation of a separate species. In this respect, we represent the exact obverse of the history of the bees and of the birds, where inbreeding and habits of strict sexual selection favored relatively rapid development of species.

Aside from the most rigorous rules of incestuous mating, the honeybee offers a lesson in the mother's determination of the sex of her offspring and of the complete subjection of the male by his sisters. The facts about bees were disclosed by Pastor Johann Dzierzon about 1835, when he discovered what caused "drone broodiness" in certain hives. He noticed that this condition, long known by beekeepers, occurred only when the queen was too old or too infirm to undertake the nuptial flight. (She had run out of stored sperm.)* During the mating flight the queen receives at one copulation all the spermatozoa she'll use during her life. By opening or closing the duct leading from her sperm receptacle she exercises what is fancily termed "facultative parthenogenesis." When she closes the duct, an egg is laid without fertilization and is destined to become a drone, or male (haploid). The egg after fertilization becomes a female (diploid), generally a worker. Not only does the queen choose in an arithmetically appropriate way the ratio of daughters to sons (a very high ratio), but when she deposits the eggs, she never fails to lay only drone eggs in drone cells and worker eggs in worker cells, all of these having been prepared beforehand by the nurse-workers of the hive. During late summer the fertilized eggs are more and more likely to become queens rather than workers but this is brought about by agreement of the nurses rather than by the queen. "Royal jelly," secreted in glands in the nurses' heads, stimulates ovarian development, while those tagged as workers receive not only a restricted diet of pollen and honey but are retarded in their femininity by the "queen's substance." In the first days of their lives both worker and queen larvae receive the royal jelly, but the diet is soon segregated. (Since the royal jelly [or "bee milk"] is very high in proteins and in B vitamins, it has been often suggested as a specific and quick cure for alcoholic hangovers, but, as the drinking man well knows, there is no magical potion for this disease in or out of the animal kingdom.)

The act of copulation in bees is conventional for aerial insects

---

* As in the case of the unfortunate Sprengel, who was so uncouth as to insist on the sexuality of plants, the learned pastor ran into the inflexible and massive stupidity of the Lutheran Church and, because of his dangerous revelations, promptly found himself out of a job.

except that it is the male's one and only useful act. The male's penis is introduced into the vagina of his queen sister and promptly breaks off. He at once bleeds to death. The broken organ serves as a plug, preventing the semen from running out again. If the plug is removed, the queen lays only unfertilized eggs and with this humiliation dies or is killed. In a highly inbred society such as this, one can expect certain gene anomalies, mostly of an undesirable nature. In some cases some of the workers suddenly begin to lay eggs, perhaps because they have accidentally or mischievously consumed royal jelly, yet because the workers cannot mate, the unfertilized eggs yield only more drones—a flagrant insult to the economy of the hive. On the other hand, there are rare cases in which unfertilized eggs from the queen have developed into workers—a mystery that has not yet been solved. There are exceptions to the tribal purity of the hive. Sometimes a fertilized queen from another hive will be welcomed, especially if the welcoming hive is low on queen candidates. This acceptance of an outsider insures that the life of the colony will last beyond the span of the original queen.

Among distant relatives of the same order as bees, certain parasitic wasps *have* been able to dispense with the male entirely. Normally they produce nothing but females. Since the number of chromosomes is not reduced by any meiosis stage, it is evident that this has been going on for a long time, yet the potentiality for male production is still curiously present. If the eggs are bombarded with X-rays, the usual abnormalities that occur after this drastic treatment are seen, and one of them, once in a long while, turns out to be a perfectly formed male. It shows no sexual interest in its sisters, however, and the females don't respond to it. Throughout the Hymenoptera, sexual congress is the general rule. The males may not always be so suppressed as in honeybee society. While the male yellow-legged mud dauber is lazy, he is nevertheless free and flies about to sip his own nectar. The male organ-pipe wasp is actually allowed to co-operate with his mate. He guards the solitary cell, while she is out gathering clay or hunting spiders. At least he has assumed the dignity of a baby-sitter.

(In general, the lot of the male improves in the more primitive insects.) The *Polistes* wasp, halfway evolved to an organized society, even has co-operating queens. It is significant that, in order to achieve a workable way of life, a pecking order has developed among these queens. There are Queens No. 1, No. 2, No. 3, etc. (As in barnyard hens, a colony with sexually active females is utterly impossible without the establishment of a pecking order.) In hornets, the fate of the nest is rather pathetic. The queen wears out at the end of the summer and stops laying eggs. Some workers desperately try to revive the colony by laying their own eggs but, as in the case of honeybees, they hatch only drones, and the nest is abandoned and all its members are dead or dispersed before the withering of the last rose of summer.

A more fatal and instant horror may befall the solitary female wasp. If she is pregnant, her one idea is to find a spider to paralyze in which she can deposit her eggs. Yet in the heat of her summer search, if spiders are scarce, the eggs hatch anyway inside her. The ferociously carnivorous grubs don't know the difference between her uterus and the succulent body of a spider, so they chew on her insides and suddenly she drops dead, wings rigid, legs curled. Since her little thin body does not offer enough nourishment, the young wasps will die too.

One of the strangest of all animal-plant relationships, one hardly to be explained by normal evolutionary processes, involves in Algeria the burrowing wasp *Scolia ciliata* and the orchid *Ophrys speculum*. The male insect emerges from his burrow a month earlier than the female. In preparation for this emergence the orchid has learned to make a flower that exactly resembles the body of the female wasp. The orchid achieves pollination by way of the false copulation of the male wasp with this uncanny blossom. (It is impossible to recount all the biological contingencies that lie behind this symbiotic association of two entirely different sexual systems of two life patterns that diverged in the formative years of the planet. It is apparent that the plants understand insects better than do our wisest entomologists.)

The ants are remote kin of the bees and perhaps developed

their highly organized systems of colony life subsequent to a period of solitary hunting much like that of the wasplike creatures that they evolved from. As in the case of honeybee drones, the winged male ants end their lives in the glory of aerial copulation with the flying females. Alone and heavy with fertilized eggs, the queen ant remains pregnant for as long as fifteen years, producing colonies of her own. Some of these communities, in the case of the *Atta* genus, may number as many as a million or more siblings. When hatched, the larvae are fed on fungus and sometimes on subsequently hatched eggs. Again we see the matriarchy and the devoted daughter slaves.

When we consider the termites, however, we are looking at a much older animal and one in no respect related to the bee, the wasp or the ant. It is said that the termite is the only colonial insect that has been able to get any work (save copulation) out of the male. And the difference in masculine status is apparent from the very start of the mating process. The swarming of winged termites of different sexes is not even a nuptial flight as it is among the Hymenoptera. The males and females do not mate in the air. Indeed, the function of the flight is simply the dissemination of the species. A species as old and wise as the termite realizes the necessity of dispersal, if only for purposes of food gathering. When the swarm has scattered far enough from the original homestead, all the flying termites cast off their wings and get down to their basic business with the things of the soil. It is only at this stage that they form pairs; they do not mate at once but live together for a while as virginal maidens and youths.* Each pair sets out on a project and as they gnaw into rotten wood or explore the soil together, they gradually attain sexual maturity and "fall in love." In the early stages of their marriage there is complete sexual equality. They build their nest, care for the eggs and feed the larvae with secretions from their glands. The larvae (the future workers and soldiers) are not exclusively female as among ants and bees.

---

* As far as I know, this protracted period of platonic engagement has no other analogy in the animal kingdom, except in certain quite bizarre human societies.

They grow into sterile workers quite slowly and it is about six months before they are able to help their parents in the great colonial project that is under way. Mama and daddy in the meantime have worked with incalculable energy and as perfect consorts. It is only when enough progeny are available (perhaps as many children as there are human beings in the city of Mamaroneck, New York) that the king and queen withdraw from the back-breaking work and retire to devote themselves now seriously and exclusively to procreation. Attended by their grateful children, the royal couple may live on for eight to twelve years and in certain species the queen, in spite of her enormous egg-swollen bulk, may live to be fifty. Aside from the water spiders, mentioned above, the termites appear to be the only arthropods which live an exemplary married life. They are positively Victorian in their virtue and their monogamous zeal.

How can we account for this? Bearing in mind the immense depth of their ancestral past, it is probably the mere fact that evolution had not equipped the female termite with facilities for storing sperm and that she was therefore in need of a constant male presence. As it did for human beings, monogamy proved a simple and elegant solution for this female deficiency. The very fact that in the more modern types of colonial insects evolution plumped for the sperm-storage process, where the male is barely tolerated and often allowed to live only long enough to perform his one little useful act, is proof that as a reproductive technique evolution is not particularly fond of monogamy.

6. Bad Flies and Pathetic Ones

We know a good deal about the sexual life of the honeybee, because she is an agricultural partner for us. For entirely different reasons, we have recently found out a lot about the mosquito and other pests—because we want to destroy them. If we are, for instance, to adopt stratagems of more subtlety and efficiency than a blast of chemicals that blows up the house to kill the villain in the cellar, we must find out how to prevent them from breeding, and to accomplish this, we must know their breeding habits. The precise studies of Jack Calvard Jones of the University of Maryland on the yellow-fever-carrying mosquito (*Aedes aegypti*) is virtually a modern classic. By the time of this study, spectacular success had been obtained in eradicating the screwworm fly by sterilizing the males with radiation and releasing them into wild populations in sufficiently saturating numbers to cause a steep drop in population. But the same ploy did not work with mosquitoes. Laboratory success was not duplicated under natural conditions. This stimulated a systematic review of *Aedes'* sex life, which is typical of nearly all mosquitoes.

In the larvae the antennae are enclosed within two small sacs in the head. If these sacs are large and well developed, the larvae will become males. The pupae, which develop from the larvae, look something like commas but in two days they shed their skin to become the adult, or imago. Sex difference is then immediately apparent. The male is smaller with large, heavy antennae and he dines only on plant nectar and water. The female has an insatiable thirst for animal blood and has the equipment to get it, while the male lacks cutting tools on his proboscis. It is important to note that in general the female mosquitoes must feed on blood in order to develop eggs. With enough blood they will lay a few eggs even if they do not find a male to impregnate them. Presumably the race might barely survive even without males. But for a lot of eggs they need a lot of blood and a lot of semen. The blood meal starts a chain of nervous and hormone-secretion events that results in swelling of the ovaries and the growth of eggs. Right after a gory meal, the female is not particularly attractive to the male but at any other time she lures him by buzzing her wings. The male will pursue sounds of this frequency (300–800 per second) even if they come from a tuning fork. The male's aggression consists of clasping. (He will clasp the cloth walls of a cage if a tuning fork is sounded outside the walls, and he may even seize a male mosquito.)

An extraordinarily complex anatomical arrangement in both male and female is necessary to make possible the events that follow the clasping. Upon achieving sexual maturity, the male's rear end has already undergone a drastic change. The last two segments have rotated and within twenty hours have made a full 180° turn, a permanent torsion that is necessary for him (and in fact all flylike insects) to be able to copulate. On reaching the object of his affections the male mosquito first seizes her back with his legs, the tips of which are equipped with little grappling hooks. Then he swings around so that he can hang face-to-face below her. His claspers grasp her cerci (two hairy paddle-shaped plates above the anus). This action causes the tonguelike platelet under her anus to move up and expose the edges of the vagina. The male then uses his anal hooks to pull the female's genitals toward him. He extends his penis so that the teeth at its tip mesh with a dorsal valve in the vagina, enlarging the opening into the bursa, or sac which is the first to receive the sperm. At that instant the penis discharges a large spurt of seminal fluid (about 2,000 sperm) into the bursa; after this intricate engineering accomplishment the pair quickly separate, the male commonly getting a parting kick by the female's hind legs. The whole act has taken about fifteen seconds.

The rear end of the male mosquito alone, immediately after being severed from the rest, can effectively inseminate a female. Moreover the rear end of an unfertilized female alone will cause the male to extend his penis and ejaculate. When, however, a female has been fertilized, she has had it for life. The sperm are transferred from the bursa to a storage sac, where they will be used when needed for fertilizing her eggs. Males will not attempt to seduce a resting female who has already been fertilized, but if she is in flight, they are still irresistibly drawn to her, whatever her condition. The male can inseminate five to six females in rapid succession. When the fury is upon him he may copulate with many more—as many as thirty within thirty minutes—but the supply of seminal fluid is exhausted after the first half-dozen. After that the females represent dry runs.

The fertilized female lays a great many more eggs than the unfertilized, probably as the result of the absorption into her body of the material from the male's accessory glands that remains behind in her bursa after migration of the sperm to the storage pouch.* It appears, however, that male accessory gland substance, in a steady diet, may have precisely the opposite effect. George B. Crafts, Jr., of the University of Notre Dame, implanted male accessory glands in virgin females of *Aedes aegypti*. When exposed to males, these females copulated eagerly but were not inseminated; they remained sterile for life and did not even produce

---

* Margaret Sanger, the well-known proponent of birth control, always claimed rather mystically that in man the seminal fluid contains material which can be absorbed in the woman's blood and which benefits her, even if actual fertilization has not been achieved. This effect has, to my knowledge, never been verified.

parthenogenetic offspring. Since the normal female will produce viable eggs, even without insemination, it would seem reasonable to focus attention on female rather than male sterilization. Crafts has found that the extract of glands from one male is sufficient to sterilize sixty-four females, in twelve different species, including such disease vectors as *Anopheles, Aedes, Culex,* etc. Even when the glandular substance of a male of one species is transplanted to the female of another species, some degree of sterilization is observed.

Hannes Laven of Johannes Gutenberg University in Mainz has discovered that the cytoplasm of the germ cells of mosquitoes of various strains may be incompatible. This represents the preservation of species type where the egg cells of one race can no longer accept the sperm cells of another and infertility ensues. In Okpo in Burma the mosquitoes transmit bilharziasis, an extremely grave oriental affliction which often leads to elephantiasis. Laven found that a strain from Fresno, California, would mate with the Burmese females but the pairings would be unfruitful. When he released 5,000 strong Fresno males per day in Okpo, they proved quicker and stronger than the native males and mated with all available Okpo females. Since the female mosquito always draws on the sperm from the first mating, even subsequent mating with Okpo males still gave no fertile eggs.

Sophisticated chemical means of sterilizing or otherwise affecting the life cycle of insect pests have become the object of intensive research within the last decade. Of course, one can also concentrate on infant-mosquito killing, and this is exactly what we do when we spray oil on summer ponds or ditches. Some species arrange the eggs in little rafts. Some lay them during flight over the water, like dive bombers. One species lays the eggs on her hind feet, then dips them into the water. The females are very choosy and won't lay until they find the right spot. Invariably all mosquitoes lay in the daytime, mostly between two and three o'clock, probably because some hormone mechanism is activated by midday light. Mainly the mothers prefer fresh water, although some like it brackish. The hairs on their legs are sensitive to salinity. It is interesting that the sex of the larvae in certain strains can be completely reversed merely by changing the water temperature at certain periods.

While we have seen that the female mosquito needs fresh blood to stimulate her sex glands, some of the carnivorous males of the Diptera order (flies) need the excitement (or nourishment) of a kill to promote the libido. The male dung fly kills and eats a smaller insect (perhaps a housefly), then he is ready for love. The corpus allatum (a hormone-producing gland) becomes enlarged, the accessory cells of the ejaculatory ducts ripen and the testicles reach their full length. Laboratory males raised on sugar and water never attempt to copulate with females. If presented with them, they first ignore them, then after a few days they *eat* them. If a live housefly is substituted for the sugar diet, the males feel so horny that they will attempt to rape another male fly or even a button.

In many flies we are taught by evolution that the object of growing up is to copulate and promptly die. This is true of both males and females among the *Ephemeridae,* who as sexually mature insects live for only a few hours. Yet in the larval state they have spent six months, a year or several years, depending on the species, living in water and feeding on all kinds of vegetable groceries. The mature fly of this family does not eat and most of its rather roughly sketched organs are without function. (That this is a relatively recent trend in evolution is shown by the fact that they should have any alimentary organs at all.) The ultimate pathos of these winged sex cells is that very few of them even succeed in copulating. Millions of these dead small flies can frequently be seen covering the summer fields. The two-hour sexual dance has brought fulfillment to at the most 1 per cent of the dancers.

Ritual dances are also popular among the more long-lived Empidae (dancing flies) as is the custom of the bridal gift and of the wedding supper. In several species of empid flies, the male presents the female, immediately before copulation, with a slaughtered insect. While she is eating this morsel he can mate her without fear of being eaten himself. (The male is smaller and less ferocious than the female.) This feast is even more ritualistic in the *Hyperborean emphis,* in which the female no longer eats flies *except* at her wedding feast. In a North American species the male spins a white balloon that attracts the female, as well it should, since it contains a few small insects, which she eats before copulation. In other species (there are 3,000 species in this great family) the males dance above the surface of the water rather like midges, but some of them spin delicate veils which they trail after them through the air, apparently to attract females.

Egg production is often a race between the layers and the egg-eaters. In some insect species the worst offender is the father. A male cricket will eat his wife's eggs while she is hunting. (It is probably to prevent such infanticide that many insect females kill their mates during or after copulation. One of the more elegant ways of preventing the father from eating his children has been invented by the great diving beetle. In the pond the female holds her mate tightly while carefully laying and cementing a mass of eggs to the horny shell of his back. He will guard the family because he cannot reach the eggs.)

The egg-producing glands of the midges in midsummer often develop faster than the rest of their bodies. Quite frequently before they can escape as adults from the pond where they were born, their bodies burst open, flooding larvae into the water. One way of coping with the tremendous consumption of eggs by predators or by members of the family is to produce even more tremendously and hope for the best. The so-called stick insects pump out half a million eggs in one afternoon and one can hear a continuous pattering on the dried leaves below their parturitional perches.

As if to point to the difference between insects of ancient lineage and the modern trend toward a short, unhappy life, the dragonflies copulate regularly and in a majestic way—about like spiders—just as they did 250 million years ago when they were as big as geese among the horsetail forests of the Carboniferous Age. (It is possible that all land arthropods at first used the gonopod technique inherited from their remote marine forebears.) The male dragonfly has a bladderlike thickening at the second and third abdominal segments, consisting of a seminal vesicle and a semen transmitter. However, the testicles are far back, beside the ninth abdominal ring, as with most insects. Therefore he must follow much the same procedure as the millipede who charges his gonopods and the spider who fills his palps with semen. He must double up his belly and bring it into contact with the third segment to discharge semen into the seminal vesicle. Now he is ready for his mate. The male seizes his partner with the claspers at the abdominal end of the body. The female twists her body until her vagina touches the male's second abdominal segment. There the semen meanwhile has flowed from this vesicle into the intromittent organ. As soon as the female's body touches this organ it straightens up like a true penis and glides into the vagina. Thus joined, the pair dart off in this peculiar position to an appropriate water plant. There the female protrudes her ovipositor and lays a single fertilized egg in each of the plant stems. She may go down the stem of the plant right to the bottom of the pond, dragging the proud male along with her. (Dragonflies diving carry so much air in their hairy bodies that they can breathe underwater for a short time without drowning.) One notes that sexual equivalence prevails here as among the equally ancient termites and perhaps for the same reason. The female not only cannot preserve semen presented to her but she insists immediately on placing the freshly fertilized eggs in plants.

We do not have space to review all the variations on a basic theme presented by the enormous class of insects. It is worthwhile emphasizing once again, however, that certain generalizations repeat themselves over and over. In a carnivorous solitary hunting species, the more advanced it is in the process of evolution, the more likely the female is to cannibalize the male. Thus while the very ancient dragonfly lives in sex equality, the more modern mantis female (a hunter of unexampled ferocity) treats the male as a combination of penis and food. In the glass terrarium (a zoo for insects) the mating of praying mantises can only be accomplished if the female's terrible forearms are tied before she is introduced to the male. This poor fellow, hypnotized and absorbed in his vital functions, can be seen holding his witch in a tight embrace. But when one looks closer, one sees that he has no head, no neck and hardly a body. With her muzzle turned over her shoulder, she continues to chomp on what remains. Yet the male will not let go until the abdomen, the seat of his procreative organs, is finally chewed out. In the course of two weeks the female mantis will mate with and eat about seven husbands. This cannibalistic habit is common among ground beetles and ant lions. The fertilized ant lion not only devours her husband but then proceeds, without sexual excuse, to eat any other male she can catch. Presumably the end of this series involving terms of increasing female domination is the disappearance of the male entirely, as in the white-fringed beetle, where females produce parthenogenetically without any mating. This appears to be a relatively modern animal.

7. Underwater Sex

Let us at last review the sex habits of the phylum to which we belong—the vertebrates. Let us not think of this phylum as a modern innovation, since its earliest familiar representatives—the fishes—go back in time before the advent of land insects or even land plants. In this great ancient class we not unexpectedly see all manner of sex phenomena, from parthenogenesis to species in which the male not only takes care of the eggs but prevents the female from eating them.

Most curiously the fishes of more ancient lineage reproduce in a manner most similar to that of mammals. The cyclostomes (literally "round mouths"), represented today only by the lampreys and the hagfishes, existed some 400 million years ago, at the beginning of the Silurian, in shallow bays. They copulate much in the manner of humans. In the temperate and sub-arctic seas, the young of the lampreys are so distinct that they have a name of their own—ammocoetes. Right after birth they burrow down headfirst into the mud floor of streams, make U-turns and come up with their heads at the surface of the mud. For two or three years before they change into adults, they are blind and sedentary. Some early cyclostomes were heavily armored and the first jawed fishes, probably similar to the present elasmobranches, such as sharks and rays, developed from them. The males of most of these later species are equipped with conical auxiliary organs which are vaguely similar to the gonopods, or false penises, of squid, octopuses, crustaceans and spiders. Originally they were pelvic fins but began to play a more specialized part than the true penis of the cyclostomes. In copulation the modified fin is poked into the female cloaca in order to widen it. When his mate is sufficiently prepared by this roughing up the male embraces her whole body like a huge ring and extrudes a tiny penislike organ from his own cloaca, thrusts it into the female vagina and releases his sperm. Thus the female selachians are mated and internally fertilized in a fashion resembling in part the spiders and in part the land vertebrates. The course of development of the offspring varies from one species to another. Many sharks hang horny egg capsules on seaweed stalks or coral branches. Often the case is draped with curious tassels and, after hatching, is washed up on the beaches to become a souvenir for beachcombers, who seldom realize what they are. In some sharks the young are not born as little fishes but in fertilized eggs, like birds. In general this corresponds to a lower number of eggs laid than when the eggs, as in the case of most fishes, must be fertilized in the water rather than in the mother's body. However, in both the viviparous and "ovoviviparous" species, where internal fertilization takes place, the embyro does not, as in placental mammals, develop in a uterus. Instead, the process takes place in the oviduct or in an internal incubatory pocket of this duct.

All such techniques are discarded with the evolution of the true bony fishes (teleosts), where the sexual invention consisted of the laying of enormous numbers of eggs which then had to be fertilized outside by milt from the male. This is, in effect, a victory of mathematics over selectivity. Although little enough is known about the possibility, it is quite obvious that when a female of one species dumps a million or so eggs around it is conceivable that the spermatozoa of a closely related species or race might fertilize them. Hybridization might then become rather common and *prevent* rather than favor the evolution of new species. Evolution does not like this. This may be one of the reasons why the taxonomy of teleost fishes is in such a state of confusion and it may also explain the insistence on the part of certain proud fishes to spawn, even if it kills them, in a selected place—usually their birthplace. It may explain why, considering the enormous time that fishes have been on the planet, there are relatively so few species, compared, for example, with insects.

Some cases of hermaphroditism are known in the fishes. Two groups, the dentate perch and the curling bream, are found with both fully developed ovaries and active testicles. The hermaphrodite perch have been seen to lay eggs and then release a cloud of sperm over them. But this is an unusual perversion. Although hermaphroditism occurs now and then among vertebrates, self-fertilization in the free state is probably unknown. In the gilthead the male organs develop first, then the testes begin to atrophy and the ovaries become active. A two-year-old gilthead is a male but a three-year-old is a female. Among the rockfish, some of the species are thought to be capable of cross-fertilization, giving rise to local hybrids—a process strongly disapproved of by evolution, which retaliates by making most of the hybrids sterile. A still more unusual reproductive technique is used by the teleost fish known as the Amazon molly, found in the streams of northeastern Mexico and Texas. There is only one sex—female, of course. But the type of parthenogenesis used is quite weird and indicates perhaps that this fish is undergoing a transition period in its phylogenetic history. The females use the sperm of other species to make their eggs hatch. True fertilization is not involved and no hybrids are produced. The female is using alien sperm in the same way that Jacques Loeb used weak acid or ether. The young are all females and in appearance, of course, take after their mothers. Some recently discovered fishes of the genus *Poeciliopsis* in northwestern New Mexico may be seized with this same rage to get away from the male sex. There are two types of females in this group, those which produce both male and female young and those which pro-

duce only daughters. The latter are probably guilty of parthenogenesis.

This may be viewed in philosophical terms as a way for fishes to
escape the hybridization trap which is implicit in external fertilization. There are more interesting and genial ways of doing it. One is
to deposit the eggs in the male's body and let him do the fertilization as well as the hatching. This we see in the pipefishes and the
sea horses. The females punctiliously lay their eggs in a pouch on
the belly of the male, where they are fertilized and remain until
they are able to swim out. At mating time both the male and female
pipefishes, swimming vertically in little S-shapes, drift past each
other, then with the S's reversed one upon the other, crossing in
three places, briefly intertwine. While he caresses her snout, she
deposits a dozen or so eggs into the opening of his pouch and simultaneously he fertilizes them. For marital relations of this kind
there must be immediate sex recognition. The male pipefish develops a yellow throat at spawning time. This is only a tiny spot of
yellow but it is enough to lure the color-visioned female. The noted
ethologist Nikolaas Tinbergen could even persuade a pipefish female at this season to follow, with intense sexual excitement, a
simple yellow marble, which did not in the least resemble a male
pipefish.

There is another, quite extreme method of avoiding hybridism
which is used only by fishes who live in the lightless abysses of the
sea and, as far as we know, only by one family of them. It is a wild
story. At the turn of the century ichthyologists recognized two distinct families of deep-sea angler fishes, the Ceratiidae and the
Aceratiidae. C. Tate Regan of the British Museum discovered one
of the Aceratiidae hanging on to the side of a female ceratiid. The
subsequent verification of many similar pairings and the fact that
no females were found in the aceratiids led to the conclusion that
the aceratiids are simply the males among the ceratiids and
that these are not two families but one species. The tiny males
fertilize the eggs as they emerge from the gigantic female. Although the relationship is close to parasitism, especially since the
male's digestive system is degenerate, it is believed instead to be a

kind of prolonged mating. The great females have "fishing rods" tipped with luminous bulbs attached to the front of the head. This is evidently to attract the pusillanimous male, since at the black depths they live the two sexes might unwittingly pass within a few inches of each other. The facts that the male's pallid luminous organs are embedded in his skin and that his alimentary system is degenerate suggest that this whole sexual technique is a relatively new evolutionary trend, degrading from a more conservative division of sexual power. The next stop obviously is parthenogenesis. Then the portly female can get rid of all her onerous electrical illuminating equipment and can enjoy the lonely splendor of aqueous nothingness.

There is a still more subtle and diverting (perhaps even delusive) method for fishes to avoid the trap of hybridization. This is territorialism. I feel that such authors as Konrad Lorenz and Robert Ardrey have fallaciously assumed that behavior of this sort represents a more profound instinct than reproduction itself. They appear to believe that the fierce property sense of cichlid fishes, for example, is behavioristically parallel to the territorial wars of nations or the racist politics of real estate brokers. Leaving aside the vast number of schooling fishes who have no territorial sense at all and whose only concern with individual distance is to avoid gulping too much carbon dioxide or other body wastes from the fish in front, it seems obvious that the "territorial imperative" in fishes is evolution's way of avoiding hybridization. If you have a place to lay eggs, the place is defended against other males because the other male may be alien. (The danger is not from males of other species but from the same species or one closely enough related so that fertilization could result—but still an alien. This is why *all* similar males are enemies at spawning time. Much has been made by the "territorialistic" authors of quirks of behavior such as the fact that the male swordtails (tropical fish), when the water is cooled to a certain degree, lose all interest in females but will continue their struggle for dominance. This action in no way proves that the fish has some mystical property sense, but simply that his way of life is framed around prospective parenthood and the need for protection of the viability and purity of future eggs.*

Among some very parental fishes such as the wrasse, the male and female pair off and remain together for at least a season. They build a nest like birds. The laying of eggs is accompanied by a charming nuptial dance. The two lift their bodies into nearly vertical position over the nest, opening and closing their mouths and waving their pectoral fins. During the dance the spawn of the female and the milt of the male are wafted down, covering the bottom of the nest. The couple never leaves the vicinity of the home until hatching and rearing are completed.

Among the family-conscious fishes are, as might be expected, some of the fiercest little fighters in the sea. The fighting fish, made famous in history by Siamese breeding and gambling, have been carefully scrutinized by ethologists, since their small size and activism make them ideal for observation and for writing books about. As Lorenz has emphasized, the fighting fish recognizes sex not simply by the appearance of the partner but by watching the way it responds to ritualized dancing movements. The male must never be allowed to glimpse the female's flank, for standing broadside is the ritual posture of masculinity and invites butting and biting. The posture of the bodies in spawning is such that the eggs as they sink are bound to drift by the directed head of the male. He releases the female (whom he has been clasping to squeeze her eggs out), glides in pursuit of the eggs, gathers them in his mouth and blows them up, be-spittled, into a floating nest. He is in somewhat of a hurry because the female, awakening from her trance of delicious catharsis, would like to eat the eggs. After ten or fifteen matings, when all the eggs have been expelled and properly stored in the floating raft of spittle, he forbids the female from even approaching the nest. (This combination of male aggressiveness and fatherliness is quite common among the vertebrate animals—among wolves, for example, although lack of maternal concern is mostly confined to creatures that lay externally fertilized eggs.)

* A more important instinctual reason for territorialism, as we shall see later, is to reduce species population explosions.

In the cichlid fishes Lorenz derives an ethologist's fond gusto from the difference in behavior of the sexes. If the male fish has the slightest fear or confusion about the posture of the prospective mate, his sexuality is extinguished. But if the female is so little inspired with proper awe of the male that her own, less fiery aggressiveness is not entirely suppressed, she does not recognize him as a potential husband. The standard female pattern (surely a cliché in the animal kingdom) is coyness and pseudo-flight. Since the male can only pair with an awe-inspired female and the female only with a dominant male, at least the trivial goal of not wasting time on members of the same sex has been attained. But Lorenz seems to see a still more subtle deployment and redirection of aggressiveness. Suppose the female in a rebellious mood assumes the broadside position. (This is equivalent to a woman throwing a cup of coffee in her husband's face.) The male assumes the same dread position, tail beating, glands pumping, and rushes at his mate —yet at the last instant he misses her and attacks another male cichlid, who happens inoffensively to be in the neighborhood. Lorenz finds this *redirection* of hostility to be much more chivalrous than the converse process in man, who, angry at his boss, takes it out on his wife when he gets home. The analogy rings false. The better analogy is a riled-up couple who take out their meanness on some neighbor who indirectly tries to be a peacemaker.

The bellicose little sticklebacks have also been aquarium favorites. It is only when he has built his nest that the male stickleback allows himself to become sexually excited and aggressive. When two males are building nests in the same tank they will almost invariably come to blows and the one farthest from his own nest will invariably lose the battle. Because of the toughness of their skin, serious wounds are seldom incurred, but in the course of a season the stronger stickleback may harry the other male to death. (Death by stress-produced insanity is a common phenomenon in the animal world. Insanity for most animals is simply a quick way to die and the fact that it can be infallibly induced by men's manipulations represents one of the cruelest forms of mastery that we have over other animals.)

whole length (lungfish, sturgeon, garpike, frog and mud puppy); or the gonads may take over the front part of the duct, leaving the kidney only the back part; or the kidney may be forced to develop a duct wholly independent of the archinephritic duct, in which case the pattern in the female even within the same species does not necessarily conform with that in the male (sharks and some salamanders). Finally, the kidney may abandon the fight in favor of the testicle, when the archinephritic duct becomes the spermatic duct, which carries the sperm from the testicle to the seminal vesicle for storage, and in the last case the kidney has to build a new duct of its own—the true ureter as it appears in the reptiles, birds and mammals. In any and all cases in vertebrates, however, there is, if not actual rivalry, undue intimacy between reproductive and excretory functions. Although this may not annoy a turtle, a dog or a bird, it is because these vertebrates do not make a moral distinction between defecation and copulation. In man the intimacy becomes truly disturbing and in certain cycles of history has contributed a major drive in the outlawing of sex, at least from the minds of "holy men" (i.e., men who are regarded as too refined to do anything with their penises except to urinate through them with their eyes closed). The disturbance may take another tack. In the extremely primitive Trobriand Islanders, although sex is indulged in exuberantly, it is not thought to have anything to do with fatherhood, but on the other hand, defecation is a secret, extremely humiliating act and, in fact, food is not looked upon as nutritional. To the Trobrianders, anal sodomy is reprehensible, not for the complex reasons that Western culture abhors it, but for the simple fact that it means "ejaculating through feces." (The direct translation of the Melanesian phrase would hardly be so pedantic, but one of the strangest linguistic effects of the "dirtiness" of sex in Western civilizations has been the development of a "secret" language, which, although commonly used in the discourse of men, is supposed, quite fallaciously, to be unknown to ladies and to men of the cloth. Thus the Anglo-Saxon equivalent of the respectable Latin word *cunnus,* which in turn can be traced back to a most ancient Indo-European root, is even now allowable only in novels by John Updike and other bold and naughty authors. The proof that sex is regarded as dirty because of its close association with acts of bodily excretion is that the common ancient words for these excretions are also regarded as within the confines of the secret or obscene language. That the "four-letter words" of graffiti and of the discourse of the common man should be held in some way to be reprehensible is one of the most unreasonable phases in man's semantic history. Also the fact that the world is full of earnest people who preach against the idea that "sex is dirty" but still recoil in horror at "four-letter words" simply attests to the fact that in their hearts they still believe that sex *is* dirty. They cannot have it both ways.)

9. Sex Halfway to the Top

Evolution, in a quandary as to how to develop a vertebrate animal that could enjoy the new richness of terrestrial vegetation, fumbled around with the amphibians, giving them an ability to breathe in the air and navigate on the land but restricting their egg laying to the water. The amphibians were neither here nor there, not only in the sense of habitat but in sexual capacity. True internal fertilization is not achieved by any of them, yet their courting antics and copulatory techniques run from the casual and sluggish to the passionate and brutal. As a phylogenetic class, they represent a way station. For example, no vertebrate above the amphibians has a larval stage. Among the newts and salamanders, who look deceptively like reptiles but are not nearly so advanced, a curious difference in sexual approach may be observed. The female salamander may do the propositioning. In the water she may move purposefully toward one of the males. He will waddle out on land, the female following. Under her watchful eye, he dutifully contracts his body and deposits a conical spermatophore wrapped in jelly on the ground. The female presses her cloaca upon the cone and allows the sperm to enter her body. In some cases she may thus absorb the entire packet of semen. If she changes her mind, she may eat it instead. In a more passionate species, a male red newt will seize his mate underwater, holding her with his feet and writhing his body violently while now and then pushing his head against hers. His tail will lash and lock with hers and the two may roll over and over in the mud. Although the observer might pardonably mistake all this for an act of copulation, it is nothing of the sort. It is courtship or heavy necking. Shortly after dawn the two separate, the male to deposit his sperm on submerged leaves, the female to wait for him to finish and then to suck the sperm cells into her body through the cloaca, at the base of her tail.

The frogs and toads, too, are physically unable to consummate a love affair in the conventional vertebrate manner but courtship may be noisy and the squeezing of eggs from the female may look like an act of violent rape. There are species, however, in which the fertilization is a sort of jolly affair engaged in communally by the males and in which care of the eggs and larvae is the father's business. When a female of one of these species has laid her twenty to thirty eggs, several males gather round the spawn, fertilize it and guard it for two weeks until tadpoles begin to move inside the eggs. At this point the males try to swallow as many eggs as possible, but not to eat them. They do not allow the eggs to slide into the stomach, but into a large throat sac which hangs from the chin to the thigh. There the spawn is nourished by the father's tissue as sedentary tadpoles and they stay there until metamorphosis occurs; then finally they hop out of the father's mouth. Another less efficient but patient effort is seen among some tree frogs and tree toads, where the females usually stick their fertilized eggs to the males' backs. If these particular tadpoles are dislodged prematurely, they find themselves helpless in the water. The male of the European *accoucheur* toad serves both as a midwife and a kind of perambulating kindergarten. He draws the eggs, which come in long strips, from the female's cloaca, fertilizes them, then winds the strings in figure eights around his hind legs. He is willing to accommodate the offspring of several wives in this way until he finds himself with eggs strung up to his thighs. (It is in cases such as this, where the larvae would otherwise be a small, helpless fish, that evolution has developed a brilliant role for fathers. In man, evolution, instead of such intimate physical rearing, has chosen to modify the father's behavior in comparison with other primates so that primitive man provides food for the mother, although cultural deviations often have modified this archetypical role, as in the practice of *couvade*, in which at the critical period the man is whimpering in bed, pretending ritualistically to be a woman or a baby.)

The normal sex act among most frogs is by no means so gentle. The rough stuff is performed by the male not, however, in order to insert a non-existent penis but to force her to disgorge her eggs. He will climb upon her and with such brutal pressure that his thumbs may bore deep into her abdomen. The embrace itself does not bring release of male sperm. Often he must sit for days upon the female and sometimes the couple hops in tight embrace over quite a track before she condescends to seek out a spawning pool. As Lazzaro Spallanzani showed in the eighteenth century with his famous experiment of putting pants on bullfrogs, even this dominating male must wait until the spawn comes welling out in order to release his sperm at the right moment. (Spallanzani found sperm-saturated pants only *after* this right moment.) The prolonged and furious embrace finally reaches its climax in the eruptive discharge of the sex cells of both, followed by the exhaustion that is usually associated in the higher vertebrates with true orgasm.

Perhaps the most ingenious ravaging is performed by the male Dactylethra (the clawed frog of Africa, in which the males are smaller than the females). After he has embraced his selected spouse, the male spins her around several times until she loses consciousness. He then proceeds with the egg squeezing—an obvious act of rape, nevertheless.*

---

* It was in 1940 that the female Dactylethra was found to be ideal for diagnosing human pregnancy in its early stages. If the urine of the pregnant woman is injected into the cloaca of the female frog, hormones in the urine cause the frogs to lay eggs within a few hours. This was later found to be true in all species of frogs, and because of its rapidity this replaced the old rabbit test.

Among the marsupial frogs of the American tropics, the male offers obstetrical assistance but the female raises her children in a broad pouch on her back. The Surinam toads embrace in normal frog-toad fashion, the male mounting the female, gripping her tightly and waiting for the eggs to emerge so he can fertilize them. But this animal is bound to be thorough. The female's cloaca finally pushes itself out as a tubelike sac, bent upward. The male seizes the tube, still swollen with spawn, pushes it beneath him, squeezes eggs out against his abdomen, fertilizes them and spreads the entire spawn over the female's back.

There is even in evolution's hesitancy about frogs the question of when a young frog knows it is either male or female. A high percentage of individuals are able to go either way, although these rather undecided young usually end up as males. If they are castrated the ovarian characteristics develop further and instead of becoming eunuchs, they turn into full-fledged females. Unfavorable conditions of environment and diet cause a swing to males.

10. The Invention of the Vertebrate Penis

When we advance to vertebrates that lay their eggs on the land (the reptiles) evolution is seen to have decided also on internal fertilization. The penis is invented by reptiles, rejected by most birds and rediscovered by mammals. Neither reptiles nor birds developed the clitoris, which is a mammalian specialty. The reptile penis can be a frightening thing, especially among lizards. It is often covered with spines, warts or hooks. The male uses the hooks to secure himself inside the female's body. Two paired lizards can scarcely be separated and when a snake, interrupted in the act of coitus, flees, it drags its partner along by the anus.

One reptile, left stranded in Australia and New Zealand by evolution, failed to develop a penis. This is the tuatara, who mates like birds, by contact of the cloacas.

In both lizards and snakes the penises are paired and housed in the base of the tail. Since normally the penis is not seen, it is difficult if not impossible in most snakes and many lizards to tell the sex at a glance. In some lizard species the males display by a throat fan or a dewlap or by a patch of color. That color vision must be possessed (perhaps only by the females) is shown by the abject behavior of the large, fierce female *Lacerta* before a male one third her size, who signals his masculinity only by faint blue shades on his throat, analogous (as Lorenz points out) to the down on a boy's face. This aggressive female, who is used to slashing and kicking around members of her own sex, literally falls on her belly before the male no matter how weak or how young he is. It is true that lizard males, perhaps having invented the true vertebrate penis, throw their weight around a good bit, but there is no rape. A good deal of biting takes place on the part of the male, but the female is always free to run away. If she stays and tolerates the bites, she is signaling her surrender.

In the reptiles evolution has introduced a theme that was found interesting and profitable in invertebrates—the ability to store sperm indefinitely. Some female snakes have been seen to lay fertile eggs five years after their last copulation with a male. Another reptile theme that is their least endearing quality is the nearly complete absence of parental concern. This probably comes from the fact that when they are viviparous they are self-reliant to the extent that they need little help and when they are hatched from eggs, the hatchlings are precocial. (Precociality, as in birds, means that the freshly hatched young are self-reliant.) Most snakes and some lizards can live for a year without any food after being born or hatched. Still a third feature of most lizards is the development of territorial aggressiveness with sexual maturity. This is by no means confined to the male. In the case of the very resourceful Cuban lizard, who is polygamous and rules a harem of three or four females, the male delegates the defense of the territory to his wives. Since he indicates a most goatish interest in every passing female, the harem responds with extreme vigilance. The female fence lizard defends her property against even would-be suitors, until her glands tell her it is time to relax and enjoy life. The chameleon female also puts up a sign: "No trespassing. This means males, too." The male hangs around nevertheless, displaying by puffing up his throat, which has a yellow mark. Far from being seductive to her, this infuriates her all the more. But when mating time comes, the yellow fades. She admits him. Such territorial boisterousness, I am convinced, is not connected with an instinct for the possession of real estate but for the *future* peace of her eggs. (It is a sort of premature motherliness. That the degree of territorial aggressiveness seems to depend on the essential safety of the eggs is shown by the fact that reptiles who deeply bury their eggs, such as marine turtles, show neither territorialism nor parental concern once the eggs are laid.)

Evolution, in making the step to egg laying on land, did not much care whether a given species of lizard or snake bore its young live or in eggs. Eggs are laid by a bare majority of snakes, the ratio of egg-laying to live-bearing species in the United States being three to two. However, a live-bearer may be very closely related to an egg-layer. The occurrence is so inconsistent that the birth habit is not even used in the classification of snakes. Some of the live-bearers, such as the skink lizard, have even developed a primitive placenta. The true chameleons, although they live in trees, descend to the ground to lay. The geckos on the other hand make arboreal nests, like birds. Laying eggs in termite nests is a popular habit among lizards, since the colony usually keeps itself at a comfortable temperature and the eggs are not acceptable termite food. The lizard identifies her eggs with the tip of her tongue. Nearly all lizards and snakes which hatch in eggs are equipped with an egg tooth; in the gecko it may be double.

There are more obvious reasons for the two penises of a snake than for those of a lizard, since the snake, having no clasping tools, must make the insertion from whichever side seems to be most handy. At rest the snake's penis is turned outside in like a glove finger drawn into the palm of a glove. When in use, the penis is forced out so that the surface that was inside now lies on the outside. Because of the frequent spininess of this surface, a reverse inside-out process is necessary to avoid injury to the female upon withdrawal. In the penises of reptiles, the semen does not move in an internal tube, as in mammals, but in a deep groove in the surface of the penis. The penises of snakes are often mistaken for "legs," forced into view by the cruel country practice of burning snakes alive. Students often take them for legs in the embryo. They are drawn into the tail shortly after hatching or birth.

Although, as mentioned, lizards and snakes would never read a book by a reptilian Dr. Spock, they do have some concern for the unhatched eggs, perhaps having learned instinctively the terrible lesson that befell their mighty ancestral kin the dinosaurs.* Thus the Indian and king cobras pair during the breeding season and take turns guarding their eggs. Two species of pythons are known to increase their body temperature while the eggs are being brooded. But after hatching, the young are on their own.

In the case of the turtle, even the eggs are on their own, simply because the mother assumes she has buried them safely. The laying and burying process is a most impressive performance. A great leatherback in the act of depositing eggs in the sand looks like an animated steam shovel. The sand whips around and she sheds copious tears to protect her eyes. The eggs are so effectively hidden that even a monitor lizard, a doctor of philosophy and his two helpers were unable to find them, in Archie Carr's experience. Buried in clutches of several dozen eggs at a time, the egg mass heats up from the low surface-to-volume ratio effect more than the eggs buried individually. The nest is flask-shaped to avoid cave-ins when the hatching young are emerging from the eggs.

We know little about the mating habits of the great marine turtles. Some male green turtles are known to go to Tortuguero at the time the females are there, but do they go *with* the females or separately? Are their cycles on a two or three year schedule, like the females, or does every mature male go to this reptilian equivalent of Niagara Falls every year? The male turtle or tortoise can mate only if the female is ready and definitely indicates her readiness. This she does by thrusting the hind end of her body with the cloaca partly out of the shell. As a rule a ritualistic quivering dance by the male (of the type noted by the poetic sex maniac D. H. Lawrence) arouses the ardor. She drops to the bottom of the water, extends her tail from the shell and awaits the male. He climbs on her back, arches himself there by his hooked feet and bends his own

* It is regarded as quite probable that the disappearance of the great reptiles was because their eggs were eaten by early mammals.

tail down so he can introduce the penis into the female's cloaca. The pair often stay united for hours. In the case of large marine terrapins, the male may ride on his wife's back for days. Some male turtles have an infallible technique for dealing with frigid females who refuse to "put out." This depends upon the fact that during the mating season the turtles are so fat that they cannot keep their heads, legs and their hindparts all under the shell at the same time. By snapping once or twice at the stubborn female's head or feet, he induces her automatically to protrude the end in which he is now interested. In zoos tortoises frequently refuse to mate, simply because the zoo-keeper does not know enough about their requirements. They have to have room and sand or soil, since the male tortoise in copulation digs his shell a short way into the ground. The usual cement floor provided simply guarantees that no fertilized eggs will be obtained.

11. The Property Singers

Because we are so well acquainted with those types of birds that possess our backyard trees and hedges (the passerines, or perchers—a relatively modern order) we have come to assume that all birds sing a song and that it is a song of territory. Thus Robert Ardrey has maintained that in the birds, as indeed in all living forms, the instinct for territorial possession is deeper than the instinct for reproduction. However, one need not apply universal Freudianism and claim, in contradiction, that *all* animal behavior is based on sex, to differ from Ardrey in certain crucial respects. Actually the way in which any animal allows sex to dominate its life may depend on how long it lives. If one is in a fever to reproduce, like the Ephemeridae, before quick death overtakes one, certainly one's whole adult life is composed entirely of seeking a mate and copulating. But the graylag goose, so fondly studied by Oskar Heinroth and by Lorenz, lives frequently to a hundred years and he may celebrate his ninety-eighth wedding anniversary with the same female, if both are fortunate. Obviously he and she have time for other social patterns related only indirectly to sex, such as the triumph ceremony, the incitement ritual, etc., which are analogous to old people's incessant bridge games, horseshoe pitching or even playing the stock market. And with the solitary carnivorous hunters, such as the eagle and the owl, the business of acquiring hunting skill and the nervous fascination of the hunt itself make overwhelming demands on the birds' time. They cannot be having erotic dreams every hour. The eagle has obviously a different sort of territorial imperative than the robin. He will share his hunting preserve, not with another eagle, but with a raven, who (smart bird that he is) makes sure that his own reconnaissances do not overlap those of the fiercer, stronger bird. Most passerines in fact have no real hunting rights. A single robin does not own all the worms in your lawn. What they are staking out, it seems to me, is the safety of the future eggs which they hope to father. The proof of the relationship between territorialism in the perching birds and their egg laying and egg concern lies in the behavior of the species who assert no real estate equities at all—most noteworthy of which are the cowbirds and the cuckoo. And what is their egg-laying pattern? *They lay their eggs in the nests of other birds.* But before we go further into this matter of territory, let us examine the sexual anatomy of the bird as a vertebrate class.

Perhaps the most spectacular link between the birds and the reptiles is the fact that the most primitive birds, such as the ostrich and the duck, do have penises. Furthermore, the penis is grooved as in the reptiles rather than having an internal tube as in mammals. We saw above that one New Zealand reptile—the tuatara —is unhappily without a penis and copulates simply by contacting the male with the female cloaca. Although this animal might be regarded as a backward reptile (sharing the penis lack of amphibians), it might also be regarded sexually as having jumped ahead to the copulating techniques of the more advanced majority of the birds, in which intercourse is a sort of penis-free sodomy. (Many psychiatrists have assumed rather wildly, it seems to me, that anal sodomy in man has its phylogenetic origin as a hold-over from cloacal animal ancestry in the remote past. However, since the birds represent a profoundly divergent class that never was in our family tree, this would mean that these cloacal tendencies derive from the ancient amphibians.) The normal way for birds to copulate is for the male to stand on the female's back and touch his cloaca to hers, although very rarely it may occur—as among the swifts—in flight. A relatively enormous number of sperm is transferred in this outwardly inefficient-looking union—200 million in the pigeon, four billion in the domestic chicken. There is no relationship whatsoever between frequency of copulation and the number of eggs laid. Since spermatozoa are very sensitive to heat, one might wonder how such a hot-blooded animal as a bird manages to preserve his sperm when the testes, for reasons of aerodynamic efficiency, are located within the body. There are several ways that this may be accomplished. First, we must assume that bird sperm are more heat-resistant than the sperm of other warm-blooded animals, such as man, in which cooling is obtained by maintaining the male seed in an outside container (the scrotum). Fortunately, during the breeding season the testicles of birds may internally migrate until they are in close contact with the abdominal air sacs, which is like moving them over the vent of an air conditioner. It is also the habit of many bird spermatozoa to develop only at night, when there is a drop in body temperature. In some species the storage region of the sperm swells into a cloacal protuberance whose temperature (as in the mammalian scrotum) may be seven degrees Fahrenheit lower than that of the body. This is true, for example, in finches.

In the female bird the ovaries were reduced from the two of the reptiles to one—the left. The right ovary and oviduct dwindle away and, if the working ovary is removed, the residual right organ, instead of assuming its responsibility for carrying on the banner of femaleness, perversely turns into a kind of testicle. Bearing in mind evolution's NASA philosophy of having stand-by organs, why is the bird short-changed on ovaries? The answer, as usual, is so simple and pragmatic that it fairly screams at you. With the streamlined body of a bird, two eggs would be carried so close together (in adjacent ovaries and oviducts) that upon being jolted by a brisk landing on a twig they would crack against each other and be broken. Even in those exceptional cases, such as some species of falcon, where the bird has two active ovaries, an egg develops only in one of them at a time.

As the moment of laying approaches, prolactin hormone from

the pituitary gland stimulates the behavior we know as "broodiness." When a follicle reaches maturity, the outer envelope of cells and blood vessels ruptures. The ovum (yolk) breaks out and heads for the oviduct. This process of ovulation takes place within a quarter of an hour to an hour after the laying of the preceding egg by the chicken and four to five hours in the pigeon. The oviduct is a long, winding tube of assembly-line character through which the ovum passes and in which it acquires layers of albumen, shell membranes, shell and pigment. Curiously enough this assembly line will accept any suitable-sized object and wrap these layers around it. Cork balls have been experimentally substituted for ova, with the result that the bird laid eggs with centers of cork instead of yolk.

Occasionally eggs may develop without fertilization. In turkeys such fatherless chicks are quite likely to occur, for some not well understood reason, after the hen has been vaccinated for fowl pox. Parthenogenesis is especially likely in certain inbred strains. Depending on what you have in mind for the turkey's future, it may or may not be a desirable habit, since all the parthenogenetic turkeys are male, with the normal diploid complement of chromosomes. They are perfectly able to fertilize females. This tendency to produce all males in bird experiments also shows up in hybridization. The turken (turkey-hen cross) is always male as is the "quailen" (a hybrid offspring of the dark Cornish roosters and Japanese quail hens), but, like the mule, these hybrids are sterile.

Some of the glamor of the male bird has been rubbed off in recent research. For example, it was once assumed that special male hormones were responsible for the usual gaudy masculine plumage. The present information points to the precise opposite. The male plumage is neutral and normal. Castrated cocks and drakes, for instance, retain their brilliant colors, but if the ovaries of a hen or pheasant are removed, she grows male plumage at the next molt. A sexless bird ends up with male plumage, while hormones from the ovaries prevent the wild colors and psychedelic feather displays from developing. Evolution obviously had a reason for making the average female bird drab. She needs protective not pompous coloration in performing her usual chore of incubation. The male, having done his job, is more expendable. In fact, the gaudiness of the male and his singing are both examples of sacrifice of the safety of the individual to the benefit of posterity. What is more suicidal in a country of predators than to perch in a prominent position in a spectacular suit of clothes and sing at the top of one's voice? But without this behavior the male would not attract a mate and would not become a father. The peacocks and the male argus pheasant are extreme examples of a degree of sexual dimorphism which has made it actually dangerous to be a male. The large cocks, with their fantastic secondary wing feathers can hardly fly, but they are so attractive to their hens that the number of their progeny is directly proportional to the length of these stupid feathers. When the parental roles of the sexes are perversely reversed, as in the polyandrous Chinese pheasant-tailed jaçana and the red-necked phalarope of Greenland, the female is the brighter-colored; she does the courting, establishes the territory and defends it, while the drab male defends the nest, incubates the eggs and takes care of the young. Evolution is by no means fussy about which sex is concerned with the eggs, once they are laid, but insists that the bird's clothing and behavior be appropriate to its role. When polygamy is the rule, the females are drab egg-incubators but when polyandry is practiced instead, each male is charged with the nest-sitting jobs and the female wears the fancy clothes. This latter condition, although natural enough from evolution's point of view, offends our puritan morality, since a loose woman is supposed to take care of her own bastards and not make every putative father solely responsible for them.

Birds are very particular about choosing a mate within the strain of their ancestry and this is one reason for the relatively rapid evolution of so many species, especially of the modern passerines. Evolution proceeds not simply when a given individual gene undergoes a mutation, but when the mutant genes are isolated within a pool of individuals. Thus evolution is peculiarly rapid when birds colonize small islands, and when they practice sexual selection to the point of inbreeding. If men had mating standards as exacting as those of birds, *Homo* would now consist of a large number of species, mutually infertile, and the converse would also be true. Man's drive for exogamy, based on universal abhorrence of incest, if implanted in birds, would have given us perhaps only a few families of birds in the whole world, dispersed according to feeding habits. Thus we might have one kind of eagle, one kind of hawk, one kind of fruit-eating bird, one kind of fish-catcher, one kind of insectivore, etc., but no diversity of genera and species. The inbreeding of wild birds, in spite of the counteracting effects of driving the young from the nest and the general failure of migrating young to return to the same nest site in the following spring, often proceeds to what we should regard as calamitous incest. Thus father and daughter mating occurs with the junco and the barn swallow. Mother and son mating is observed among barn swallows and tree swallows, while brother and sister marriages are quite popular with the yellow-eyed penguin, the mallard, the downy woodpecker, the great tit, the yellow wagtail, the song sparrow and probably a lot more, where observation under wild conditions is inadequate.

Sexual drives are quite transferable among birds when the glands are active. Although it is difficult to conceive of masturbation among birds, their sexual play may involve the female mounting the male (a trivial diversity, when one remembers that except for a few species like ducks, it is immaterial in the mechanics of the sex act which one of the sexes is on top), females mounting females, males mounting males, males or females copulating with stuffed birds or even with the hand of a bird-keeper. The latter behavior is usually the result of imprinting, when the keeper is the first moving object to have been seen by a precocial hatchling. Birds may even become imprinted on toy locomotives.* A five-foot African shoebill stork in a zoo preferred his keeper, with whom he had fallen in love, to a female provided for him at considerable cost.

---

* Imprinting to *sound* can actually occur when the bird is still in the egg. This is one of the reasons why duck eggs hatched among chicken eggs always result in ducklings perfectly satisfied with their clucking mother.

However, these are psychic perversions which seldom are observed in a natural environment. As emphasized, when serious mating takes place the bird is quite racist and segregationist in its pairing and is against any suspicion of hybridizing. Perhaps the most loose in this respect are certain species of migrating birds, such as ducks with circumpolar traveling habits. Thus up in the arctic tundra a drake from Madagascar may date a duck from Bolivia and this may result in some semi-hybridizing. In addition to the inborn selectivity of a bird's mating choice, the sex glands of different but related species often mature at separate times, providing a seasonal barrier to cross-breeding. The finicky, even cruel intolerance of birds to those that don't look as if they lived on the right side of the tracks is seen in their treatment of the occasional albino, who is always attacked and thus rarely survives to maturity. Cases of normally monogamous birds are reported in which, due to some acquired deformity, the marriage broke up. Thus the husband of a long-mated pair of ringed plovers returned hopefully to the spring nesting site with one foot missing. His wife immediately abandoned him.

The mate must not only be free of deformities but must show the marks of the race and of the sex. Since birds are eye-minded, odor does not play its usual role. Male and female flickers are colored alike, except for a pair of barely perceptible moustache marks on the male's cheeks. When the female is painted with an artificial moustache, the male attacks her as a rival. A mere tuft of red feathers placed in a robin's territory during the fighting and breeding season will cause him to go into a tantrum of rage, while an entire stuffed robin colored brown, like an immature bird, is ignored. The sexual habits of the lovebirds, which occur in nine species of *Agapornis,* have been patiently studied by ornithologists. Here pair formation, as is not uncommonly the case, occurs before maturity, yet it lasts for life. For so serious a project the birds, once having spotted the barely perceptible markings of sex and species, take surprisingly little time to form their partnerships. They test each other by attempting to preen mutually and quickly discover by this mild petting whether they are compatible. It is only after sexual maturity has arrived that the male member of this child marriage has a rough time. Among all the species the female professes indifference and even hostility to her young husband's advances, which consist of such patterned behavior as "switch-sidling" and "squeak-twitterings." The male, in the anguish of his desire, sometimes gets a sharp peck on the foot for his trouble. He is constantly scratching his head with his foot, a universal sign of frustration. Things get a little warmer when the stage of court-ship feeding (the transfer of regurgitated food to the lover), which is common to all species, arrives. In the more primitive types the female often offers such food to the male, but in the advanced species it is always the male who gives. Finally the females of most lovebird species show a "maybe-yes" mood by the subtle adjust-ment of their plumage, especially the head feathers. The more she fluffs, the more encouragement the male assumes. At length she will brazenly solicit copulation by leaning forward and raising her head and tail. For an evolutionary reason, the females of the more primitive species don't fluff, since they are obviously different in appearance from the males. It is only in the advanced species, whose male and female look alike, that some supplementary ges-ture is thought to be necessary, signaling in effect, "I am a female and I am about to say 'yes.'" When the newly married pair have had a little more experience with this sort of thing, the awkward period of female frigidity and male frustrations disappears from their lives. There is no longer so much squeak-twittering and head scratching.

A good deal of debunking of birds has taken place in the last few decades. For some reason more superstition surrounded the stork than any other bird, perhaps because he was common in the northern European countries of great fairy story tellers. Far from being faithful to the same female year after year, the male' stork is not even faithful to her in any one year. After having com-pleted the carpentry work on his nest, he accepts the first female that comes along. The fable used to be that it was Mrs. Stork who was occasionally caught in adultery and that the male could detect this sinfulness by his sense of smell. (He has none.) It is true that marital quarrels break out in the great high nest when a third stork makes its appearance before brooding time. But the intruders are not seductive males; they are always females who have not yet been able to find a male with a nest. The in-house wife naturally does not wish to share the single-room apartment with another female, although the male does not object to the idea of a *ménage à trois*.

Where this kind of ménage is notably successful is in the strange society of two homosexual graylag ganders, as observed by Lorenz. What happens is a singular example of feminine pertinacity. A young goose falls in love with one of the inverts, standing and swimming patiently beside the scandalous pair as they superciliously ignore her. When the ganders make their unsuccessful attempts at copulation, she learns to push herself between them in an attitude of readiness at the critical moment when the male she admires is trying to mount the other: suddenly the female cloaca is there and he mates almost impatiently with her but, immediately afterward, he turns to his friend and addresses to him instead of to her the usual ceremony of post-copulatory display.* The success story in all this is that finally the female becomes a steady part of the pair's life. Both males copulate with her and all three go through the precopulatory and postcopulatory display together, as well as sharing the thrill of the triumph rite. According to Lorenz, such triangular marriages constitute a brilliant biological success. The three are always at the top of the ranking order of their colony; they have the best of the nesting grounds and year after year they raise a large number of healthy goslings. It does not seem that the perverted ganders morally deserve such a happy fate, but evolution in dealing with the long-lived geese is obviously willing to wink at what Anatole France termed grammatical mistakes in gender, provided that the mistakes are ultimately rectified.

The marriages of birds with which we are all familiar vary

* This formalized gaiety and ritualism *after* copulation appears to be peculiar to the family Anatidae (ducks, geese, swans), whereas most animals show exhaustion or depression, or at least they do not see any reason to celebrate.

greatly in style. The wrens are blandly polygamous. While the male and female woodpeckers spend a life of mean bickering at each other, the cockatoos, except at breeding time, sit in sentimental pairs, almost too sweetly embracing each other with wings and beak. In colonial birds, such as the jackdaws, marriage is a serious social matter since one has to reckon with the pecking order. No male may marry a female that ranks above him. When the female mates, consequently, it is always a promotion for her and the news gets around fast. Jackdaws, like wild geese and dabbling ducks, become engaged in the spring following their birth but neither species becomes sexually mature until a year later. (In the case of the dabbling ducks actual "dry" copulation may take place between the youthful couple, although the duck's penis delivers no sperm.) The affection of married jackdaws is nearly as cloying as that of cockatoos and seems to increase with the years. The male starts his serious courtship by feeding his sweetheart, as she begs and quivers and babbles a sort of baby talk which the adults use on these occasions and he replies in kind. This baby talk and feeding continues for life, and jackdaws live nearly as long as humans. Thus even in old age the male is still saying the equivalent of, "Woodum sweetums like a wormie," and she is babbling back, "My big brave snookie-wookums!" She is not always the recipient of favors. She is the only one that can clean those parts of his head feathers he cannot reach.

Among the pigeons, mating is by no means such a dedicated business, and the courting gestures which the cock makes to every single female he encounters are not necessarily serious. As with an incorrigible old roué, many of these passes he makes are simply courtesies of habit, as one would say, "Good morning, Mrs. Johnson." Among bullfinches there is an unexpected reversal of the usual pecking order. The female is once and for all superior in rank to the male. Although their marriages are permanent, the husband is literally henpecked for life. This, however, does not affect his tenderness. Instead of assuming a submissive attitude, he seems to glow and expand and the more she scolds, the more he professes his love.

One, of course, must not pretend that birds choose their temperaments, their moods and their times for love and for combat. Poor things, they are under the most infallible control of the chemicals within their veins and these molecular messengers are controlled in turn mostly by the sun. Only the spring increase in the length of the day influences the migratory and breeding habits of birds in the temperate and boreal zones. (The effect of temperature is quite minor.) In the case of equatorial birds, where the day is the same length the year round, the rainfall is important and photoperiodic responses are weak. It is not known exactly how rain affects the breeding cycles. For centuries the Japanese art of *Yogai* has been practiced, whereby caged birds are encouraged to sing in midwinter by lengthening the days with candlelight. Poultry raisers have long learned the trick of stimulating winter laying by illuminating the coops for added hours at night. Young ducks show a maximum response in growth of the testicles to red light, a feeble response to blue and none to infrared. Radiation of the eye itself is not essential. Light, somehow filtering through to the hypothalamus in the brain, stimulates the anterior pituitary gland, which in turn triggers off the sex glands. When the eyes are masked or removed, the blue light becomes as effective as the red.

The glandular effects may change with age. An old hen goes through a rather revolting menopause. As her left ovary degenerates, she stops laying and the hitherto dormant right ovary transforms itself into a pseudo-testicle. She usually shows signs of the growth of a comb and wattles and some male behavior. (This ugly metamorphosis is not unknown among mammals, including men.) The partial sex reversal is sufficiently common that in the Middle Ages crowing hens were considered bewitched and immediately had their necks wrung, their bodies burned and the ashes scattered over water.*

---

* Medieval thought considered animals to be either individually responsible for bad behavior or responsible by virtue of possession by evil spirits. Thus it was not at all unusual to hold pompous trials in which animals were solemnly accused and defended with due process. For some reason hogs were constantly in trouble with the law.

Although hormones are directly responsible for many patterns of action, psychological conditioning is nevertheless powerful and sometimes inflexible. In colonial birds, the establishment of the pecking order determines the sexual success of the male. The alpha rooster (or number one) of the flock is most successful with hens, while the omega rooster (lowest on the totem pole) may be psychologically castrated. Hens treated with male hormone, testosterone, revolt against their pecking-order superiors and achieve top status in henhood, and this status is retained, even though the injections are stopped and the secondary effects of the treatment have disappeared. On the other hand, hens whose ovaries are removed (so that they become poulards) take a nose dive in the pecking order. Unless they receive male hormones, they are lower than the dust. In the case of starlings, neither castration nor injection of testosterone affect social status. Some other facet of personality is dominant. The European robin doesn't begin to breed until territorial possession is established. (There is nothing in all the varieties of territorial defense, however, to deny the plausibility of the egg-protecting thesis as compared with the idea that ownership of a piece of property subsumes the whole reproduction of the species.) In the Lucifer hummingbird of Mexico, male and female stake out and defend *separate* territories. In all cases where the male carries out counteroffensive tactics (by chasing an intruder), if he carries his pursuit into the region of which the pursued is owner, the roles are automatically reversed, and the pursuer is fiercely pursued. In the case of the polygamous red-winged blackbird, the male defends against intruding males but lets females pass unchallenged. Each member of the harem, however, defends her nest not only against intruding females but against other members of the harem. In monogamous species with pronounced sex dichromatism (different colors) such as the American goldfinch and the cardinal, the males defend the territory against males and the females against females. (So pardonably red-conscious is the cardinal that he will waste a good deal of time and energy in fighting an image of himself in a kitchen window or in the shiny bumper of an automobile. Thus man and his things incalculably affect the lives of wild animals that live near him.)

Sometimes, among birds who are not very air-minded and nest far apart in sparsely endowed semidesert country, the only way to make a date is to have a kind of "singles party." Sage grouse, for example, mate invariably in the same breeding ground, generation after generation. In one case a highway ran through these grounds and in another a small airfield was constructed but the birds kept trying to get back to the same mass rendezvous. The mating procedure among such birds will involve a good deal of prancing and display, with the chances very good that only the top males will be able to father future chicks. After the erotic festival is over, the females scatter widely to build their nests. In such societies formalized fighting between males is such a biologically stringent rule that successful reproduction is probably impossible without it.*

When patterned behavior sets in, it is dangerous or impossible to try to divert the direction of the pattern. One drive will assure that a couple of married birds builds a nest and a completely separate drive takes over in the process of incubation. The iron primacy of the instant drive is shown by the fact that when a married couple starts building a nest they are utterly invulnerable to any untimely suggestion. If the clamorous hatchlings from another couple are placed in the half-built nest, instead of becoming foster parents, they will incorporate these baby birds into the nest. A nest is completed consisting partly of pieces of dead hatchlings.

Territory may indeed mean many things. Contrast, for example, the collared flycatcher with the glaucous winged gull. The male flycatcher is unjustifiably proud of his nest-hole and shows it as insistently to passing females as a car salesman displaying his wares. He may carry things too far. After he has obtained a mate and ensconced her in the nest-hole, he may display *another* nest while his female is incubating eggs in the first. This salesmanship may prove

---

* This is quite analogous to the backbone criticality of certain customs among primitive people. If the male habits of initiation and ritual of head hunting are abolished by missionaries, for instance, the whole society falls to pieces. You have on your conscience a dead culture.

so ardent that the wife deserts her eggs and starts afresh in the new hole. The glaucous winged gull takes possession of fishing boats. On the return from the voyage the boat will be boarded by the same bird. Cape pigeons show great pride. A single male may lay claim, in a real estate rather than a food sense, to the smoking carcass of a beached whale.

The psychological factor is undoubtedly important in stimulating the chemical and sexual nervous system. The female pigeon will lay eggs readily if placed in a cage where she can see a male, somewhat less readily if she can see a female and not at all if she is alone. With a mirror in the cage, she begins to lay at once. Among large brooding colonies of sea birds, wavelike spasms of copulation overrun the colony, yet in the case of most wild ducks, the precise opposite is true. Mating pairs of ducks are so bashful that they must have separate ponds in which to conduct their amours. Perhaps the most agile motherhood skills of all are demonstrated by the cuckoo and the cowbird. Although she has not the faintest intention of incubating her own eggs, the female can control within a few seconds the time when she surreptitiously lays an egg or two in the nest of the host bird. She has to perform this act when the host female is momentarily absent but when some of her eggs are present. This is as if a pregnant woman had to decide to give birth just during the commercial of a TV program.

12. The Triumph of Momism

Aside from warm-bloodedness (a talent which some of the reptiles were about to achieve, and, in the case of their descendants the birds, developed to an even dangerous extent) the dizziest, most profound change from reptile to mammal is the rise of motherliness. When a female not only nourishes its unborn young with her own blood but feeds it, when born, from the juices of her own body, a quantum jump has been made in the life pattern of both mother and child. It is true that parental care is common among altricial birds, but this is because flying is not as natural for a bird as it is for a metamorphizing insect; the nestling's period of food dependency is quite analogous to the food dependency of a human child as it goes through the relatively long period of developing an adult brain. But bringing worms or field mice to the gaping maws of nestlings is quite different, both physiologically and psychologically, from feeding the infant milk from one's own body. Momism or the Oedipus complex is not a sole luxury of humans in the age of Freud. Everyone who has had adult cats as pets is familiar with their occasional relapse into unweaned kittenhood as, kneading at an absent teat, they paw rhythmically at you when ensconced on your lap. The youngster with the security blanket is figuratively carrying around his mother, whose breast has become his own thumb. The triple transfer of love object from mother to blanket to adult female is surprisingly efficient, and in view of the intrinsic complexity of being a mammal, it is really surprising that so few mistakes in gender or even in species are made along the rocky road.

The drama of achieving full motherliness was not performed overnight in evolution's rather long and cautious experiments with the class of mammals. In the monotremes (which means "one-holed") one sees a half-reptile, half-mammal. The male of the platypus has a kind of penis on the hind wall of the cloaca, but it is more like a duck's or an alligator's penis than a wolf's. It is tube-shaped but is not pierced by a urethra. As in reptiles, the semen flows through external grooves. The monotremes make themselves doubly ambiguous by having bills and cloacae like birds and laying eggs. However, the egg tissues have a firm connection between mother and embryo. Remarkably enough, in the platypus and echidnas only the left ovary functions, and here the animal does not have the bird's aeromechanical justification. The first mammals of the Mesozoic probably looked like monotremes. Monotremes incubate their eggs, echidnas in the maternal pouch and platypuses in holes they dig by the shores of rivers. During the incubation period the males are not admitted to these underground huts.

One step farther along in momism, with the marsupials, birth becomes a kind of miscarriage. The embryo leaves the womb as what can only be considered a larval form; it is born (in the opossum) as few as twelve days after conception. The way from the birth duct to the pouch is torturous for a tiny creature barely an inch long, with no functioning senses and barely a flyspeck as a brain. It looks like an animated bean, but it usually succeeds in its adventurous journey.

The first crude mammalian placenta was seen in the koala bear, another of the weird and uncompetitive animals for which Australia acted as a continental refuge (a sort of grand-scale institution for evolution's retarded children). The placenta, called the allantois in this case, is seen somewhat better designed in the bandicoot—it is now definitely a sac attached to the embryo's abdomen. From this point on all mammals are alike in having an "afterbirth" attached to their navel cord—the expelled placenta. In most mammals the navel cord tears during birth. Some animals bite it off. Practically all land mammals except women eat the afterbirth while cleaning the baby. It contains valuable hormones which promote the production of milk. However, aquatic mammals (whales, porpoises, etc.) let the placenta drift away untouched.

With the placenta, a mechanism by means of which the embryo shares the blood of the mother, we arrive at a chemical problem of the most serious nature. It is known that the natural female hormones of the mother are contained in this flow of blood. What do these hormones do to a male embryo? Here we are at the heart of mammalian sex. We have seen at the start of this book that sex is determined by the X or Y chromosomes,* but we have also seen that reinforcements and even reversals of sex arrive with the hormones. B. P. Wiesner in 1934 announced the now accepted theory of sex maintenance in the embryo of placental mammals. Although in mammalian embryos as young as four days after conception (in rabbits) one can determine the sex by the appearance of the female chromatin, this doesn't mean that the organism will defend its sexual integrity against chemical intrusion. In simple language, this theory states that *the female embryo develops without hormones, while the male embryo produces its own male hormones.* One sees the reasonableness of this doctrine in the case of a male fed by the blood of its mother. If female hormones were necessary to insure that a genetic female developed in that direction, then since the female sex hormone is always present by placental transmission, only females would be possible. The theory is

* If you have access to a good microscope, you can readily determine whether you are a male or female by painlessly scraping out a little tissue from the inside of your cheek with your fingernail and fixing the scraping on a slide mixed with a drop of methylene blue or other dye. You will detect so-called satellite chromatin adhering to the edge of the nuclear membrane in female but not in male tissue.

proved by the experimental facts that in mammals normal and castrated female fetuses and castrated male fetuses all develop essentially alike—as females. The phenomenon of the freemartin shows, on the other hand, the power of testosterone. This is a female calf which had a male calf as twin and which is born with undeveloped or maldeveloped reproductive organs although its brother is normal. In such cases the placentas of each twin are so closely joined in the womb that there is vascular interconnection permitting blood and hormones from the male to reach the female.

Thus at a crucial period in development the male hormone testosterone is the key to sexual differentiation. The female way, so to speak, is the natural way, but evolution says to the embryo with the X-Y chromosome pairs, "Take a sip of this, my little man." By a complex sequence the hypothalamus in the brain regulates the anterior pituitary gland, which in turn regulates and is regulated by the gonadal glands. Thus the hypothalamus is either male or female but not both. The critical sip of testosterone which turns a female hypothalamus to a male one may take place in the womb before birth but in rats, where the effect has been most thoroughly studied, it occurs right after birth. If castrated, a newborn male rat grows up to show effeminate behavior. It indulges in the posture of *lordosis* (the normal female crouch which makes the vagina readily accessible), even though it has no vagina. On the other hand, the injection of the long-acting testosterone propionate in the *newborn* female produces the same effect as the implantation *at this time* of testes. The effect is on the brain not the pituitary. This is shown by the fact that when the pituitary gland of a male rat is transplanted under the hypothalamus of a female, her reproductive functioning and behavior remain female.

Although human homosexuality is a mental deformity which is crusted over with layers of cultural lard, one can see how it could arise by hormone influences at a critical period of brain development. If the still female-tending hypothalamus did not get the sip of testosterone in time, the brain would stay female.

We have been talking of the brain as if it consisted only of that primitive but absolutely essential part of it, the hypothalamus. Is there a male and a female cerebral cortex? Do women act the way they do not only because their hypothalamuses are female but because their higher brain lobes are also effeminate? There is very little evidence of this, although in mammals who have only a "neo-cortex," or bare little attic of higher brain, such as rats, the removal of this gray matter in the female releases any sexual inhibitions that she might have scraped together. On the other hand, surgical lesion of the neocortex in rat males abolishes mounting behavior, a demasculinizing effect which is not counteracted by injections of testosterone. Thus there is some evidence that in the female mammal the upper brain may be playing its typical role as a prudent moderator (to keep her behavior within ladylike limits), while in the male mammal some sex-stimulating effect is lost when the cortex is removed. (Bearing in mind the classical sex-differentiating effect of alcohol on the brain, the female's looseness and approach-ability is nullified by the male's diminution in performance.) It appears also that even in mammals as primitive as rats, the pattern of maternal behavior (retrieving the pups, crouching, licking, nest building) is not dictated by the glands or even by the hypothala-mus. Non-pregnant and ovary-less females and females without a hypothalamus and castrated and normal males—all show maternal response to newborn rat pups. This is perhaps unusual among mammalian species, although maternal response on the part of non-pregnant females is common in the mouse, the hamster, the wolf, the elephant and the primate.

In discussing birds, we mentioned the effect of light on the whole life cycle. There is a potent sex effect of light in mammals, so clearly decisive in certain species that it has been commercially exploited. Thus blue light, appropriately enough, has been found to increase the number of females in a chinchilla litter. Minks (when the male pelt is the most valuable) are born under a pink-ish light. This sex-determining effect was discovered in time-lapse photographs of plants, where it was found that blue inhibited the development of stamens (the male organ) while pink delayed the formation of pistils. The photochemistry involved in these effects is not understood. However, it is unquestionably a hormone change. In the adult female animals that show periodic estrus, or "heat," artificial increase of the hours of daylight will bring them into estrus even in the dead of winter. (This is notably so in the case of rabbits.) We may understand female periods and their dependence on light more clearly if we review the main effects produced by estrogen from the ovaries. First of all, the estrogen stimulates the growth of the cells which line the vagina and the uterus. Estrogen encourages the growth of the milk-secreting ducts of the mammary glands and otherwise enhances secondary sexual characteristics (smoothing out the contours with fat, for example, in women so that no matter how strong they are, they never *look* as muscular as a man). Estrogen makes females *act* like females. (In rodents, for example, females are generally more placid and explore new territory without the constant nervous defecation of the male). This hormone stimulates the anterior pituitary to secrete luteinizing hormone (LH), which triggers the release of eggs from the follicles and stimulates the growth of corpora lutea. Finally it also *inhibits* the secretion of follicle-stimulating hormone in the pituitary. Here is a strange chemical ritual, for in so doing, the estrogen saws off the limb that supports it, for once the follicle-stimulating hormone from the pituitary is no longer present in the bloodstream, the follicles in the ovary dry up and the concentration of estrogen falls sharply. At some lower-limit concentration (when the essence of femaleness has almost vanished) the pituitary automatically starts forming follicle-stimulating hormone again, to enter another repetition of the cycle. In chemical engineering terms, this is a feedback control system. The anterior pituitary and ovary form a self-sustaining oscillatory system. Without outside interference this cycle would continue like a chemical clock. But evolution found that for many animals this would be imprudent. The eyes (to receive light) and the light-correlating pineal gland (which in earlier animals was actually furnished with a private eye) act as switches to turn the oscillation on or off in such a way that the pituitary and sex hormones dance according to the tune of the seasons or the time of day. The female mammal's periods of estrus dictate the sex hormonal behavior of the male. He is a secondary clock, who sets his oscillations according to the time of the master (female) clock. The testicles also receive LH from the pituitary but, although it is precisely the same chemical, it is now known as "interstitial-cell stimulating hormone" (ICSH) because it causes the interstitial cells of the testes to secrete testosterone. However, the actual production of sperm in hamsters has been found to require at least twelve and a half hours of light per day, hence breeding in the winter would be unfruitful.

The important condition for an animal family to survive is to have food available at the time of birth. Thus, whether a mammal is monestrous (coming into heat once a year) or polyestrous (several times a year) depends on the way an animal makes a living. Animals that depend on grass for grazing commonly are monestrous. The female sheep, for example, shows willingness to mate only for one day in the autumn and, if fertilized, will immediately lose all interest in rams until the following year, again for one day only. In some mammals, the seasonal imperative is moderated by a valuable ability to suspend the growth of the fertilized egg. This is not the same as the storage of sperm, as in a host of lower animals we have discussed, but it has much the same desirable effect. Martens, weasels and others of their musk-bearing relatives are able to make the fertilized egg go into a kind of summer or autumn sleep, so that birth is postponed for from nine to twelve months, a remarkably long gestation for small animals. (Normally the length of gestation is proportional to the size of the animal and for a very good reason. The size of the egg cell of a mouse as it rolls fertilized down into the uterus is precisely the same as that of an elephant. The huge difference between the adults is in the *number* of cells that the egg zygote develops into. Naturally it takes longer to accumulate in proper form the vast population of elephant cells than of mouse cells, a discrepancy which enables the white-footed mouse, for example, gaily to bear as many as fifteen litters a year.)

In tropical martens, on the other hand, the time between mating and birth may be barely one and a half months. If those species of martens who live in the temperate or sub-arctic zones and take nearly a year for gestation are exposed to light in a cage for twenty-four hours a day, they will bear young only a little over four months from the time of mating.

The length of the mating season also depends on the animal's living habits. The female sheep's habit of being in the mood for love only one day of the year is all right for such a gregarious animal but it would never do for the grumpy and solitary creatures, such as moles and gophers. Boy has a hard enough time meeting girl, as it is. Both sexes of the gopher live as recluses but by some sense (probably odor) the male finds the female, patiently waiting, holed up in her burrow. After mating, the male returns promptly to his own burrow, never sees his children and couldn't care less. For an unknown reason, great and mysterious surpluses of female gophers occur every few years. However, the gopher's bashful nature is such that she is unable to go out and look for a male. She must sit and wait and may die as an old maid. In such a species, the occurrence of sexual readiness for only a week or so each year would result in quick extinction. The kangaroo rat is a similar hermit with an accordingly prolonged breeding season. Moles are in the same class in that very few of them live together. The males are somewhat more amicable than the females. In one observed case two females occupied a tunnel but the inevitable quarrel took place. They plugged up the passageway with a wall so they could live in separate quarters. Moles propagate only once a year and bear from one to five in a litter in special birth chambers in the lower tunnels. This low replacement rate is adequate because the mole has few enemies.

Such a modest rate of propagation would be disastrous for small rodents under a thousand guns from the air, the ground and poisoned bait. Yet even in species such as the previously mentioned white-footed mouse, where fecundity is alarming and almost incredible, each mating involves a certain ritual. The female fights off the male but only for the extremely short time necessary to prove that she is a lady. As soon as she gives in and begins such gestures as the lordosis response, the male becomes suddenly coy, then she has to chase *him*. The two occupy the nest for a few days, then he leaves or is thrown out. Within a few hours of the birth of her litter, she will mate instantly again. In many rodents the female shows sex desire only a few hours immediately prior to ovulation, which insures that the egg will become fertilized in the best condition.* House mice are ready to breed at the age of two months while house rats will mate at three months. They have to start early, for they lead short violent lives. At two years a rat is past sexual maturity. A very exceptional rat may live three years but is blind, toothless and hairless. (He would never survive to that age and condition in the wild state.)

In social rodents a peculiar phenomenon is observed which obviously cannot have any significance for animals, such as the sheep, who go in for one-shot couplings. This is the *stimulation* of ovulation by coitus. Normally one expects that ovulation spontaneously occurs, the female in heat seeks (or wants) a male and the sequence ends by fertilization. M. X. Zarrow and collaborators at Purdue University have found that what they call "reflex ovulation" occurs in rats not only after intercourse, but even if the uterine cervix is electrically or mechanically stimulated. They suggest that this may also occur in primates, where the release of luteinizing hormone could follow copulation. (The indirect conclusion is also that deep vaginal masturbation in female primates, including women, could produce ovulation.) This hitherto unnoticed complication may have some connection with the improper behavior of various female mammals in heat. Female guinea pigs in heat go around mounting females or males, if they are present. The "bulling" cow and the "horsing" mare are familiar to breeders and invariably indicate the female estrus.

---

* We also shall see the importance of this fresh-egg condition in humans for avoiding such distressing gene degredations as those that result in mongolism in the infant.

Since the dog has been with us so long, men are naturally quite familiar with his sexual habits, many of which are shocking to human morality. The most objectionable is his blithe disregard of the human laws against incest, which probably gave rise to use of the names "dog," "son of a bitch," etc. as terms of opprobrium.* However, his ancestor the wolf is a model husband and father as is his cousin the coyote. The fox is such a faithful husband that fox breeders find it very difficult to get a male fox to copulate with more than one vixen.

The nostalgia of the dog for his less friendly forebear the wolf is shown by the exasperating tendency (to owners and breeders) of the female terrier or dachshund to prefer as a mate a large wolfish-type dog rather than one of her own little strain. Probably the small male dog would also prefer such a miscegenation but realizes its mechanical difficulties. Dogs, bears, martens, seals and the relatives of all four do not complete their copulations very quickly, for two very important anatomical reasons. The penis is stiffened with a bone and is also protected with erectile nodes. After ejaculation these bulbous structures swell until they fill the entire vagina and prevent the sperm from flowing out. Thus the couple is forced to cling together until the erectile nodes subside. Mink and sable, bound alike with such impedimenta, may copulate for eight hours at a time. The immortal Kinsey reports that the blood pressure rise and fall in both male and female dogs during copulation indicate that a true orgasm takes place in both sexes. There are other ways than by prolonged insertion of the penis in which the backwash of sperm may be discouraged. Thus in guinea pigs, when fluid from the accessory sex glands is ejaculated, this

* In spite of common aversion to the dog's incest, it is noteworthy that the historical notion of primitive peoples accepts various animals as physical forebears. This is indeed one of the mythologies that supported a nearly universal totemism, the belief that certain ancestors were descended from various important animals. According to Knud Rasmussen, there is a fable among the Copper Eskimos about a woman who did not like men. Her family let dogs copulate with her and she gave birth to the first white man.

coagulates to form a hard plug which closes up the vagina for a considerable period.*

One rather ambiguous sex organ which makes its appearance in mammals for the first time is the clitoris. In cats and civets it is a very complicated structure reinforced with bone. (Its prominence in cats may be chiefly responsible for the convulsive twisting and curvetting antics of female cats at the end of copulation.) If the clitoris and other sexual parts are desensitized with Novocaine, these post-coital antics disappear. Among certain insectivores and rodents the clitoris has a hairy tip and protrudes so far that the females may be mistaken for males. This organ in the female hyena is often as prominent as the male's penis. In the spider monkey the clitoris is so large that it is virtually a non-ejaculating phallus. Although in more advanced primates the organ is more modest in proportions, the verified sex reversals of women into men involve the transformation of the clitoris into a penis. As evidenced also by the existence of inoperative teats in men, evolution was prepared to accept such reversals with equanimity.

Among many animals, selective polygamy or complete promiscuity with a strong ranking of males analogous to the pecking order of birds, make it likely that only a few males become the fathers of the community. This has advantages (in encouraging the endurance of strong genes) but possible hazards (in permitting excessive inbreeding, with the consequent preservation of defective genes). An example of this kind of sexual society is the kob antelope of Uganda. Here twelve to fifteen dominant males out of a total colony or herd of 800 to 1,000 do all the copulating. We see the emergence of a strong professional husband or professional father class. The females have no regular season to go into heat, but become receptive whenever the latest offspring are weaned. All mating takes place in a common stamping ground,

---

* The semen of other animals, including man, contains a lower percentage of coagulant that has the same purpose. It is the belief of many gynecologists that one of the reasons why lower-class or primitive people have more children than the civilized or refined is that the more fastidious women insist on washing themselves meticulously after intercourse, thus defeating the function of the coagulant.

where the professional husbands shove the boys and the shoe clerks out of the way to get to the females recently in estrus. As far as these master bucks are concerned, selection is completely promiscuous. The only thing they ask is that the does be in a receptive mood. This kind of behavior is carried to a pathetic comedy in the case of the roe deer, where the husband gets married after the doe is already pregnant by some more adventurous and domineering personality. This patient buck defends his soiled bride and his foster fawns with the utmost fierceness. In actuality the forest trees take the brunt of the embattled antlers, since when angry roebucks face each other they usually attack the trees in a typical act of redirected spite. This is not true in the case of all antlered species, since the antlers are designed purely for fencing and locking with the antlers of a rival. In defending himself against a predator a buck of any deer species would never think of using anything except his front hooves. Harem behavior varies from the absurdly large herds of wives that a powerful elk tries to defend to the purely promiscuous but non-possessive habits of the white-tailed deer. The caribou, like the elk, is a collector. The bull rushes around guarding his cows and looking for new ones but seldom keeping more than a dozen at a time. Weaned calves and even yearlings are attached to successive harems and although they get in the way, as long as their mothers are of interest they are kept in the harem, well guarded. During this time of fury, the bull eats little or nothing. Thus the successful bull loses all his fat reserve by wintertime. Things are quite different with the moose. The cow is much bolder, when in heat, than the roe deer. She plunges around in fretful circles, inviting with a hoarse, lascivious call any male. When he comes, she pretends to be shy and runs away but not very far. The bull moose is not ambitious enough to try for a harem. He stays with one cow for about ten days and then plays around. Often, when in her days of heat, the cow is still being followed around by a calf. She tries only half-heartedly to drive it away when her paramour arrives on the scene, but the bull generally tolerates its presence.

In small herds of water buffalo (an important farm animal in

Southeastern Asia) it is sometimes found that one bull in a man-arranged harem is not able to service all of the cows. When this is the situation, the owner may bring in one or even two additional bulls. What commonly happens next is a peculiar example of male psychology. The original bull dominates the new ones so they become entirely impotent. And he is now able to mount successfully all the cows. The act of mounting and of penis erection is not much of a problem to the domestic bull. He is never satisfied. He will repeatedly mount receptive cows for hours at a time even after his semen is completely exhausted.

The parallel nature of polygamy in such widely spaced mammals as elk, fur seals and Mohammedans is evident. But on the whole the fur seals do a better job of making things come out even. Much emphasis has been placed on the overwhelming role of the great bull—the beachmaster—who arrives at the northern islands ahead of all the rest—the less experienced males as well as females—and prepares his seraglio. Late-arriving males ("idle seals") must be satisfied with a bachelor ghetto farther from the beach. The females arrive in two waves. The first are pregnant and give birth to their pups, while symbolically under the protection of the great bull. A six-year-old bull may hold four cows but it usually takes a ten-year-old to sultanize over one hundred. Most master bulls that last until August are worn out and half starved, since they have never left their domains. In the meantime the cows have been allowed to go back to the water to give their pups swimming lessons and to catch fish. In this interval a suspicious amount of hanky-panky with the bachelors goes on (although one would never suspect it from a Disney movie), since the masters cannot leave their posts to chastise the seducers. Just at the end of the beachmaster's punishing husbandhood and vigil another wave of females arrives —all virgins. The great exhausted bulls, seeing this rippling mass approach of eager femininity, in effect say, "Oh, *no!*" The maidens are not disappointed, however, for out of the ghetto come the idle seals, glad to take care of them. Thus the books are balanced.

From the review so far of sex among the animals, one might assume that it is a rather grim affair. Male and female are under the

mastery of hormones that dictate unlovely and even dismal con-
catenations. Actually it is not so with all creatures, and the exceptions where sex seems to be fun perhaps significantly occur where
the female is a self-reliant and brilliant animal. A. Strachan's classical description of the attitude of a Bengal tigress toward her mate
has always fascinated animal lovers. The male strides slowly in
her direction while her body seems to sink into the ground as if
she were flattening herself in the presence of a prey. Her eyes are
blazing, ears laid back, tail twitching. She waits until the tiger is
within killing distance, then springs at him (an attack he pretends
to ignore totally); she lifts a powerful forepaw and . . . gently
pats him on the side of the face. Then she raises her head and obviously kisses him. This is the prelude to a necking sequence of
the utmost delicacy and controlled passion, but the ending, of
course, is in triple dots . . .

Perhaps the secret of such polished affairs is that the sexes normally have little to do with each other. (This is not the case with
all felines. The African lion in practicing polygamy is simply relying on a pride of females to see that he gets fed. He is not regarded
with any degree of romantic tenderness by the lionesses.) Among
all solitary and intimidating animals, whether carnivorous or not,
the female never expects any fatherliness on the part of her mate
and in fact desperately protects her small young from a confronta-
tion with him. Thus we see the gulf between the pack-minded
wolves, where family life keeps the community together, and the
bears, where love is a sometimes thing. Like the black bear, the
grizzly female enjoys male society only once every two or three
years. This is a very full-blooded romance, however. The two
wrestle passionately, paw each other interminably and are insepa-
rable for about a month. Occasionally another male may show up
in the middle of the honeymoon. The female immediately runs
away but (as is usual in such cases) she has not exactly disappeared forever. If the rude visitor is big and persistent enough, he
is able to expand the romance into a threesome. It does not matter
to the female bear which one becomes the father of her cubs, since
she will in all probability never see either of them again. With

bears of extraordinary endurance and vitality, the bearing of young may take place in the middle of an arctic blizzard. The polar bear, unlike the martens and the rest of the sissies, does not have to time her parturition to the seasons. The winter is preferred. With the heat of her great body she bears, nourishes and rears a litter of cubs that start out about the size of guinea pigs.

In colonial or gregarious mammals (where the unit of togetherness may be a monogamous pair, their children and relatives—or may consist of a whole animal town) there is often a segregation etiquette. Thus bat mothers retire to a sort of maternity ward, while in most species the prospective father goes to a bachelor club. Beavers marry for life. Shortly before giving birth the mother drives out of the crowded lodge the two-year-old children but allows the one-year-olds to stay. The father leaves the lodge to take up temporary headquarters in a den on the bank of the river. The mature male prairie dogs, after mating, take up residence together in a special part of the great town—quite analogous to the "men's house" of human savages.

Maternity is not always a smooth process. Due perhaps to a slight miscalculation on evolution's part, the otter young are born in an unusually large, mature state and death during parturition is not uncommon. The elephant mother suffers a good deal and is often helped during her birth pangs by her sisters and grown daughters, who support her and act as much like midwives as their limited manipulative equipment allows. The situation is very grave if elephant twins are born (an exceedingly rare occurrence).

Too little is known about the sex lives of whales but if that of the toothed species can be regarded as simply an extrapolation from the better-known eroticism of their smaller relatives the dolphins, it must be intense and fairly continuous. The large whales are known to copulate belly to belly. Two blue whales have been seen to shoot high above the water, bellies pressed together. In this passionate second or two actual mating is believed to take place. The female is usually larger than the male and does not permit her husband to disport with other females. On the other hand, the dolphins that have been studied closely are mostly semitropical and, in Dr. John Lilly's experience, indulge in promiscuous sex play or in actual copulation whenever they have nothing else to do. They do pair, with sexual selection strictly up to the female, but one can scarcely regard a male dolphin as a faithful husband or doting father. The willingness of a young dolphin to attempt an impractical copulation with a woman has been shown in Lilly's experiments. So anxious was the young lady in the interest of science to give him relief that she fondled his penis and allowed him to ejaculate against her leg.

Many animals masturbate and some of them in rather peculiar ways by no means influenced necessarily by incarceration. The mature red deer is the oddest. He masturbates by lowering his head and gently drawing the tips of his antlers to and fro through thick herbage. Apparently this part of the stag's body is as sex-related as a woman's breast, since erection and extrusion of the penis from the sheath follow in five to seven seconds. There is little protrusion and retraction of the penis and oscillatory movement of the pelvis. Ejaculation ensues about five seconds after the penis is erected, hence the whole act takes place within the time a fast man can run a 100-meter dash. Clellan S. Ford and Frank A. Beach have discussed other odd masturbatory habits, of elephants, dolphins, carnivores, ruminants and rodents. (As might be expected, the primates are even more versatile, especially in zoos. Baboons and macaques will attempt to couple with all sorts of cage-mates—with apes or monkeys of other species, dogs, cats and foxes, even with snakes.) Hypersexuality can arise, especially among tomcats, without any evidence of brain damage or other abnormality. One respectable tom, who had sired several litters in his neighborhood, took to mounting and attempting copulation with a child's toy rabbit, from which sperm could later be recovered. This perversion is quite analogous to fetishism in human beings and appears to be associated with the temporal lobe of the brain.

It is tempting to say something about the special loves and marriages of more of the dear and eccentric animals that belong to the great group of sub-primate mammals, but we have time for only two more instances. The female porcupine is nearly unique in that when she says "No," she can readily enforce the negative. Since mating doesn't take place unless the female agrees, the male lets her make the first advance. When ready, she is very aggressive and chases her chosen husband around the blackberry bush. She lays her prickles flat and curls her tail upward. For reasons that will be elaborated in another place, the armadillo is a peculiarly interesting mammal. Although the love-making habits are not exceptional in any way, the reproductive mechanisms are. The female gives birth to exactly four offspring, all of the same sex, and for a good reason, because they are always *identical quadruplets*. The original egg cell when fertilized splits into equal quarters. The children are precisely alike even to the smallest details of their scales and the number of hairs on the belly. That this has been going on for a long time is shown by the fact that the mother has exactly four teats. Although the armadillo thus has a technique of completely avoiding sibling incest, it can hardly be pointed out as a smashing success as an animal. Nevertheless we must bear in mind, for future cogitation, this remarkably entrenched way of creating four identical beings from one egg.

Man, as a keeper and breeder of animals, has recently applied chemical and biological engineering in controlling or modifying their reproductive habits. Synthetic hormones are given to cattle to synchronize their estrous cycles and consequently to program the births of calves for a movable market price. Chemical birth-control techniques vary from the simple use in coyote bait of synthetic stilbestrol during the breeding season (analogous to "the pill") to the permanent chemical sterilization of rats by feeding them sex hormones at infancy. "Mestranal" (the estrogen component of the human oral contraceptive), if given to pregnant or nursing rats, is passed on to the offspring and sterilizes the latter for the rest of their lives. This trick is also being tried on pocket gophers and kangaroo rats. How about intrauterine devices (IUD's) in animals as well as in the human females of India and other overpopulated areas? A curious variety of reactions has been observed. To be effective, the device must be designed for the shape of the uterus, which is commonly *bicornuate* (or double-lobed) in most mammals. Since we are not sure how the thing works in women (the most plausible theory being that it over-accelerates the transport of eggs from the ovary to the uterus, so that the eggs don't have time to implant themselves) it is not surprising that the results in lower animals are ambiguous and of varying efficiency. In cows fertilization by artificial insemination is inhibited by IUD's, but not fertilization by natural mating. For large animals the IUD's used successfully have been spirals of polyethylene plastic. For rodents and rabbits, they may be threads of silk or nylon or even glass beads. The IUD's decrease the amount of secretion of luteinizing hormone in sheep or rabbits—an effect not seen in humans. On the other hand in these species the rate of egg transport through the oviduct is not affected, nor is it in rats. To show the diversity of reaction, in mice and chickens the rate is actually reduced.

Improvement in sex ratio and eugenic breeding can be achieved by a bioengineering technique which is already common among pig and sheep breeders and, as will be more thoroughly discussed later, seems practical for women. The females are treated with hormones that lead to multiple conceptions, the fertilized eggs are removed and inspected microscopically and those that are deemed worthy of continued existence in the universe are transferred to the wombs of "host" mothers. Since the sex can readily be determined before transplantation, this is an effective way of obtaining more of one sex than of the other. Just as in the stud system of animal breeding, it is a means of insuring that one superior parent can pass on her genes to hundreds of young rather than a few. When it is combined with stud breeding (or perhaps with frozen semen storage) it represents the acme of eugenics.

13. The Curse of Eve

It would be insulting to a spinster lady of fine sensibility to realize that, of all physiological processes that bind us in evolution to monkeys and apes, the most dramatic and convincing is the fact that she shares the disabilities of menstrual bleeding with every female primate, from the spider monkey to the gorilla. Why the bleeding occurs only in this kind of mammal is not clear but it probably is connected with life in the trees and the year-around availability of food in the geography which favored primate development. Where food can be had all the year around, there is no good reason for having only one season set aside for mating and the timing of gestation adjusted so that the young are born in good weather.

Let us review the process of menstruation. It took embryologists a long time to work out the chemical details and, in fact, Gustav Born of Breslau on his deathbed dramatically outlined a theory that he was never to live to see confirmed. Born's key proposal was that the corpora lutea (literally "yellow bodies"), the masses of cells formed in the ovary from the follicle cells after they have discharged their eggs, are endocrine glands and are necessary in the life of an embryo. We now know the full sequence of the menstrual cycle to be as follows: from the ovary, estrone, which stimulates the growth of cells lining the uterus, also triggers the pituitary gland to secrete luteinizing hormone, LH. The LH sets the process of ovulation going and also accelerates the growth of the corpora lutea, which in turn secrete progesterone. This hormone encourages the *final* stage of growth of the lining of the uterus, making it ready for implantation of the egg and nourishment of the embryo. If the egg fails to be fertilized, the corpora lutea degenerate and this makes the concentration of progesterone fall. Lacking its hormone support, the lining of the uterus gives up the struggle and sloughs off in the form of bloody tissue. Menstruation can therefore be prevented by injections of progesterone. It is only in primates that this bloody tissue, instead of being internally absorbed, is rejected through the vagina. This complex cycle varies little in any primate, only the time between menstruation and ovulation differing in various species. (If pregnancy occurs, the placenta itself acts as an endocrine gland, for it secretes both estrone and luteinizing hormone. The additional supply of LH saves the corpora lutea from degenerating; thus the supply of progesterone is maintained and the lining of the uterus, rather than sloughing off, is ready for business.)

In chimpanzees the period is thirty-four to thirty-five days, in the rhesus monkey twenty-eight days, in the baboon thirty to forty days. Although theoretically this crucial change in the primates from a definite period of estrus (heat) to year-long sexuality with monthly periods should do away with rutting seasons, it has not in all species, since in certain colonial animals, such as the *Callicebus* monkey, practically all the females seem to come in heat at the same time, a synchronization of periods which turns the society upside down for a week or so. The conjugal bonds and the ties which unite the individual families of the band in defense of their territory are torn up in a riotous carnival of indiscriminate mating. After the wild party is over, as Ardrey remarks, the community settles down to raising bastards.*

* It appears that synchronization or at least regularization of cycles of estrus depends on the presence of males. Even a group of female mice will show wildly diverse and irregular cycles but these will be straightened out

During the menstruation of the female all male primates scrupulously avoid serious copulation. The male may mount the female but he doesn't try to penetrate. The mounting designates no more than a friendly gesture. The signals of sexual readiness in the female primate are loud and clear and, if males are not attracted, she will go after them. In some monkeys the skin of the anus region and vulva become bright red, but this sometimes extends in a curious sympathetic transformation to the male. Thus the male's hindquarters, and in the mandrill even his face, echo the ruby glow of the female's behind and he displays as insistently as she does. The copulatory approach is, of course, from behind, as in dogs, but in the higher apes there is a good deal of variation from the four-legged posture of the female. In the gorilla (where the female is much smaller than the male) she may sit on his lap as the penis is inserted. Although, judging from George Schaller's extremely accurate observations in the wild, the male gorilla goes through a good many strenuous copulatory motions and appears to achieve a true orgasm, there is no reason to assume that the female shares in this climax. In fact, this mightiest of the apes is strangely lacking in virility (his penis is much smaller in proportion to body size than in any other primate) and he much prefers eating to love-making. (Probably no thrill in the cheap movies or fake literature is as completely bogus as the scene in which a sex-crazed male gorilla abducts a lovely blonde woman.)

Chimpanzees, adventurous as well as more virile when young, apparently do a good deal of sexual experimenting. They embrace sitting or lying down, apparently testing to find out which position they like best. As they grow older, however, the interest in sexual yoga fades away and they fall back on the classic from-behind method of all lower mammals. As a species the chimpanzee, in both male and female, is conceivably even more highly sexed than man. Of all the primates, the chimpanzee's genitals are the largest and even the play of the immature apes has a sexual bias. As is well known to apologetic zoo-keepers, the chimp shifts blithely

---

by the presence of a male, even if separated by a fine mesh cage. Since even the used bedding from the male cage has the same effect, it is evidently a male hormone odor that is responsible.

from heterosexual to homosexual to masturbational activities and even to pranks of sheer sexual exhibitionism. In a puritan society the chimpanzee would have been in the stocks all the time, if not burned alive. Quite unlike the gorilla or other anthropoids, the chimpanzee is gaily inspired by the presence not only of his own kind but by other higher primates, including man, and hence is at his liveliest and most scandalous in the presence of company. Although he observes the taboo of menstruation, sexual intercourse continues during pregnancy but stops between the time the baby is born and is weaned. Thus the status of lactation determines the sexual availability of the female, and the female's functions alternate as mother and mate. It is probably this alternation that makes the chimpanzee a less faithful husband than the gibbon. The gibbon lives in a single-family group, nearly always paired for life. Unlike most other apes and monkeys, both male and female are extremely belligerent to members of their own sex—either a cause or effect of the solitary family arrangement. There is a good deal of watchfulness and suspicion in the gibbon's personality and, being a good husband and father, he is on this earth likely to outlast both the chimpanzee and the gorilla as a wild animal.

As befits their tree-mindedness, the orangutans commonly make love off the ground. With his body dangling, the male swings toward his mate, who embraces him enthusiastically. He clasps her with his thighs, his feet twine around her back and, breast to breast, hanging by their hands, they rock back and forth in a romantic interlude which will last as long as their powerful fingers can sustain them. For the actual moment of coitus, however, they generally drop to the ground and proceed in classical fashion.

It is generally agreed that, among all primates, the baboons are most likely to survive. They have that certain combination of ferocity and cunning that, tied in with their society of closely knit bands, is hard to sink in the erosive river of mammalian life. It is hard to tell the true sexual temper of the baboon, since in captivity he seems to behave quite madly at variance with his natural character. (This is only to be expected when he is extracted from his roaming band society.) Cases have been cited in which jealousy between two male rivals has been so fierce that the female over whom they were contending was literally torn to pieces. Yet Eugène Marais in his three-year observations of a troop of South African baboons never saw a single sexual outbreak of this sort. It is possible that baboons vary in monogamous behavior not only from one species to the other but from one troop to the other. In general, the male is much bigger and more belligerent. He is a surprisingly powerful animal for his size and his canine teeth are fierce daggers. A horde, or troop, usually consists of several males with attendant females and young, each adult keeping a soldierly distance from the others. In a troop where rank prevails, the chief each day has his pick of those females who show by their enormously swollen red behinds that they are in the mood for love. Yet since, like all primate females, the others are also ready for mating at practically any time, the lower-ranked lieutenants and bachelors find sexual comfort among the unswollen females. (This sort of "rhythm" exclusion tends towards the same sort of sexual selection that we see among the kob antelope.)

Perhaps incarceration affects female as well as male baboons. In the famous London Zoo riot of 1929 one hundred strong young male baboons went berserk and nearly tore up the joint, but were pacified when the zoo-keeper (evidently a complete moron) was finally persuaded to sweeten the baboon yard with forty females. But females under such conditions behave much more licentiously than they do in the comforting restrictions of the wild troop. Niels Bolwig reported seeing one estrous female copulate thirty times in less than an hour with six different males, then disappear into the bush with the youngest and evidently least satiated.* There is some degree of homosexuality among baboons. The smaller, younger male can obtain political advantages by submitting his behind to a more powerful male. In turn the superior male protects him against the attacks and indignities of others. When either a female or a homosexual male is eating and is suddenly interrupted by a strong male who craves the same food, the weaker animal will as a reflex

---

* Among primitive human societies such female voracity in sex is regarded with suspicion and even fearfulness. The Trobriand Islanders expect a good deal of copulative enthusiasm from their women but the nymphomaniac is regarded as a dangerous witch.

gesture turn its behind invitingly toward the intruder, who may be interested enough in this diversion to allow the weaker one to keep the food.

In confinement, many apes (with the exception of gorillas) show sexual reactions when humans of the opposite sex approach them. This is not so true of baboons because of the discrepancy of size. However, the uncanny astuteness with which a gang of baboons can evaluate the sex character of a human being is attested to by many South African farmers. If the baboons are interrupted in their depredations in the orchard or garden by the appearance of the farmer's wife in the door of the farmhouse, they pay her no attention. If the farmer himself appears, they scatter immediately for the hills. Even if the farmer appears *with a woman's dress on,* they scatter for the hills. (Come to think of it, I see no very good reason, at least outside the pages of Truman Capote-type literature, why the farmer should appear in his wife's dress, but apparently they do a lot of experimenting—or perhaps a lot of drinking —in South Africa.)

It appears that, as sophisticated as they may seem, monkeys have to learn the mechanics of copulation. The famous primatologist H. F. Harlow raised young monkeys in isolation from their elders, so they never observed an act of coitus. When they reached maturity, they did not mate, even though they showed signs of sexual tension and the sexes engaged in mutual grooming. (Grooming is the petting or necking equivalent of teen-age humans, except that it is reciprocally more useful, since lice are often picked off the lover's body and eaten. This amorous habit incidentally persists among primitive human races who don't get around to bathing very often.) When these virgin female monkeys are introduced to more sophisticated males, they defend their virtue with the utmost ferocity. It is quite likely that human children would show the same behavior, unless there were wise guys among them— older brothers or sisters who had been tipped off as to the nature of sexual involvement. Possibly this then points to another gulf between the primates and other animals. Sex is no longer instinctual but depends upon cultural environment.

sians, who view our man-on-woman pattern as impractical, disgusting and unfair to the woman. Among such tribes the favored procedure is for the man to kneel, with his body nearly erect, draw the woman (lying on her back) toward him so that her legs are around his hips and complete the insertion while she is still horizontal and he is barely crouching. The Melanesians maintain that such a position favors a woman's orgasm because of her freedom of movement.

The permanence of the woman's breast seems natural in a species which does not as a rule refrain from copulation either during pregnancy or during lactation. Extended nursing again is a consequence (or a cause) of the unusually long infancy in the human child, which in turn relates to the fact that the baby is born with a large skull and takes time to fill it with brains. Thus the permanent breast of the woman developed in the sudden evolutionary spring that saw man's brain capacity double or triple in a mere wink of geologic time. Simply because modern jet society regards the bottle as a source of food and the breast as sexual titillation does not mean that the permanent breast in primitive man had anything to do with sexual allurement; rather it was a convenience to assure the baby of a source of food during a time when its mother was interested also in acting as a wife. The breast in fact may at first have been a source of dissatisfaction to the lusting male, just as it is a "keep off" sign to the male chimpanzee.

The breast-observant traveler can see a wide variety through the races of the globe. The Mongoloids, especially the American Indians, tend toward very small breasts. Among the photogenic Balinese, the breast is small and high so that the baby, resting on the mother's hip, can lean over to drink at his pleasure. In Balinese myths the witch has abundant body hair and pendent breasts. (In other words, she is as unlike a Balinese woman as can be imagined.) Among certain African races the breast is not regarded as worth having unless it is long and droopy enough to throw over the shoulder. Margaret Mead in a survey of seven diverse South Pacific cultures has concluded that there is a rather perverse connection between emphasis upon suckling in the society and the amount of sex distinction, sex envy, ritual mimicry of the other sex, etc. Where suckling is continued until the child is three or even four years old, the men begin to grow restive and satirical. Although Sigmund Freud, in a study of a small neurotic section of middle-class Vienna at the turn of the century, erroneously assumed that "penis envy" was gnawing at the souls of all girls and that all boys and men were obsessed with their mother's genitals, most of the normal primitive people in the world show quite the opposite tendencies.* The man envies the woman her capacity for motherhood, and the Oedipus complex is notable for its absence, although the taboo against incest sometimes reaches almost frightening intensity, especially as regards brother-sister relationships.

Because modern anthropology has been horribly handicapped by the misguided invasion of virgin cultures by missionaries, it has sometimes been nearly impossible to relate man's earliest ideas about sex to the notions of present-day primitives. Just as modern man destroys a forlorn animal species about every month of the year, so in the past the missionaries in their despicable self-righteousness, destroyed whole cultures overnight. The *men's house,* an institution in many southern Pacific societies, where men and initiated boys could take refuge from the women, was regarded by Margaret Mead as one of the strongest and healthiest of customs, serving to bolster the morale of every tribe. When the cold-eyed missionaries insisted that the men and boys tear down their houses and come to church, to sing ghastly hymns, the societies broke at the backbone. The natives became mere lackadaisical hangers-on in a white Protestant world. The Iatmul of the Pacific once had a charming and invigorating custom of sacred male flutes. These were played on the fringes of the village on certain occasions, and a supermasculine monster was supposed to roam about, the women all fleeing toward the beach in ritualistic but satisfying

* Dr. Karen Horney, a former disciple of Freud, neatly disposed of his theory of penis envy, in concluding after a wide psychiatric practice in both Europe and America, that girls envied boys only their ability to see themselves urinate. Moreover, the boy can inspect himself to see whether the supposed dreadful consequences of onanism are catching up with him, while the masturbating girl is always in the dark.

terror. Afterward the women would return to trace in awe where the testicles of the monster had supposedly bounced on the ground as the sacred flutes played. When the missionaries came in, this happy monster was immediately exorcised. In tearful rage, the Iatmul men threatened to do the unthinkable—to bring down the whole structure of society by showing these flutes to the women. So ended another unique culture. In some of the East African tribes a type of polygamy was practiced which was based on a peculiar and effective system of woman labor shoring up the whole agricultural economy. Although the women themselves resisted successfully some of the attempts of busybody missionaries to change this economy to a respectable Western form of misery, other attempts unhappily succeeded and both tribesman and tribeswoman alike became useless beggars. Fortunately, in some cases the efforts of religious fanatics have led to their own biological degradation. The Hutterites, a hot-eyed sect forming small communities in North America, have so long practiced first-cousin marriage that they average two inches shorter in height than even the poor white unbelievers who are their nearest neighbors. One must conclude that this is a much lower order of sinfulness, since, unlike the missionaries' sins, it is not inflicted on innocent outsiders.

We cannot even accept the word of the missionaries in regard to the condition of the people when they descended upon them. When double-checked by professional anthropologists, their reports or diaries seem always to have consisted of pious fabrications or slanted half-truths. Perhaps the intrinsic guiltiness of their acts prevented them from any clear-eyed observation—another proof, if any is needed, that truth is in the eye of the beholder. Moreover, one does not become a useful anthropologist by merely spending thousands of hours among the books of the British Museum, as did Sir James Frazer and Karl Marx. The result of such lucubrations is that you come up with such theories as the dictatorship of the proletariat or, in Frazer's case, the idea that the central Melanesian food taboos are the result of the cravings and sickly imaginings of pregnant women (whereas such cravings are a European invention and do not even apply to all of twentieth-century Western women). From what valiant and dedicated field workmen, such as Franz Boas and Bronislaw Malinowsky and Margaret Mead and many others, have been able to glean from the leftovers of the moral slaughter by the missionaries, and by avoiding the pre-formed academic attitudes of the stay-at-homes, we can advance certain cautious generalizations about the sexual ideas of primitive man:

As seems to be proved by the paleolithic cave drawings, early man knew of the connection between copulation and birth. Thus the noteworthy exceptions to this knowledge, such as the Melane-sians of the Trobriand Islands studied by Malinowsky, must be assumed to represent cultural deviation or regression. This is not an unusual contingency even in our own culture. If, for example, the Church of Christ or most of the Southern Baptists had their way, we would go back to interpreting the origin of man according to the literal words of Genesis. Evolution, which is as plentifully proved as the sexual origin of babies, would be as unthinkable as is the latter to the Trobriander mind. The mind of the religious fanatic is very similar, in fact, to that of the primitive; it revels in small triumphs of inverted logic. When one asks one of the higher doctors of theology in the fundamentalist sects how Cain was able to marry and beget offspring the answer is that Cain had sisters which the Lord forgot to mention. The descent of all mankind from an incestuous union would be a double jolt to the Trobri-ander, who, although insistent that reproduction is purely meta-physical, since the soul of the baby at its own whim comes from the shadow world to occupy the mother's belly, is even more in-sistent on the awful sinfulness of brother-sister union. The Tro-briander's pathetic little triumphs of logic lie in such facts as that both women and men have sexual discharges, so why should one fluid be any more potent than the other? Also a Trobriander will solemnly report that while he was away on a two-year trip to Sa-moa, his wife had a baby now one year old. How could he have procreated at such a distance?

Women beyond the age of menopause and infirm old men were

allowed to live in those races of men who developed language. Just as the old female buffalo is the one who gives the signal to run, the opinions of old women were taken seriously in matriarchal and matrilinear societies and old men were solicited for their advice and for their knowledge of songs and myths. Curiously the menopause is an invention of man, since (possibly because of shorter life) it is not observed in apes or monkeys.* (We have noted the equivalent of menopause, however, in hens.) Menopause assuredly is a time marker for women, but when in the same sense is a man old? According to the rather brutal criteria of primitive societies such as the Samoans, he is senile when he has the capacity of only one act of sexual intercourse per night. In actual years, measured against Western standards, sexual senility may vary greatly with the culture. Among the Australian aborigines and other primitives the older man is given exceptional sexual privileges and, as long as he can give a reasonable account of himself, practically any sexually mature woman not protected by totemistic taboos is available to him. (Among the natives of Brazil, even children are considered bound to yield their bodies to the "dirty

---

* The existence in human females simultaneously of menopause and of sexuality continuing *after* menopause introduces a seemingly insoluble dilemma for some of the more stubborn policy makers of the Catholic Church. The arguments against artificial contraception are based on the so-called "natural law," i.e., that the act of sex was designed to create babies and that any hampering of this purpose is therefore a crime against the "natural law." Since some of the birth control techniques, such as the condom or coitus interruptus, function in a way that is morally the same as mutual masturbation, they are held to be against the natural law. Yet the same harsh objection is obviously applicable to the intercourse of a woman beyond the menopause or even to the intercourse of a woman of child-bearing age during those periods of her monthly cycle in which she is unlikely to conceive (the "rhythm method"). In such cases the man is theologically doing the same thing as going through the motions of copulating with another man, an animal of another species or even with a pillow. It is obvious that in refusing to look upon intercourse as an act of love the Church has, in effect, renounced the idea of love between the sexes and reduced intercourse to a purely biological transaction which we share with all bisexual animals. In other words, the Church, originally founded upon the idea of the unique spirituality of man, has now painted itself and its faithful flocks into a corner with the monkeys and the squirrels.

old man.") Among the Mentawei of Indonesia, in fact, a man has to be well along in years before he can get married, if at all. Among these people marriage is a religious and very expensive business. When he has put aside enough property he can go through the marriage ceremony and accept the very serious job of head of the household—including the many grown-up and teen-age children that he has already accumulated. After marriage there is no time for his wife and him to do otherwise than hold their exalted positions and let their children support them. Somewhat similar dilemmas are often faced by poor South American Catholic couples, who, surrounded by their children of all ages, finally attain respectability by the visit of some peripatetic priest. Among the rural Irish of the same faith, on the other hand, the man may wait as a middle-aged virgin until his father or elder brother or uncle has died and left him enough property to support a wife and family. In the Bantu system of Africa, the mother-in-law is greedy and eager rather than tearful when she gives her son to a young woman, because daughters-in-law form a labor pool she gets to boss around. As Margaret Mead has so cogently pointed out, the rise of Naziism was undoubtedly encouraged by a colossal psychological mistake on the part of the Weimar Republic, in which the only jobs available during the Great Depression were given to older men, leaving young men unable to compete for women's favors.

This is a great continuing source of antagonism (the old man with the money getting the beautiful young doll) and it remains underground only when custom rigorously dictates. (Aborigines, after all, are much more devoted to ritual courtesy and amenities than were Nazi Germans.) The antagonism may, however, have ugly family repercussions, as among the Mundugumor of the Pacific, where the mother tries to save her son's sisters for him to exchange for a wife in order to keep the father from exchanging these same daughters for another wife for himself.

Such matters as female orgasm and the functioning of the clitoris are much better understood in some primitive societies than they have been in modern Western culture, in spite of all the innumerable libraries of sex science and the floods of explicit pornography to which we are exposed. This does not mean that female orgasm was common among early man and became less respectable or less fashionable as civilization crystallized. In general, the opposite may be more generally the case. It is true today that whole societies of primitive people ignore female orgasm. Since it is obviously less closely related to the biology of conception than the male orgasm (and in fact could be regarded as a relatively irrelevant phenomenon), one would not expect a clear neurological history of improved pleasure for the female primate. Yet even when orgasm is definitely lacking, as in the Arapesh of New Guinea, the sexual appetite is nevertheless demanding to the extent that the husbands complain of their wives' insatiability. It is noteworthy that among cultures where female orgasm is unknown there is usually what we would now call feminism. Among the Ngyars of Malabar, for example, the custom of *ciscisbeism,* the taking of male concubines ("male mistresses") is allowable to women of quality, yet orgasm is apparently not achieved or even heard of. Yet we must juxtapose to this and to the great polyandrous matriarchies of early Indian civilization (circa 5000 B.C.) the nineteenth-century Victorian Englishwoman, quite submissive to the males, where orgasm would have been a scandal to live down and where young girls were cautioned that it was unladylike to take a nap in the fields because certain snakes creep easily into the genitalia but cannot be pulled out on account of their scales.

The Melanesians and Polynesians are experts on feminine pleasure. As noted by both Margaret Mead and Malinowsky, an act of sexual intercourse is regarded by the men of these races as not only incomplete but farcical if the woman does not experience a full orgasm. It is significant that among most of these peoples childhood is riotously filled with sexual play during the so-called period of "latency." When they grow into puberty both sexes are thus already quite sophisticated. (It is probable that, except where religious taboos intrude, this would have been the normal life habit of primitive man anywhere as he advanced to the stage of living in bands or small societies, whether these were based on agriculture

or persisted in the hunting or pastoral ways of earning a living.)
At the period of uncontrolled adolescent love, the participants are
by no means blasé, however. Among the Trobriand Islanders, pre-
climactic intercourse includes a lot of scratching, tongue-sucking,
even the biting off of eyelashes. (As Malinowsky notes, young
men and women of a tribe who would ordinarily have long attractive eyelashes have short ones, because they have been bitten off
in the frenzy of love. Albinos, who are regarded as unthinkable
as love partners, have lashes of normal length.) In the amorous
scratching and body-biting behavior, the girl is invariably the more
aggressive.* Among people where sexuality is so well understood
(except for its function in procreation) it is only natural that the
female organs are familiar to the point of sassiness. The clitoris
becomes a delightful, funny thing—the word being used in folk
sayings, jokes and figures of speech. (Compare this easy slangi-
ness with the colossal misconceptions of Freud brooding on the
same subject, based on the observations of a neurotic Western
social group. Some of his women disciples tried in vain to disabuse
him of his stubborn notion that clitoral rather than vaginal masturbation was primary among all little girls.)

Yet, in spite of the intrinsic frankness of the South Sea Islanders
and the masterly studies of modern anthropologists, there remain
two mysteries of primitive human sex which have not been un-
raveled. How did *Homo sapiens* develop the incest taboo? This is
immensely strong, and universal, and seems to be as peculiarly
characteristic of our species as the gift of speech. Among the only
known exceptions were the Inca nobility of Peru, the Egyptian
Pharaohs, some early Middle Eastern cultures, and princes of the

---

* This appears to be a rule of the sexes, particularly where the male is
definitely more powerful than the female. The male hamster, relatively a
great brute with dangerous incisors, allows the much smaller female to bully
him incessantly with irritable nips and the lion puts up with a lot of ragging
from his small wives. In an experiment at the University of Massachusetts a
group of boy and girl students were allowed to subject each other (anony-
mously) to electric shocks. The girls would invariably direct the maximum
possible jolts at boys, but not at girls. Thus with masculine gallantry prevail-
ing in spite of vehement threats ("Baby, this time you're going to get it but
good!") none of the girls received any but gentle shocks.

blood and, most curiously, certain royal groups of the Polynesians. These exceptions indeed certify that incest was only allowable by a sort of divine right to perpetuate a lineage or property rights—a perverse privilege of a few godly people who could hardly be regarded as mere men and women. Among most human societies the mother-son incestuous union is viewed as the most wicked, yet among many natives it is regarded as so unlikely as to have little scare value. Brother-sister incest, as we have noted, is among most of the South Sea Islanders held in such horror that early separation of the siblings according to sex is practiced. In the "old days" of the Trobriand Islanders ("old" referring to pre-missionary), the emotional shock of a man seeing his sister in the arms of her lover on some enchanted evening was the end of all things. The three were supposed promptly to climb to the top of coconut trees and hurl themselves to destruction. So charged with taboo is the whole relationship that the ultimate insult (atonable only by immediate conflict to the death) is for one man to tell another, "Copulate with your sister!" (or plainer words to that effect). Yet the creation myth of these people had a brother and sister emerging from a hole in the ground to become the first men on earth.*

Since the long-term biological consequences of the world-wide incest taboo are, in effect, to make man what he is—a highly hybridized animal in which even the superficially most distinct races easily interbreed—one can only assume that it is a true specific instinct of man, a cultural instinct true enough, but, like language, a part of the basic tissue of humanness. That the taboo may come from "religious" rather than rational compulsions (as in the Trobriand Islanders, who even castrate all male pigs in order to make

---

* The intense glare of purely religious taboo in this case is heightened by the fact that the Trobriander boy is encouraged to court the *daughter* of his father's sister. This is, by all odds, the marriage surrounded by the most favorable auguries. Furthermore, intercourse of a boy with his paternal aunt is a jolly and quite acceptable diversion, and indeed she always appears as a sort of roughhouse, tough-talking seductive Auntie Mame, but she is Auntie Mame only to the boy. She must not even be seen in the same room with the boy's sisters, perhaps because the boy and his sisters are never allowed together with such a non-chaperone figure.

them fatter and point to the continuing pregnancies of sows as evidence of the unimportance of the male in procreation, neglecting the presence on the island of numerous wild boars) does not make it any less a specific instinct, mysteriously and variously manifesting itself according to the cultural style of the natives or of the civilization. (As an example of a strange rationalization of the instinct, the Arapesh man asks, if he married his sister, how could he get along without a brother-in-law? Who would accompany him on the hunt, and to whom could he turn for help in getting drunk?) Where the taboo is violated, it is generally with a clear knowledge that an inhuman act is being committed and in some perverse cases of civilized people it is committed only *because* it is an inhuman act and therefore has the feverish charm of the unnatural, like a form of sexual perversion.

While incest is hardly a problem of any substance in modern civilization, being only a minor police irritation in overcrowded tenements, the other mystery of primitive sex is one that carries with it a whole complex of high horsepower implications for the art of modern living. We have noted that among the Samoans and especially among certain primitive Melanesians, sexual relations among boys and girls who have reached puberty are completely uninhibited. By the time she has married, a Samoan or Trobriand Island girl may have had scores of affairs in which (in the stilted language of the 1930's) she "went all the way." No techniques of contraception are used or even heard of—not even the most ancient and natural one of coitus interruptus. Yet it is extremely unusual to the point of freakiness—that the girl would ever be pregnant until an appropriate time after she is finally married—an end, it is important to note, of her period of unquestioned promiscuity. *After* marriage, her fertility makes itself known. She bears healthy children with commendable regularity. How has she remained unpregnant through all the days of wine and roses? Concerning this there is a good deal of dispute among anthropologists and gynecologists and even among moralists. Margaret Mead stands alone among a lot of men theorizers. She points to the fact that the unmarried Samoan girl is able to time her own affairs, whereas when she is married it is her husband that does the timing. In other words, the Samoan girl is unconsciously (and a great deal more successfully than Catholic couples) practicing the "rhythm method."

Much as I respect Margaret Mead's views on anything, this seems to me a highly implausible hypothesis. It is especially so among the Trobriand Islanders where passionate sexual consummation is believed to have no connection with pregnancy. Furthermore, why should the girl avoid times (during ovulation) when her body is most urgently requesting her to get mated? I think we can avoid this theory as purely romantic. Among the masculine notions, one first has to deal with a rather crude and, on the face of it, improbable idea that when a human egg is confronted with a number of sperm cells from different male individuals, the result is that the egg is not fertilized at all. At the prospect of rival fathers the egg, in effect, becomes alarmed and makes its membrane impermeable to all the rivals. This notion places a good deal of responsibility on the discrimination of the egg, which is generally not supposed to be sensible of the presence of any sperm until the sperm, like a tiny missile, bursts into her protoplasm, more or less at random. There may be something to this rather rough theory (since it is backed up to some extent by the known infertility of careless prostitutes) but so far there have been to my knowledge no proofs at the cellular level.

The most promising approach is Ashley Montagu's doctrine of the natural infertility of young adolescent girls. Although, judging from the large number of illegitimate children born these days in modern cultures by girls of fifteen or younger, the doctrine would appear to be anemic, it must be emphasized that what also has changed among Western girls in the last few decades is the rate of sexual maturing. The average of menarche (the first menstruation) has taken an almost incredible nose dive. Thus we should perhaps compare a primitive girl of sixteen with a modern Western girl of about twelve. If this comparison is valid, the relative rate of illegitimate childbearing by young girls depends on how far the period of promiscuity is removed from the menarche. If it is true that in virtually all the primitive South Sea Island societies which we have been considering (where teen-age promiscuity is a way of life) the girl goes through the period of playing the field of young bachelors right after the menarche and, after such a short and wild period, she gets married, the facts begin to fall in line. Montagu's older data on the infertility of young Western girls then make sense, if they are corrected by subtracting from the age of his typical young girl the average number of years by which the age of menarche has decreased since the time of his survey.

In the middle and upper classes of American and European cultures the average age of menarche has diminished in a few decades from sixteen to 12.3. A few centuries ago it was about 18.8 and that is the average today of certain South Pacific peoples, the Bundi of New Guinea. That this very critical life marker depends in some way on community behavior is shown by the extraordinary fact that, while menarche among the nomadic Lapps remained at 16.5 from 1870 to 1930, that of the nearby farm communities decreased along with the rest of northern Europe. Some part of this fantastic change is obviously related to diet. The girls of the poorly nourished Bantu of South Africa, like the Nigerians and many Indian nations, do not menstruate until well over fifteen or sixteen. In Slovenia it was found that girls who ate meat twice a day during childhood reached menarche at the average of eleven years, eight months; those who ate meat once a week or less first began to menstruate at the age of fourteen or over. Yet even where people have the same food habits, the girls of upper-income families show a trend toward lower menarche ages than those of middle-income families and the poor, and this is paralleled by a lower age of menarche in small families as compared with large families. It is a curious corollary of these statistics that the parents who have most biological reason to worry about having their thirteen- or fourteen-year-old daughters become unwed mothers are the luxuriating three-car-owning suburbanites rather than, as is so often fallaciously assumed, the parents of the ghetto. Of course, as a matter of family style, it is also the mothers among the well-to-do who are most vigilant (in spite of the movie clichés), or at least more so-phisticated.

It is of incidental interest that along with these changes in the female development cycle, a further consequence of higher pro-tein intake during childhood and adolescence has been the increase in adult size of both sexes and the earlier attainment of maximum size. While in 1900 the average European or American attained his full height at the age of twenty-six, the modern youth of nine-teen is as tall as he is ever going to be and this is a great deal taller than his ancestors.

The question of varying sex ratio in births has been a cause of perplexity. In a general sense most of the anomalies can be ex-plained by the basic and reasonable assumption that the male hu-man, from the fertilized egg on to senescence, is essentially weaker (except muscularly) than the female. Boys react more quickly to malnutrition and even to radiation, as in Hiroshima. During the 1940's the average height of the thirteen-year-old Russian boy de-creased by a full inch, while the girls remained relatively stable. The boy/girl ratio at birth always goes upward toward the end of major wars—a fact which has been mystically and inappropriately attributed to "Nature's attempt to redress the balance." The fact seems to be irrefutable that younger mothers (of which there are a superabundance during wartime) tend to have more boys than older mothers. If we continue our assumption that the greater fra-gility of boys is true from conception to birth, then, for some rea-son, younger mothers provide a better womb environment than older mothers. This ameliorates the disadvantage of being con-ceived as a male and increases the proportion of male fetuses which survive until birth.

A recent discovery about "old" mothers has served to dispel some of the guilt complexes of women bearing mongoloid-idiot children as they approach the menopause. The occurrence of such chromosomal defectives turns out to be connected not with the sexual age of the mother but rather with the loss of virility or at least of enthusiasm of her husband. Basically it now appears that the chromosome arrangement associated with mongolism is caused by egg deterioration. The egg, having left the ovary, remains fertilizable for twenty-four hours. It begins to deteriorate, however, before it becomes infertile. Male spermatozoa within the female maintain their fertilizing power for about forty-eight hours. Therefore, if intercourse occurs at least every two days, the egg entering the fallopian tube is likely to be met by fresh spermatozoa and fertilized before deterioration. Thus the declining frequency of sexual relations as a couple grows older greatly increases the chances of mongolism in the child (the ratio of mongolism varies from 1/300 in women under thirty to 1/40 in women over forty-five). The lesson, for even young couples, is that if they want to be sure of having a normal child, they should, at least during the period of the woman's ovulation, have frequent intercourse: they should, in other words, practice the rhythm system vigorously in reverse.

There is a good deal more to be said about human sexuality, but in fact all of it has been said, since the essence of the human species has been either an expression or a perverse denial of it, and in the denial of normal sympathy between the sexes (as in classical Greece) has come forth the most powerful if indirect affirmation of sexual obsession. When one lounges by one of the typically Olympian swimming pools that are perhaps the answer that normal modern youth has to perverted youth, one realizes at last the delphinic affinities that so fascinated Dr. Lilly. Give some healthy adolescent males and females a plastic swimming raft to play with and they will react to it as to an aphrodisiac. Tanned legs and arms touch and pat and slap; patterned squeals of the female follow the hoarse watery intimidations of the male as he overturns the raft with a brawny shoulder. Mutual ducking, underwater allegiances and saucy rebuffs are like the antics of amorous dolphins —also a sex-haunted species. One has to remind oneself of the total extent of this obsession throughout the world and throughout the history of this species. A Luvala boy is allowed to urinate only against a certain restricted list of trees—all of them hardwoods; otherwise his penis would lose its virtue and become incapable of valiant erection. Among the paramount chiefs of the Melanesians was a man whose penis was reported, upon insertion, to have the property of phenomenal further bulbing out, a capacity which redounded greatly to his credit in the archives of his village.

Yet in going through history and anthropology, one is constantly impressed by the pathos of the male. It is true that polygamy was combined in certain societies with the killing of female infants. This irrational behavior was shared by the Eskimos and by the equatorial Laotians, who had the nasty habit of leaving girl babies in the mud to be trampled to death by water buffaloes. And in ancient Japan a four-year-old male was a vicious little dictator who tyrannized over every female member of the household. Yet for the most part this appears to be a demonic revolt against the superior substantiality of the female—against the fact that it is she who creates life. Among Polynesians there is never any worry about whether a girl will become a woman. This is as gracefully inevitable as the sequence of night and day but there is considerable doubt whether a boy will make it as a man. Among the American Indians the fretfulness about the fate of the boy shows itself in the unblinking constant stares of concern of both parents toward their boy child. Can he accept the mysterious challenge of becoming a man, warlike, impassive, tough? Much more often than is realized, there was a youthful revolt which headed not in the direction of wildness but of deviation—of homosexuality. The boy could not face the tensions of prideful Indian manhood. In the ritual called the berdache the young man dresses and thereafter lives as a woman. Among the Mohaves transvestism is carried to the fanatic extreme that the man not only dresses like a woman and uses a woman's gestures and tone of voice but mimics pregnancy and childbirth, going aside from the camp to be ceremonially delivered of stones, which are named. Female homosexuality, on the other hand, seems to have been unusual among primitive peoples, being primarily a Grecian invention, significantly at a time when male pederasty was viewed as an ideal rite of love.

15. Is Sex Worthwhile?

Earlier in this part of the book we pointed out that since artificial parthenogenesis (the development of the egg without spermatozoa) had been shown to be feasible for rabbits, it would in
the course of time be found practicable for higher mammals, such
as man. In a species so sex-obsessed this might constitute the most
basic revolution since man learned to talk. Since this and other
techniques of biological and genetic engineering pose special problems of politics and of sociology, we shall reserve more detailed
discussion of them, but in the meantime a few pros and cons are
in order in regard to the desirability of an essentially non-sexual
society.

Man was the first voyeur. It is only among men that one finds
an absorption in sex so overwhelming that it exceeds the orbit of
personal interest and overflows into the keen observation of the
copulatory activities of other men, of one's relations, friends, or
the moral habits of the community as a whole. Literature may be
said to have originated from this voyeurism, since literature ceased
being a personal diary (whether written or not) when the notes of
the voyeur were shared by the village. The dramatization in high
style of such desperate episodes as that of the Trobriander youth
who stumbles upon his sister and her lover culminates in the works
of Shakespeare and, as its epitome in our time, where sexuality

becomes, like alcoholism, a disease in the writing of Updike. In its long, wary, contingent preparation for the mastership of the planet, did evolution have in mind a culture in which wife-swapping and pot-crazy group sex were the terminal targets of man's hopes and desires? Quite evidently a mere revulsion—a return to a new puritanism—is not the answer, since the puritan ethic itself is simply the obverse side of the coin and denotes an even more sickly and abominable preoccupation with sex. During times of extreme intellectual stress, when new philosophies, new systems of mathematics, of music and of natural science were being built up (as in the sixteenth and seventeenth centuries in Europe) it is noteworthy that among a similarly sex-crazed upper class, the pioneers in thought fled prudently into bachelorhood (Spinoza, Leibniz, Bayle, Kant, etc.) and Milton could cry in anguish:

> O why did God
> . . . create at last
> This novelty on Earth, this pair defect
> Of Nature, and not fill the World at once
> With men as angels without feminine,
> Or find some other way to generate
> Mankind?

All of the singular retreats from sexuality occurred during a time when the upper-class Frenchwoman was perhaps one of the most intelligent of any feminine group in history—yet also the most alluring, the most lascivious. The natural reaction in a masculine society—to blame everything on the invention of women—misses the point by 180 degrees, since modern biological discoveries have found that it is the man that is, futuristically speaking, a redundant gender. It is the male that can be eliminated from the human species to form a more tranquil, sexless, yet more productive world.

The satires, such as those of Aldous Huxley in *Brave New World,* which equate a sexless system to a sort of glorified automobile factory where persons of different model and purpose are turned out to feed the maw of a dreary society of robots, may be precisely wrong. Man, in regulating the sweaty clamor of sex, may find that love is more than the mutual friction of mucous membranes.

PART II
Living and Dying Together

Having taken a sight-seeing tour of sex throughout the animal kingdom, it is now time to examine the social rather than the merely familial repercussions of the sexual way of reproduction. In scrutinizing the ways in which various animal groups and societies behave, we shall also give some attention to behavior such as the acquisition of food, since in many cases animals flock together not to mate but to eat or prevent themselves from being eaten. And we shall discover what seems to be a very profound connection between community eating and sex. We shall find ourselves accepting a revolutionary principle: that the behavior of animals in societies—indeed perhaps the real reason for society formation—is to avoid overpopulation and thus to escape mass starvation. We shall see that this deep instinct has been disastrously lost in man.

1. The Essential Problem

In discussing population control, there are viewpoints as wildly variant as those of the eminent Catholic spokesman Colin Clark, who believes there is no problem at all (the more souls, the merrier God's feast), to the angry Professor Paul Ehrlich of Stanford, who thinks (with some reason) that we are already lost: unavoidable and catastrophic population explosion, along with the pollutions and social pus and diseases of malnutrition that go with it, is already beyond hope of restraint by any means less drastic than vast wars of extermination or colossal famine.

That there *is* a fixed limit to the number of human animals that can be allowed to pullulate on the surface or in honeycombs *under* the surface of the planet is proved, however, by an ingenious and unexpected mathematical extrapolation by the English physicist J. H. Tremlin. This assumes that by some miracle of chemistry or of manna from heaven the planet can support the nutrition of some sixty *trillion* people by the year 2855. Curiously this is the end point, not because of food, but because of lack of power for refrigeration—assuming even the development of astronomical amounts of power from the deuterium oxide (heavy water) in the oceans. It is at this density of packed bodies that the heat produced by these bodies exceeds the thermal radiation capacity of the earth. The ground temperature becomes that of Venus, where lead melts. Everybody burns to death. Thus, in order to attain a population of this magnitude, a new sort of animal would have to be developed—in effect, a disembodied wraith or a frictionless thinking machine or a very small human being, perhaps the size of a rat. (These are not inconceivable developments by the year 2855 and will be discussed in another book.)

In considering the mess we are in through lack of the automatic instinctual population restraints of the lower animals, we propose to consider some of the societies and the social habits and ecological peculiarities of organisms in general.

2. Equilibrium Population

Because man is threatened directly by no other living creatures than bacteria (although his food supply is endangered by many insects and nematodes) or viruses, he is nearly unique in a world in which the object of society is generally protection against formidable predators. A solitary ant is meaningless unless considered as part of a colony of ants. It is, in fact, a debatable theory that the flocking of birds and the schooling of fishes is a tactic of protection against fiercer birds and bigger fishes. As we shall see, however, such societies have an even more profound, seemingly converse reason for existence—the automatic *limitation* of the species. Since this reason for social behavior in animals has only recently been recognized, we shall defer discussion and consider at first some of the quirks of ecology—a word that is becoming a guilty one, since the ecology of a biological system has now come almost to mean the property of a pattern of life which can most easily and disastrously be distorted by the acts of man.

Consider, for the moment, a modest ecological situation in balance, and involving several kinds of animals, including man, that was knocked cockeyed by an imprudent act of humans. Some years ago the World Health Organization launched one of its mosquito control programs in Borneo and squirted DDT all over the place. The mosquitoes suffered vast casualties all right, but the thatched roofs of the natives began to fall to pieces, eaten by caterpillars relatively immune to DDT but previously held in check by a certain kind of wasp who was killed off by the DDT. In rural Borneo the housefly is normally kept under control by a small lizard, the gecko, which the natives welcome as a useful pet. When the geckos snapped up flies saturated with DDT, they weakened and died. Household cats ate them, were in turn poisoned and also died. The fearful end result was that the chief prey of the cats, rats, underwent a population explosion and bubonic plague promptly invaded this part of Borneo. Panic reigned and fresh cats were parachuted into the region to hold off the rats. Eventually some semblance of the original ecological equilibrium was restored, including cats, geckos, wasps, caterpillars, flies—and mosquitoes. The natives decided they preferred malaria to plague.

Our planet is complexed with such ecological networks, associations and equilibria.

From the standpoint of self-sufficiency and imperturbability perhaps the most perfect social organism on earth is the lichen, which one sees in small or large grayish disks or plates on trees, rocks and everywhere in the forest or woods when some degree of moisture is present. The lichen is composed of a peculiar and unique association of two organisms much more different essentially than an elephant and a clam. Part of the lichen is a fungus and part is an alga capable of photosynthesis, like any green plant. Unlike the elephant and clam, the two components of the lichen do not even belong to the same *kingdom,* if one accepts the modern interpretation of that term. The fabric of the lichen is made from fungus threads so densely knit they look like tough leather. The green cells of the alga occupy a particular spot just beneath the upper surface of leathery fungus. The fungus threads absorb and hold water like cotton and they hug the algal chains, which make food for both by means of the chlorophyll they contain.

Older even than the ancient balsam, the lichens represent the most indestructible form of life known on land. In spite of the hundreds of millions of years of this weird symbiosis that created a new kind of being, the alga and the fungus do not lose their identities. If separated by laboratory botanists, and properly nourished, they can preserve their separate lives.

A lichen is a colony in a state of passionately serene equilibrium. As such, a lichen has no descendants. It resorts instead to a kind of statistical marriage. Spores in inconceivable numbers may float off the fungus "person" and meet in the forest air with individual cells of algae of the kind necessary to go through a sexless mating, the start of another lichen colony. But a colony may be, under stable atmospheric cycles, more resistant to death or even to change than a rock.

Nobody can tell how old a given lichen is. Man's span of botanical curiosity has been far too brief to chronicle the lichen's years or centuries and, unlike the case of the redwoods, there is no way of estimating the lichen's age. A lichen in a lonely place may have outlived the individuality of the continent which was its native land. Initials were carved in lichens on boulders in North Greenland when explorers were frozen in for the winter of 1925, and these initials were found unchanged in 1950, with no growth or the slightest change in the carving. For the lichen twenty-five years is a wink in the night and probably the boulder would decompose, under the influence of the strong acids secreted by lichens, before this superb association of organic entities would show the slightest change in its ever mature, ever full-grown majesty of existence. It is true that a lichen never does anything except live. It has no prey, no predators, no sex life, no philosophical questions. It has solved the problem of the universe by a unique social invention. (The reason I bring up the subject of the lichen is that symbiosis must be considered in the future of man, possibly the symbiosis of man and robot or even symbiosis of man and some super pet animal.)

Some colonies of creatures escape the predator problem by managing to exist under circumstances which most predators cannot tolerate. Thomas and Louise Brock have made a specialty of studying the kinds of life that can exist in the hot springs of Yellowstone National Park, where the water may come out of the earth at 200 degrees Fahrenheit—the temperature at which water boils at this altitude.* Simpler organisms, such as bacteria, were seen to resist temperatures near the boiling point. The blue-green algae (which, like bacteria, have no nucleus) survive at 170° F. True algae (with a nucleus) can stand up to 140° F, while the ephydrid fly, a unique predator for this rich soup of hot springs flora, can tolerate 124° F.

Obviously the fly can eat only the micro-organisms that allow themselves to grow at the lower temperature levels of the springs. Ecologically this is shown by an optimum temperature for algae, above which they are killed by temperature and below which they are eaten by the ephydrid fly. This family of flies is a specialist in peculiar places. It thrives in hot springs, even at 15,000 feet in the Himalayas; one genus prefers the bitter brine of the Great Salt Lake, while the genus *Psillopa* likes to mess around in pools of petroleum oil. All of them find as food single-celled creatures who also live in such unfragrant places.

Yet the ingeniously perverted fly is also preyed upon. Larger flies of the family Dolochopodidae eat their larvae. Spiders are common at the edges of hot springs and scamper audaciously out to grab the adult ephydrid, who seldom rises off the surface of the hot water. Dragonflies restlessly patrol the banks. Occasionally one swoops too close to the surface, becomes wetted and dies instantly.

Let us take another ecological society—that of the human skin. Living on this surface, a small animal is subject to embarrassment, since the flat squames of the outer skin made of keratin are always being shed and the environment must be that of huge boulders and plots of ground being lifted, curled up or scraped away—a land of perpetual catastrophe. The only safe refuge for an animal that insists on this as his native habitat is in a cave, and there are two types in the skin. One is the duct of a sweat gland, which resembles (as Mary J. Maples, the New Zealand ecologist, has pointed out)

* The average temperature of the earth's surface is about 54° F. The presence of living organisms in hot springs demonstrates that life could persist at the supposed temperatures of a young earth, and in fact the bacteria and blue-green algae found are likely candidates for the first kind of life on earth.

a pool at the edge of a sea with frequent changes of water level and salinity. The other cave is the hair follicle, a cylindrical infolding of skin from which projects the hair, a tall tree of hard keratin. The follicle exudes sebum, made by the sebaceous gland. This is rich food, with a high proportion of fat. Free amino acids are present as the result of by-products of the process that forms the keratin. In spite of this opulence of food, there is only one steady animal inhabitant—the follicle mite. It lives, mates and breeds in and around the eyelashes, the hair follicles of the outer nose folds and chin. The other inhabitants are yeasts, bacteria and some viruses. With an upset in equilibrium of the body, some of the single-celled species can multiply and penetrate the horny layer. Fungi thus produce athlete's foot. These same fungi, however, often form communities without damage on the sole of the foot or the spaces between the toes.

Bacteria thrive on the skin. Normal inhabitants are the cocci (sphere-shaped) and the diphtheroid (rodlike). The cocci are harmless, except for one species, *Staphylococcus aureus,* which causes boils. One diphtheroid is the acne bacillus, which lives in the depths of hair follicles. Some areas of the skin are as densely populated with micro-organisms as natural soil. Some people have a high skin bacteria count (regardless of bathing habits), others low. (This differential attractiveness of the skin may be analogous to the fact that some people attract ticks, chiggers, fleas and mosquitoes, while other people seem to exude some subtle repellent for such pests.) It is noteworthy that a greater variety of potentially disease-causing bacteria is attracted to the soft skin of babies than to that of adults. Contact with other humans, and to a lesser extent with other mammals, is far more important in the transfer of micro-organisms than contact with an inanimate object, however dirty. In such a transfer staphylococci, for example, are transmitted on the tiny squames, or rafts of shed skin. This displacement of heavily loaded rafts of staphylococci goes on almost constantly, even in the simple acts of dressing and undressing. Undamaged human skin, however, is a highly perfected armor against most pathogenic micro-organisms. The skin is too acid for most species, while the constant shedding, although providing free transportation, hinders the establishment of the invaders on a single body. It is certainly no secret to TV commercial fans that underarm odor is primarily due to the by-products of metabolism of certain, so-called "gram positive" skin bacteria, who feed on the rich secretions of the special apocrine sweat glands that are located in the coarse hair follicles of the underarm area.

On the whole, animal skin is not as reliable a country for small creatures as the surface of the earth, where enormous societies and complex ecological relations of societies exist in varying states of slowly swinging equilibrium. Theodore H. Savory, the English expert on *cryptozoa,* the animals that live in the *cryptosphere*—the immediate neighborhood of the earth's crust, where there are leaves and humus, mosses and stones, fungi and soil and salts—has pointed out that this place to live is so favorable that it houses stupefying numbers of little creatures, many of whom have not had to make any spectacular evolutionary adventures in several hundred million years. It has been estimated that insects alone (and they are in an astonishing minority) in an average temperate-zone soil occur in numbers of the order of one billion per acre. Most of such insects are without wings, belonging to the subclass Apterygota, representatives undoubtedly of the first insects that emerged from the sea and came into existence on earth. If one excludes micro-organisms, five phyla creep or squirm in this fertile twilight—arthropods, platyhelminths (flatworms), nematodes (roundworms), annelids (earthworms) and mollusks.

The average population breakdown is amazing. Worms of all three phyla represent only 3 per cent of the cryptozoa. Snails (mollusks) and wood lice (crustaceans) account for 4 per cent each. About half of the remaining 90 per cent are arachnids (spider mites), one third insects and the rest are myriopods of various kinds. Because of the vast numbers involved in this place to live, it is evident that arachnids (mites), although deficient in numbers of species, may outnumber the earth's total insects with its million or more species. The mite is a very primitive organism. It is small, its exoskeleton is thin, and it thus solves one of the first problems confronting an animal emerging from the sea: how to get around without expending an undue amount of energy. The thin cuticle is permeable to gases and allows the diffusion of oxygen directly into the body and the escape of carbon dioxide in the same way without bothering about such complications as tracheae, book lungs and the other refinements of the mite's more highly evolved arthropod cousins, such as the true spiders. This simplified method of breathing is not efficient enough for an active creature who has to climb or jump, but it is no handicap in the cryptosphere, where things do not happen often or very fast. The problem is not food, for the soil is rich in microscopic flora and fauna. The problem is heat. The cryptozoans in a densely populated cryptosphere face precisely the same ultimate problem that we mentioned at the beginning of the chapter (for the year 2855): population control is determined by the rate at which heat can be removed. If too much heat is evolved from too many thickly packed bodies, water evaporates. Every student of physiology is told that a ton of mice eat ten times as much food as a ton of horses. Yet for the cryptozoa, who seldom exceed five millimeters in size and per ton eat even more than mice, the desperate need is to keep heat out, because a rise of temperature hastens evaporation. For some cryptozoans, such as slugs, exposure to wind is as fatal as heat. This is why they are seldom seen in the daytime but emerge in monstrous numbers after sunset. A windy night keeps them at home.

The precise ecology of these enormous hidden, heat-limited populations has not been very well analyzed. We do not know, for example, how one species reacts to another from the standpoint of food competition, pollution by excess carbon dioxide or other body wastes, resistance to pathogenic micro-organisms, evolutionary punches and counterpunches. It is obvious, however, that these myriads of small creatures must be regarded as living soil. If the equilibrium is dramatically disturbed world-wide as, for example, by massive chemical applications by man, the change in nature of the cryptozoan population might be unpredictably disastrous. For one thing, this unimaginably large accumulation of creatures is now dormant from an evolutionary standpoint. It is pullulating harmlessly and, to some extent, helpfully. But it is an inconceivably monstrous *reserve* of possible mutations. If you jab at it with a chemical poker, who knows what might come swarming out of the devastated cryptosphere? Wingless and flaccid and half-blind creatures by the trillions upon trillions could develop wings and venomous vigor and regain the impassive stare of compound eyes, and could descend upon us in who knows what new, irresistible cloud of terror. Best leave alone this slowly panting, sleepy hidden reservoir of immemorial life. If it is in equilibrium, let it stay in equilibrium.

Most of the generalizations or laws of populations have been derived by the observation of more simplified societies than those of the cryptozoa—for example, fruit flies and other animals that have short enough lives to follow the fate of generations and which can be put in a bottle or a cage. From a large number of studies, such biologists as Francisco J. Ayala of Rockefeller University have made some deductions, most of which are probably only remotely applicable to human beings.

One of the most practical findings in the statistics of small animals is that the "Malthusian parameter" (also variously called the "intrinsic rate of natural increase" or the "innate capacity for increase") depends very intimately on specific conditions of temperatures, humidity, quality of food, etc. In some experiments with insects the strain with the highest capacity of increase at fifteen degrees Centigrade had the lowest at twenty-five degrees. Furthermore, natural populations seldom have a stable age distribution. The R. A. Fisher theorem of evolution by natural selection is that the rate of increase of *fitness* of any organism at any time is equal to the genetic *variance* in fitness at that time. What this means in lay language, noting that the term "fitness" in biology has the special meaning of *ability to survive,* is that those animals with greatest ability to change or mutate also have the greatest likelihood of increasing in number. This is illustrated clearly in the case of fruit flies. When one population of flies is irradiated (in order to increase the number of genetic mutations) it adapts to a new environment (say a change in average temperature) much faster than a population of the same flies not subjected to radiation. In competition, the irradiated flies—the mutants—would take over the scene, and the others would disappear. (This conclusion is definitely one that is not applicable to man, with his long generation time and his limited production capacity.)

Astonishing as it may seem, there is little agreement among biologists as to whether food or the lack of it is a major factor in increase or decrease in natural animal populations. Temperature is definitely more important, at least in the case of flies. The number of flies produced at a temperature of twenty-five degrees Centigrade is slightly larger than at nineteen degrees, but the flies born at the higher temperature are smaller, hence the biomass (or total weight of flies) produced per unit of available food is the same at either temperature. Furthermore, the average longevity is 40 per cent greater at the lower temperature. If one greatly increases the food supply, the rate of births jumps by 50 per cent, but the population increase is only 17 per cent, since the amply fed animals live shorter lives, presumably on account of overcrowding. Yet *undercrowding* in the fruit flies can be as harmful as overcrowding. The larvae survive better at some intermediate density of population. (For one thing, female flies prefer to deposit their eggs near places where eggs have already been laid by other females. This female sociability or gregariousness has been found to be genetically inherited.)

It was found that when two species of fruit fly, *D. nebulosa* and *D. serrata,* were made to live together at a temperature of twenty-five degrees Centigrade, the former eliminated the latter within four or five generations. This was to be expected and illustrates the well-known principle of "competitive exclusion." But imagine the consternation of the biologists when it was found that by decreasing the temperature to nineteen degrees Centigrade, both species coexisted happily until the experiment was finally stopped after sixty generations. The explanation seems to be this (and it proves that in animals, like insects, that have different forms in the young and in the adult stages, the competitive exclusion principle is by no means a sacred fiat): at the temperature of nineteen degrees one species is at an advantage in the larval (food) stage, while the other is less affected by overcrowding in the adult stage. The relative advantages cancel each other out at certain stable ratios of the two species. Thus, although they rely on the same food, they can reach a stable equilibrium. Obviously the equilibrium is easily disturbed by unpredictable factors, just as the equilibrium between American Indians and Caucasians was grossly disarranged by the crucial fact that the Indians had developed little or no resistance to smallpox.

3. Birth Control among the Small Animals

The response of the fruit fly to overcrowding is mysterious and important and we shall see echoes of this complex of instincts as we climb down and up the ladder of evolution. If we go about as low as we can, Hans Kalmus of the University of London has called attention to such an instinct in viruses, or at least in that type of virus known as a bacteriophage, which lives by invading and taking over the minute body of a bacterium. Such a virus can be viewed as a mere splinter of life consisting of a DNA or RNA molecule covered with a protein sheath. Yet it has an instinct for time and breeding activity much more sophisticated than that of a Pakistani farmer. The great rate of multiplication of bacteriophages, which divide once every few minutes, causes them to exhaust rather quickly the material of their more slowly growing bacterial hosts, leading to the death of the host (lysis). If it were not for the occurrence of latent non-multiplying bacteriophages, unchecked bacteriolysis would have long ago resulted in the extinction of all phage-sensitive bacteria together with the extinction of the phage. This seems to have been avoided by an automatic mutation of the phage *enabling it to suppress its own multiplication under certain conditions.* (Thus we see a universal instinct, extending down to the tiniest living thing, to avoid destruction of the species by the instrument *of birth limitation* of the species.) These mutated phages have survived and their favorite hosts along with them. Throughout the history of life on the planet, undoubtedly millions of species of phages have become extinct because the instinct did not develop. In their mutation in the direction of lowered rate of multiplication, the phages may indirectly have caused genetic changes in the host bacteria. To this is ascribed, for example, by Kalmus, the sudden and mysterious decrease in the virulence of scarlet fever streptococcus just before World War I. The myxomatosis virus was brought to Australia to reduce the population of European rabbits, which had been imprudently introduced into a habitat where there were no efficient predators. A lot of rabbits died off but today the virus has lost its oomph. It seems that in this adjustment between the virus and the rabbit, weaker strains of virus evolved and tended to replace the virulent strains, for the same reason that bacteriophages of slower multiplication power evolved—so that the virus would not be obliterated along with the rabbit. Simultaneously rabbits developed immunity but in this situation the gentling of the virus was more crucial.

This instinct for limitation of numbers in more complicated animals may take shape in a variety of acts or suppressions. The fruit flies, above a certain population density, simply reduce their rate of egg laying. In flour beetles cannibalism rears its head among some species and egg production drops off. In one beetle species crowding results in the female puncturing some of the eggs she has produced. The frequency of copulation also slows down. Some kinds of flour beetles have glands that produce a gas that is released as they find themselves stumbling over too many neighbors. The gas is lethal to the beetle's own larvae and acts also as an anti-aphrodisiac (the two sexes find each other disagreeable). Flour contamination with beetle excrement inhibits the egg production of another closely related species.

In some spider crabs and spiders fratricide with or without cannibalism among larvae is a common reaction to excessive population. Density-dependent controls in the small animals thus vary immensely, even from one species of a genus to another. In some species these controls are iron-clad, inflexible, holding the population steady or locked in predictable oscillations. In others the control may be lax or even entirely absent over long periods of time, with the result that such external factors as the weather dominate the rate of increase or decrease of the numbers of a given animal in a given place. The oscillations of the gray larch bud moth in the Engadine Valley of Switzerland are peculiarly instructive. At low population densities a "strong" form of this animal gains advantage by virtue of its higher reproductive powers and greater tendency to scatter and explore. But when its numbers reach a certain concentration, it tends to be attacked by the so-called "granulosis virus"—a social disease peculiar only to this strain of moth. The "weak" form, being resistant to this disease, then begins to predominate, but its density in turn is limited by a microscopic wasp which becomes a parasite only on the "weak" form under crowding conditions. Thus the cycle endlessly swings back and forth in the Engadine Valley.

All bets are off when a given species makes its way, usually by man's help, into a new land with a new ecology. Commonly it fails to make the grade. (It must be continually borne in mind that *living* species represent a small percentage—about 1 per cent—of all the species that have once existed upon the earth.) When the animal is suited to the strange land, it is suddenly set free from the controls that confined it in its native habitat and undergoes an orgy of feeding and reproduction. Examples in the United States are the Japanese beetle, the European gypsy moth, the South American fire ants, the Asiatic chestnut blight (a fungus), the European starling and the English sparrow. The outbreak of chestnut blight was so ravening that it practically rendered the American chestnut extinct. After vast increases in the number of Japanese beetles, a social disease (a bacterial epidemic) spread through the armies of this beetle and still remains the chief control upon their mass depredations.

In considering the effect of food supply in controlling populations, the question is an important one as to what proportion of animals feeds on living or non-living matter. The animal kingdom feeds in an overwhelming majority on other living organisms. Herbivores, parasites, predators vastly outnumber truly *saprophytic* species (those that eat excrement or carrion). Many of the animals that are popularly supposed to feed on dead plant matter are actually getting their nourishment from the living bacteria that swarm in such matter, in other words, the animals are not saprophytic but herbivorous or fungivorous. For example, nematodes do not eat humus but they eat the bacteria or yeasts that themselves fatten on the humus. Fruit flies do not like a diet of decaying fruit. What they are after is yeasts and other micro-organisms inhabiting the dead fruit.

The way in which plants are able to cope with herbivorous animals determines to a great degree the survival of both the plants and the population of the animals. High population densities of plant-eating animals created a strong selective evolutionary pressure on the plants to develop nastiness or repellency or subtle poisons. The animals in turn may develop new offensive techniques. In time some degree of equilibrium may be reached under natural conditions. An example years ago was the near ruin that the Hessian fly brought upon Kansas wheat. By the help of man (specifically R. H. Painter) a fly-resistant strain of wheat was developed and the fly population dropped to a harmlessly low equilibrium level. When young pea aphids are placed on a common crop variety of alfalfa, they produce an average of 290 offspring per female every ten days. When the same aphids are allowed to settle upon a special resistant strain of alfalfa, the average offspring is only two per female. Similar differences are seen in ordinary and resistant strains of sorghum.

The interminable contest between species can be a shot in the arm for subtle evolutionary improvements. Entomologists have observed the endless cycles of dominance between caged populations of the housefly and the blowfly. During eighty generations (160 weeks) there was a persistent alternation of dominance of first the blowfly and then the housefly. Once having achieved temporary rule, one species becomes genetically lazy, while the "under-fly" is making mutational experiments and as a result of the statistical success of such experiments evolves a kind of fly that can carry out a successful revolt. This newly dominant variety rests on its laurels, while evolution prods the new "under-fly," and so it goes. So far such experiments have shown no damping of the oscillations between the dominance of one species and the other. Apparently this is an example of a rather strange kind of equilibrium—a steady swinging of the pendulum, provided ecological conditions otherwise remain the same (of course they do not ordinarily in nature, save in exceptional cases such as the "strong" and "weak" bud moths of the Engadine Valley).

However, what we are now more concerned about is the fact that the danger of too dense a population of an animal species settling in one part of the land, exhausting all its sources of nutrition and so starving, can and is prevented by a mutual repulsion acting on the animals of the same species, making them space out or lower their rate of increase, or destroy each other.

Let us examine in this connection societies that are peculiarly similar to human societies—those of the ants. In a good ant year one sees a large number of thriving colonies but these numbers never become excessive, because they are regulated in a tyrannical and remorseless way during the time of colonization. The vast majority of swarming sexual pairs do not survive and if they happen to land in the territory of an established colony of the same species they will be attacked and devoured. Thus in a given territory only a certain number of ant colonies can be established. This instinct to limit population density finds its most refined embodiment in the advanced species of property-conscious (food-storing or food-raising) harvester ants, who carry out systematic wars of decimation between colonies. (We must necessarily call this behavior advanced, since the only other animal on the planet that deliberately wages war between the colonies of his own species is man.) Many historic ant battles, much bloodier than Verdun, have been observed or remarked upon. Thoreau was especially interested in the chronicles of ant wars.

The mystique of such societies deserves further attention. Why and how did they become social in the first place? Since it is known that they are relatively recent (100 million years of society) and are descended from wasplike Hymenoptera, it is perhaps only courteous to examine first some social traits of the wasps. The studies of the *Polistes* wasps by Mary Jane West of the University of Michigan have thrown light on the remarkable "foundress" association in this genus, which meets the strictest biological criterion of social or altruistic behavior: that is, *it is an activity of an individual that benefits the young of others of the same species.*

The one-comb, primitive nests of *Polistes* wasps are started by a single determined female, which in some species may be joined by from one to ten other "foundresses" (females on a nest before the brood hatches). This female sociality—the co-operation of females in rearing the brood before the emergence of offspring *workers*—is common in *Polistes* despite the resultant sterility of a large number of fertilized females. (This is as if in a group of pregnant women all but one decided to abort their own children in order to become nursemaids.) Only one foundress of each colony ultimately becomes a queen, or egg-layer. The others become idle or, more commonly, sterile workers which care for the queen's brood but don't lay eggs.

What is the motive for this basic and extraordinary unselfishness? Is the foundress association (which is really a sort of voluntary pecking order) designed to limit the number of the species or to improve the *quality* of the species? Some biologists claim that joining a foundress association would be advantageous to the species if by making the sacrifice of her own fertility and becoming a nursemaid, more replicas of good genes could be produced than the sacrificial wasp could expect to make on her own. The sterility of *daughter* worker wasps on a parental nest is theoretically explainable on the grounds of gene stability, since in insects such as *Polistes,* where the males have only one set of genes (haploidy), sisters have more genes "identical by descent" than do sisters and daughters. However, it is hard to explain on this basis the ready acceptance of sterility by sisters of the queen, since their nieces would have less closely related genes than their own daughters, which they have sacrificed.

These arguments and questions seem somehow rather thin and ghostly. The ghostliness disappears, however, if one assumes that foundress associations are formed to *prevent* an excess population of *Polistes* wasps, which would certainly occur if all fertilized females produced to their capacity. As mentioned, there can actually be perceived a pecking order among the foundresses, possibly correlated with degree of ovary development but also significantly associated (as Mary Jane West has noted) with the time of joining the foundress nest. In other words, the first female to arrive became top banana, not only because her ovaries were about to disgorge eggs but also because she was there first. The subsequent arrivals took their place as helpers in a linear hierarchy in the order of their arrival.

This is not invariably the case in all species of *Polistes*. In three cases observed in *P. canadensis,* later arriving females usurped the queen's place, possibly because these Mary Queen of Scots were closer to egg laying. One of the ousted queens sat forlorn near her former nest, while two philosophically unflappable displaced queens set out to form other foundress colonies. In *P. furcatus* five changes in residence led to two nest-starters and egg-bearers becoming workers in the nests of other females.

It is possible to see in the *Polistes* foundress habit a foreshadowing of the queen-worker-drone hives of the bees and the immensely complicated caste colonies of ants, in all cases the tendency being to limit egg laying to one female of a group of varying size. This is not only the beginning of true insect sociality but it is the establishment of a clear-cut, foolproof mechanism of population control which may, however, require additional help, such as the murdering of intrusive young, fertilized females. (It is of incidental interest that the nests of the *Polistes* wasp are constructed of plant fiber mixed with saliva. This fiber is notably tough and was once a favorite material for the wadding of the muzzle-loading guns of American pioneers.)

The degree of sociality of wasps varies greatly. Some species are tiny parasites on other animals and are thus no more social than fleas or ticks. The tiny fig wasp has established a symbiotic relationship so inflexible that all species of figs must be pollinated by chalcid wasps (no other means of pollination will do) and the wasp cannot hatch anywhere except in the receptacles of the fig. There are some rather peculiar associations of an unclassified kind between certain wasps and certain birds. Mostly the bird seeks the wasps' nest and may decide to live in it. The wasps do not object to the birds but do attack humans and other animals that come too close. While the bird gets rent-free lodging, it is not clear what benefit the wasps get in return. (We shall see later that many ants tolerate and even protect a variety of intruders into their nests.) Some wasps are solitary and fierce predators (e.g., the tarantula hawk).

According to entomologists, sociality among the Hymenoptera has been achieved independently at least ten times in the course of evolution. Quite recently social organization of some complexity has been discovered among the sphecid wasps of Puerto Rico by Robert W. Matthew of Harvard. Here the development of the absolute queen has not yet been achieved. Baglike, pendent nests are made only from the wax scraped from the underside of the fronds of the Crysophila palm tree, and the colonies are found nowhere except near these palms. In nearly every case one female in the nest was found to have unhatched eggs, or oöcytes, much more developed than her nest-mates and she lays most but not all of the eggs. However, the nests are more like apartment houses than bungalows. No two cells in a given nest are ever in the same stage of development, so, regardless of the number of females, only one mature egg is available in the colony at any time. Foraging females from each nest co-operate in bringing food to one cell at a time. Someone always stays home to guard the nest, which is protected fiercely against intruders. Very few new nests are built and when they are they tend to be close by so the offspring usually live at home—or next-door, a fact which promotes a high population viscosity and the probability of nest-mates being relatives. This may, in fact, be a necessary genetic preliminary in the evolution of true social behavior. If we stick to the rigorous biological definition of sociality as the activity of an individual benefitting the young of another of the same species, a different genus of the same sphecid wasps is not social.* Its nests consist of husband and wife, the male guarding the entrance while the female is out shopping for food. This idyllic family pair is unusual in the insect world to the point of perversion.

The evolution of ants from wasps has been demonstrated by the discovery of ants preserved for 100 million years in amber, found recently in New Jersey. The noted Harvard biologist E. O. Wilson and co-workers are of the opinion that, although social in nature, these were members of a new subfamily of ants representing a link between the non-social tiphiid wasp and the most primitive Myrmoecoil ants. The presence of a metapleural gland in this and all other primitive ants points to the evolution of ants from the ancestors of today's wasps. This organ may, in fact, be a kind of "socializing" organ, its secretions being necessary to the development of ant colonization. The heads of these ancient New Jersey ants are remarkably wasplike.

In some modern ants sociality has proceeded to the point of the specialization of castes as gardeners for growing food. One may truly say that the fungus-growing New World tribe of myrmicine ants, the Attini, were the world's first farmers. As described so delicately by Neal Weber of Swarthmore College, these ants eat only the fungus that they culture and *this kind of fungus is not found outside of an ant's nest*. In this remarkably skilled and complicated process of gardening a flourishing growth of the one fungus is produced and of this fungus only, although the medium on which it grows is suitable for the growth of many other kinds of organisms. When the ants are removed these other organisms multiply and replace the fungus. The garden becomes a foul mess. It is evident that the ant castes responsible for the vegetable garden are very diligent at removing "weeds."

* As we shall see in numerous further examples, I am much more inclined to accept V. C. Wynne-Edward's viewpoint on sociality *as a means of checking uncontrolled reproduction of the species.*

The vital part of the attine nest is, in fact, the fungus garden, which is also the abode of the queen and the brood, understandably so, since they are the heartiest eaters. All members of the tribe subsist solely on this special fungus but some are soldiers, some are leaf-cutters (bringing in food for the fungus), some never leave the garden but continuously cultivate it. These ants seem to have been a source of distress to the early Spanish explorers, since Bartolome de las Casas in 1559 described the failure of the Spaniards in Hispaniola to grow cassava and citrus trees because of leaf-cutting ants whose nests were "white as snow" (probably because of the fungus gardens and the brood). Argentina in 1909 by legal edict considered *"hormigas coloradas"* and *"hormigas negras"* to be plagues on account of the leaf cutting. These were later identified as attine ants of the species *Atta sexdens* and *Acromyrmex lundi*. The Indians of Central and South America used to eat the large *Atta* queens, since their egg-filled gasters were as nutritious and tasty as caviar.

Such ants can do more good than harm in forming deep soil in the tropical rain forests. In such areas few animals and few roots of trees go much below the soil surface. A large *Atta* nest contains far more organic matter, in the form of hundreds of fungus gardens, than any other soil agency. This makes possible the multiplication of bacteria and other organisms that can exist deep underground, only because the ants have carried the surface humus and soil there. On the pampas of Argentina the presence of nests of *Acromyrmex* is in fact detectable by the richer growth of plant life above and around them. An *Atta* colony starts, as do all ant societies, with one productive female. In the forty to sixty days before a worker caste develops, she has kept herself alive by eating 90 per cent of her eggs ("alimentary eggs") or feeding them to the first larvae. She is richly endowed since the newly fertilized female stores in her spermatheca some 300 million sperm as the result of mating probably with as many as eight males, who die right after the nuptial flight. A full range of worker castes appears between the fourth and tenth months of the queen's reign, the soldier caste not showing up until the twenty-second month. A typical mature nest may have about 2,000 chambers, 300 containing trash, 150 with loose soil, 250 with gardens and 1,200 empty. (The empty chambers are for sheltering the sexual forms after they have matured and before they leave on the nuptial flight.)

The caste system is graduated according to size. If ants are noticed in files of different-sized individuals, the chances are very good that they belong to *Acromyrmex* or *Atta.* The size spectrum is continuous from the smallest, or *minima,* caste through a series of intermediate, or *media,* to the largest workers, or *maxima,* and the giants, the soldiers, with very big heads. A large number of soldiers is characteristic of a mature colony. They tend to remain in the garden and come out mostly when the nest is disturbed. Their jaws will with one slash produce a five-millimeter cut in the human skin. They can cut half-moon sections out of a man's leather boots. The *minima* caste is largely confined to the gardens, culturing the fungus and caring for the eggs and the small larvae. The *media* tend the garden and the brood but also go out to cut leaves. The *maxima* cut leaves and gather other material and protect the colony.

Although the queen alone is able to start a colony, the odds are she will not make it. Of young nests 99.95 per cent are destroyed by predators or other causes within fifteen months. After the workers mature and the society is well under way, the odds become more favorable for survival. The queen, unassisted in her first laying, now receives fussy attention. The workers remove the eggs as soon as they appear at the cloaca. (The queen of more primitive species lays eggs unassisted during her whole life.) The larvae lie on their side with their mouth parts pouting for food and the nursing workers respond by placing clusters of fungus threads on them. In the pupal stage, ants of such an advanced society cannot emerge without the help of the nurses. They have been in continual attendance, licking the skin and grooming it. They continue these services to the young sexual forms, but the callow worker is on its own. It quickly learns to feed on strands of fungus. The individual workers (as among bees) have short, busy lives, seldom lasting beyond eighteen months; the males live only the few weeks of maturity through the nuptial flight, while the fertilized females have about the same life expectancy as a woman of ancient Rome (about twenty years) and doubtless would live as long as a turtle if they were not subject to so much predation.

Let us examine in a little more detail the agricultural technique of this marvelous insect. When the cut leaf sections are brought into the nest they are recut by other specialists into much smaller pieces and licked all over. The gardener ants then press along the edges of these pieces with their sharp little jaws so that the fragments become wet and pulpy. The ants then deposit a clear anal droplet on the mashed leaf, which is then carried into the garden and forced into a prearranged place. A gardener ant picks up tufts of fungus and places them at intervals on the prepared leaf. Branches, or hyphae, grow out in all directions from the tuft. Some of the worker ants, instead of cutting leaves, specialize in gathering woody particles or other organic trash or even white cassava starch granules, which they drag to the garden, defecate upon and plant alongside the fungus mycelium. They may drag parts of insect carcasses to the nest and scatter them over the garden. These, too, acquire luxuriant islands of fungus growth.

All attine ants have the same technique for tending the gardens. The ants walk over all of the exposed parts and even down into the mycelial cells, using their antennae as probes to test the condition of the crop. They lick the hyphae (branches) and occasionally eat them. Anal droplets are normally deposited only on the garden. These and the saliva must be remarkably selective weed-killers, because the spores of all fungi except their chosen food crop, although constantly brought by accident, never proliferate. The brood, like the garden, is continually licked and presumably protected in this way against harmful parasites. Enough saliva is applied to the queen to keep her in glistening health and much of the spare time of the workers is spent in grooming each other.

Mycologists (fungus experts) have been puzzled in trying to classify the crops raised by such ants, since they have no recognized wild relatives. The currently accepted names are *Leucocoprimus gongylophora* and the genus *Lepiata* (many species).

It is noteworthy that, in spite of all the aggressive hygiene and precision pest control of the gardens, *Attini* tolerate a houseguest —a wingless cockroach which feeds on scraps. When the virgin females leave the parent nest on their nuptial flight, these tiny cockroaches attach themselves to such potential queens and thus share their fate in new colonies. It is as if a marrying girl took her pet dog along with her on the honeymoon.

Ant colonies of many kinds keep pets (known as myrmecophiles) and in fact this may be one of the offbeat peculiarities of all social life. The formidable harvester ants allow tiny wingless crickets in the nest, who, like lap dogs, have reached an evolutionary stage at which they can no longer make their own living. The crickets nibble at the bodies and legs of the ants to obtain oily secretions as their only food. Another kind of ant associate, more of a vagrant and tramp than a pet, the *Scottinella* beetle, occasionally runs along with the ants during the day. Some live in the ant nest and are tolerated—an amazing act of benevolence since they often feed upon the ant pupae. Their safety may lie in the fact that they live in little silken cells semi-isolated from the ant colony even when in its midst. The carpenter ants (so called because they can tunnel through dead wood) also have beetle houseguests (*Atemeles*), but in this case there is some degree of mutual benefit. These tiny beetles secrete a drug upon which the ants feed voraciously. The beetle larvae are tended and fed along with the ant larvae by the ant nursemaid workers. So passionate is the attachment of the ants for the beetles that, although *Atemeles* frequently gobbles up ant larvae when the nursemaids are not looking, the ants dash to the defense of the beetle larvae in preference to their own when the nest is broken into or grossly disturbed. The carpenter ants also have small crickets as pets. The toleration of pets is seen also among bumblebees, who apparently control their own population by periodic periods of lethal hysterical fighting among members even of the same nest. In the midst of such a family ruckus, a fly that through past ages has grown to resemble the bumblebee closely, although having no stinger, casually makes his way to the honey pot in the burrow's chamber, skirting struggling bodies. This fly stays with the bees through at least one summer and is welcomed in this house of discord, much in the fashion of the "man who came to dinner." After he has taken a deep draught of the bees' hard-won nectar, worker bees may examine him and help clean up his disarranged fur. The fly does no work but has an honorable status in the hive. He will witness strange fights between the queen bumblebee and other hive bees while she tries to lay eggs. The workers may even eat the eggs but she will persist. It is probable that this cannibalism and family hostility is connected with the fact that bumblebees have no predators and thus adopt a rather Celtic method of controlling their own numbers.

In such intricately braided-together societies as the ants and bees, ideal communism prevails in regard to food. The colony's economics is based not only on the primacy of the queen and the brood as food consumers but on complete exchange of food between the workers. If a given worker ant is well fed, it may be solicited by another (hungry) ant. The two of them will raise the foreparts of their bodies and one will produce from its mouth a drop which the other eagerly swallows. This liquid food comes up from the crop, which has been aptly called the "social stomach." It is a large reservoir in the front of the ant's belly between the gullet and the true stomach, and only when food passes a valve from the crop to the true stomach does the food become the private property of the individual ant. Until this act of digestion the food always belongs to anybody that requires it. It is "collectivized" food.

Ant society is, in fact, military communism. Although the mighty harvesters are known to wage systematic colonial wars, the soldier caste in other species is important and is, from the standpoint of biology, perhaps the most "altruistic" of the castes. Unlike the food-storing harvesters, most ant colonies cannot afford universal military service and gigantic mass offensives. Conceivably a given ant queen might secure herself a better chance of surviving by a greater production of soldiers, even though most or all of the individual soldiers were killed in their acts of devotion to the nest.

But ant soldiers are big and must be fed, in most cases by the labor of other ant castes, so there is an economic limit to professional ant militarism. One therefore seldom sees more than a modest proportion of the soldier caste, as, for example, in human terms in modern Switzerland or Denmark. The harvester colonies are more like Russia. In some cases military ants may attach themselves to certain trees and protect them against the leaf-cutting hordes of *Atta* and other leaf-destroying insects. Anybody who has climbed an acacia tree as a child is familiar with its population of defenders. The acacia provides its personal ant army with food in the form of sweet honeydew exuded near the base of each leaf petiole. The acacia's cunning does not stop here. In order to make the protective ants patrol the whole leaf, it has developed an additional source of food at the tips of the leaves in the form of the so-called "Beltian bodies." One sees here a form of symbiosis which charmingly proves the point that trees are no fools.

We have mentioned before that, since it is a much older and physiologically simpler animal, the termite or "white ant" has received less respect for its social behavior than such marvels as the harvester or *Atta* ants. It is true that Maurice Maeterlinck sold millions of copies of books about this creature but most of his material seems to have been copied, in some cases word for word, from the obscure works of the young naturalist Eugène Marais, who developed the mystical idea of the termite colony as a single organism, distributed in small functional particles, but was unable to put together enough money to sue the great Maeterlinck for plagiarism.

In terms of ancient ancestry the termite is a sort of tiny socialistic cockroach with no genetic connections whatsoever with the ants or other Hymenoptera. It is thus utterly astounding that in its societies it should have developed such nearly exact parallels of behavior with the ant, although preceding it on earth by at least a hundred million years. It is more gracious to the termite to concede that the ants (unconsciously) imitated the termites' colonial systems and in many respects failed to equal them in complexity or efficiency. Like the cow with its rumen, the termite solved a food problem and made it unnecessary to worry about famine, since as long as wood was available it could eat. Like ants, termites are able to regurgitate some partly digested food from the anus, some nutritious portions being passed out for the consumption of other termites. One reason for this is the wood or cellulose diet. To break down the cellulose requires, as in the cow's rumen, special microorganisms, some of which are also consumed as high-value protein food. These are not present in the gut of the young termite but he promptly acquires them through eating the feces of older termites.

We have mentioned that the presence of the king and queen inhibits, by chemical pheromones, the development of additional reproductive individuals, except in parts of the nest distant from the royal chamber. If a colony is deprived of the king and queen, substitute monarchs of either sex will develop within a short time from undifferentiated nymphs. If an orphaned termite colony is separated from a normal one by fine wire screens which prevent all contact and all transfer of secretions, the isolated group will develop a king and queen in the normal manner. If only a single screen separates the groups, preventing transfer of secretions but allowing members of the two colonies to touch each other with their antennae, a peculiar thing happens. The orphaned group will develop substitute kings and queens but will kill them as fast as they appear. The orphaned colony, in physical contact with another of its species, seems to be aware that another royal couple is in the vicinity and is not sure two sets of royalty are proper.

At first glance it would appear that population control of the termite species (or at least of the relative number of the different castes) is entirely at the discretion of the king and queen. Recent research indicates this may not be the whole story. There seems to be little doubt that the young king and queen inhibit the sexual development of larvae, but when enough workers have appeared, the workers themselves secrete pheromones to promote the development of soldiers and, in some species, of winged sexual adults. The soldiers themselves secrete social hormones which inhibit the formation of more soldiers. The orderly layering of a society with exquisite balance is thus instinctually achieved by the castes themselves. There is no such marvel of equilibrium in any other society on earth.

At least originally, before the evolution of the ants, the termite soldier was probably not so much a military creature as a member of a corps of engineers. They still repair broken places in the nest and carry out other construction jobs. Probably when the termites' mortal enemies, the ants, appeared on earth the soldiers became specialized fighters. Many species have several types of soldiers, each with his special task. There are large, medium and small soldiers, some with normal heads, some with snouts like beaks or sabers. The latter, the nasuti, use these snouts to spray enemies with a liquid which is more annoying than lethal—a sort of Mace—and it can also serve as a glue in repairing the nest. There is a limit to the proportion of soldiers, more specific than in the case of ants, since, because of the shape of their mouths, the nasuti cannot feed themselves. The workers thus exert an inflexible citizens' control on the number and vigor of the military.

Soldier termites strike the alarm by striking their heads rapidly against the tunnel floor. This usually means: "The ants are coming!" In most cases a termites' nest is in the long run overrun by the larger, more aggressive ants, but they will know they have been in a fight. The embattled nest is often so full of glue from the termite soldiers' squirting that the ants may retire in disgust and are often trapped and destroyed by brave termite defenders.

Although we have always thought of the spider as a solitary hunter, a number of species of social spiders have been discovered and some significant points of interest for the theory of sociality emerge from the study of their laying habits. Most of these gregarious spiders are in the tropics, where food is ample so that populations of small carnivores are unlikely to be limited by lack of insect prey. Among the tropical uloborids are many species that spin immense webs where large numbers of males and females live amicably together (another sign of abundant food, since the male is often on the menu of the female in less productive climates). B. Kullmann of the University of Bonn has shown movies of social eresid spiders in West Pakistan. If an insect is thrown into the giant web, it will be attacked from all sides. The spiders feed on the carcass together. It is the duty of the last spider left sucking to remove the dried carcass from the web. B. Krafft of the University of Strasbourg has established in his own laboratory a colony of *Agelena socialis* spiders from Gabon (South Equatorial Africa). These spiders hunt large insects together in the communal web like a pack of wolves bringing down a caribou. The spiders fight each other only if the web is too small. In the case of the Pakistan spiders, numerous colonies may be interconnected, the individuals moving from one colony to another at their pleasure (probably for mating). The salient point is this: these social spiders, in laying, average only forty eggs per sac, whereas a closely related non-social species has as many as 600 eggs per sac. Although more information is needed on these abnormal animals, it seems very likely that socialization in this case is a clear route to limitation of the rate of population growth.

In some cases primitive people depend on social spiders, just as the natives of Borneo depended on gecko lizards, to protect them against flies. The villagers of mountainous parts of Michoacán, in Mexico, are plagued during the rainy season by immense swarms of flies that invade their homes. The defense is the *mosquero* (*Coenothele gregaris*), a tiny crebellate spider one eighth of an inch long which lives in vast colonies on scrub oaks at an altitude of 8,000 feet or more. The nest of the *mosquero* community surrounds each branch of a tree with a spongy inner layer of dry silken line and with an outer envelope of sticky hackled-band threads. The mountain villagers of Michoacán cut such an invested branch from a tree and suspend it as an animated fly trap from their ceilings. They dispose of immense quantities of flies. These colonies of fierce little *mosqueros* tolerate another animal in the web, a still smaller insect, a beetle of the genus *Melanophthalura*, who cleans the nest of debris and lives on microscopic bits of food discarded by the spiders. Also living in curious harmony with the *mosquero* colony is one of the running spiders, *Poecilochroa convictrix*, although the precise status of this rather ominous guest is not known. It would be rather like keeping an ape around the house. Pets (or commensals) are quite common among social animals and, as we learn more about the colonial spiders, we shall doubtless discover more associations where the guest species perform some useful function as garbage disposers or the like or have lived so long in the colony without invitation that the host species has simply forgotten that they once were strangers.

Man often finds himself unknowingly helped by an invisible hand of predation. During 1923 and 1924 there was an incredible increase in the numbers of bedbugs in Athens—an embarrassment to this seat of classical splendor, then anxious to build up tourist trade. The then available pesticides did no good, but as if by a miracle a tremendously efficient predator—the crab spider (*Thanatus flavidus*)—suddenly appeared in great numbers and by 1925 had eradicated the Athenian bedbug population. As the bedbugs disappeared, the crab spiders retired, shrank in numbers and resumed more normal predatory habits. (In retrospect it would now be useful to know why 1923 and 1924 were the years of the bedbug in Athens but it is almost as impossible now to reconstruct this ecological situation as it is to guess what virus or bacillus was responsible for the "sweating sickness" that decimated the armies of Henry VII of England, killed many important people of that time but never returned.) The large jumping spider *Ascyltus pterygodes* has similarly saved, time after time, the ravaging of coconut palms in the Fiji Islands by moths. There is also the ladybird who saved the California citrus crops from aphids. We shall see that larger animals are often controlled in population explosions by disease organisms.

We cannot leave the subject of arthropod sociality without considering the pollinating relationship of plants and insects. Although bee colonies are controlled to a major extent, as in other colonial Hymenoptera, by the queen's instinct in limiting the production of sexual forms, the bee is peculiarly dependent on plants and their structure. Insects and plants existed many million years before insect pollination but the honeybees evolved only as flowering plants evolved. The first insect-pollinated flower was probably a generalized type, such as the ancestor of the buttercup and the magnolia. "Bee flowers" are yellow or blue, since bees are color-blind to red. Butterflies can pollinate orange and red flowers, such as the carnation, the catchfly and the day lily. Night-blooming flowers such as the datura, the tobacco, yucca and most orchids rely on moths for pollination. The flowering plants have shown a good deal of evolutionary ingenuity in developing attractants for various other pollinators. Some plants, for example, develop "perfumes" that resemble decaying flesh or dung. The starfish cactus smells like carrion. The giant arum in Sumatra generates heat at the time of blooming to volatilize its carrion odor, thus attracting beetles. The foxglove and some orchids have throats marked with lines leading into the nectar-holding flower tube, functioning as landing platforms. Without moth larvae the yucca would not be pollinated and yucca is the sole host for its particular moth. We have here a tight symbiosis in which neither plant nor animal can live without the other.

Some plants, by a sinister extrapolation of the insect attractant theme, have become carnivorous. It seems so easy to get the pollinating insects within the flower or the hollow leaf—why not *eat* some of them? Thus the Venus's-flytrap and the sundew. The leaves are covered by setae, each tipped with adhesive so that gnats are stuck and are slowly digested. In the pitcher plant, insects are lured into leaf tubes by odor and cannot escape because the inner walls are covered with slippery scales and spines. A gaseous narcotic kills the prisoners. In *Nepenthes* cup-shaped containers contain water. Insects falling in are killed and digested. (Some sly insects, however, immune to the poisoned water, live happily in the pools and feed on the trapped insects.)

Although the flea as an animal is not an especially successful one, the drama and terror of his association with man in the plagues of earlier centuries makes it advisable to examine his habits—which are purely parasitical. As pointed out by Miriam Rothschild, mammals have been available as possible hosts for parasitic insects for some 180 million years. A fossil flea, scarcely different from living species, was found in Baltic amber dating from fifty million years ago. It is thought that fleas evolved first as winged scavenging flies, feeding on larvae or excrement in the homes of burrowing animals. Countless generations later a pioneer flea decided to creep into the fur of a passing mammal (a small one) and pierce the skin to live on blood—an exciting leap forward from the not dissimilar act of piercing the crust of weathered feces. Mammalian blood is a very rich and attractive food and to imbibe it, a host of desperate animals will make themselves dangerously dependent and overspecialized. It is possible, in fact, that parasitic animals may be more numerous than all others but the flea is not a great success statistically. There are some 300,000 kinds of beetles but only 1,500 species of fleas. There are many more kinds of bird lice than there are kinds of birds. On the other hand the number of mammalian species is much greater than the number of species of fleas, many kinds of which have undoubtedly been exterminated in the past.

It is not often realized that the rat flea itself was the chief sufferer from the plague bacillus. The rat flea that carried the Black Death germ from one sick rat to another, and then moved on to the next available host—man—was responsible for pandemics that exterminated one quarter of the human population of Europe. Yet for every rat or man that died, ten times as many fleas perished. In South America both the native rabbits and their fleas have become adapted to the myxoma virus and both recover smoothly from infections. In Britain the rabbit population is not immune and an ideal vector was another rabbit-specific flea, one of the most successful fleas known. An epizootic swept the British rabbit population, perhaps 100 million rabbits dying during the first outbreak. Each rabbit carried about seventy-five fleas, who perished with their hosts (since, unlike the rat flea, the rabbit flea was entirely overspecialized and could not live on other animals). Thus the epizootic must have killed a billion fleas in Britain alone.

Flea larvae can be indifferent to cold but cannot stand dryness. A species of bird flea parasitizes an antarctic petrel. There the fleas are found alive in the nests of the petrel, buried for nine months of the year under yards of ice and snow. Even the adult rabbit flea can take the cold. They can be kept for nine months in a refrigerator at slightly below the freezing point of water, rattling around like pebbles in a glass container, yet able to feed and jump only a few minutes after defrosting. Wings are a nuisance to a flea living in fur, but that they once had wings is suggested by wing rudiments in the pupal stage. In place of wings they developed outrageously powerful jumping legs.

A rabbit flea jumping onto a rabbit from the ground has a job of real engineering difficulty. In a meadow he is like a man in a forest of 600-foot trees. In his jump he usually turns over at least once in midair but manages to hold one of his three pairs of legs aloft for grabbing. Once on the rabbit the fleas make their way to the ears, where they attach themselves with sawtooth mouth parts. A very strange chemical symbiosis takes place. The fleas that settle on a rabbit's ear can never breed unless the rabbit is a female *and they breed only when she is pregnant*. Thus the breeding cycle of the flea is geared to the sex hormones secreted by the host. Ten days before young rabbits are born the eggs of female fleas begin to develop and by the last day of the doe's pregnancy they are ripe. After the rabbits are born the fleas move from the doe's ears to her face. While the mother is tending her young and eating the placenta the fleas pass on to the nestlings, on which they feed fiercely. It is there that they mate and lay eggs. After twelve days of egg laying on the little rabbits the fleas abandon the young and return to the mother. As she becomes pregnant again, they begin a new breeding cycle.

Actually the fleas come under the influence of changes in the rabbit's glandular chemistry the moment the buck sets eye on the doe. The temperature of the pairing rabbits' ears rises suddenly, so that the fleas become as excited as their hosts and hop about, moving from buck to doe and back again. The rabbit is a peculiar animal in that female ovulation *follows* coitus. Within a few hours the pituitary gland releases hormones into the blood. These hormones in turn stimulate the ovaries and the adrenal glands to secrete other hormones. One of the first effects on fleas is to make them grab on more fiercely to the skin of the doe. Hence once a flea has moved onto a pregnant doe it will stay there.

Many bird fleas, if slightly warmed, will copulate on emerging from the pupae, without a blood meal. In most species, however, the female must eat blood before her ovaries mature. The rabbit flea is an exceptional case in that the female will mate only after she has fed on the blood of newborn rabbits. In spite of the fact that rabbit fleas will make their active rendezvous only on the rabbit young, there is evidence that another hormone in the expectant mother rabbit prepares the fleas for copulation. (This material—somatotropin—is from the pituitary [a growth substance] and is one of the hormones used to increase fertility in women, and which, when it works, often results in multiple births.) Even then the female flea apparently must be subdued by an elaborate and fearsome male copulatory apparatus, including a sort of feather-duster penis and clasping organs armed with all manner of spines, struts and hooks. Considered as a whole this contraption is the most elaborate genital organ in the animal kingdom, not excepting that of the mosquito. (It may be that making copulation extraordinarily complex and even dangerous is one way of controlling population.)

The breeding behavior of the plague-carrying oriental rat flea, however, does *not* depend on the hormones of the rat. This versatile flea copulates and lays eggs even on a rat that has been castrated and had its pituitary gland removed. The number of fleas on female bats increases in the spring just before migratory bats take off for their summer breeding places, so in this case the hormones of the host may play the part of attractants.

In the literature of the seventeenth and eighteenth centuries it is repeatedly stated that women are attacked more frequently by fleas than are men. In old books it is always a woman pictured as wearing the latest design of flea trap. Although this sex difference has usually been attributed to the greater delicacy of the female skin, it is quite possible that the human flea (*Pulex irritans*) responds to ovarian hormones.

4. Population Controls Higher Up the Ladder

The theory of V. C. Wynne-Edwards of the University of Aberdeen that all social behavior, including the "territorial imperative," the pecking order and even the swarming of locusts and flocking of starlings, is designed primarily to limit the population of the species, seems to be one of those simple but immensely fruitful ideas that come out of biological thinking once every few decades. It is much more persuasive than the assumption of the mere "territorial" instinct itself, which can be twisted by dramatic amateurs to prove the inevitability of human wars and the like; and, in fact, sociality is a concept that lies much older and deeper than that of territoriality.

Consider the schooling fish. Although much has been made over the fact that a school is less vulnerable to predator fish because a shark, for example, is easily diverted from the single-minded pursuit of one fish when he is surrounded by innumerable darting prey, the argument is a rather tenuous one, since one seldom sees a shark emerge from a school of herring without a catch. Schooling has, in fact, led to the near extinction of anchovies off the coast of Peru because of the fact that bigger catches by fishermen equipped with efficient netting gear always depend on schooling habits. Neither the natural nor the unnatural (human) predator argument, however, is really relevant. The more basic fact probably is that schooling fish do not pause long enough to guard their eggs. One could thus argue that schooling is a device to increase the mortality of fish eggs and hatchlings and thus to limit the productivity of the species. Is there a leader of a school of fish? If so, it is a geometrical rather than a dictatorial figure—a mere symbol to get the fishes going together. Erich von Holst, a German neurologist, removed from a common minnow the tiny forebrain, which in this species is the site of all schooling reactions. If this brain-deficient fish saw food or had any other reason for doing so, it swam unhesitatingly in a certain direction and the whole school promptly followed it. Schooling fishes labor under conditions of contamination which may result in death or weakness, since those in the middle of the formation have less oxygen and are exposed to more carbon dioxide than the leaders or the ones on the fringes. Although shifts in position are common, there may nevertheless be a sort of mild pecking order in which the less aggressive members of the pool in the long run come out with less oxygen and more water pollution, just as people who stay all the time in New York City and never attain the suburbs have more emphysema. Some more advanced schooling fishes, such as gray mullet, definitely have a hierarchy, in which the school leaders are usually bigger than the others. This is unimportant unless, as seems improbable, the *progeny* of these leaders have a quite definitely higher chance of survival.

Animal sociality, as Wynne-Edwards has emphasized, is based on an instinctual dread of the future, not of the present. In animals below man, the only way evolution has of making them realize the importance of the future or even of its existence is by pure adaptive instincts, based on transcendental memory of the past. In most animal communities starvation is rare. No individual starves since the population does not outgrow the food supply available in its habitat. It is the unconscious threat of starvation *tomorrow* not hunger itself today that instinctively makes an animal species limit its population density, which it does by various expedients—for example, territorial defense. For birds that feed on seeds or berries in the fall or chickadees living on hibernating insects in the winter, the food supply to begin with is so huge that it could feed an enormous population—for a few hours. But the birds must depend on this supply for weeks or months. Hence social restrictions are set up. We have "territorial imperatives." We have pecking orders. Even in sea birds, there is a token nesting place on the shore or cliff that represents each bird's fishing rights. This place may occupy only a few square feet but, since the number of places is limited, so also the overall size of the colony is limited.

Wynne-Edwards got his inspiration from observation of the grouse on the Scottish heather moor. Here the dominant males hold territories almost all the year round. Occasionally the community may admit some socially subordinate males and unmated hens that have no territory of their own but with the onset of winter these barely tolerated supernumeraries get kicked out in the cold. The red grouse males, like barnyard roosters, do their crowing and threatening only on fine mornings between first light and two or three hours later. Once the morning threats are over, the same bird leaders will feed amicably side by side for the rest of the day. The convention of competing at dawn or at dusk is quite common. Ducks take flight at dusk and the massed squawky maneuvers of starlings take place as darkness is falling. Wynne-Edwards believes that these massings of birds or even of locusts are primarily for the purpose of "taking a census." The flocks can realize they are building up too much population only when they see themselves all together.

In addition to population limitation by fiercely self-enforced laws against the formation of bird tenement districts, David Lack and co-workers find that bird fecundity itself can be automatically limited by overcrowding. (Biologists distinguish between *fecundity*—the ability to reproduce—and *fertility*—the actual reproduction accomplished. In this sense the modern woman can be fecund without being fertile.) There are a large number of animal instances where overcrowding affects fecundity by a glandular mechanism which operates through the brain-connected pituitary gland.

In birds it is particularly important to realize that crowding can be either of the *habitat* or of the *niche*. A habitat, so to speak, is a bird's address; his niche is his profession. If the profession is digging grubs out of trees, it is obvious that there is room in a given area for only a certain number of woodpeckers, whatever their precise species. One species will generally drive the other out entirely and the remaining species will resort to territoriality to control its numbers. "I pick grubs in *these* trees. They are mine. Get the hell out!" Since there are only a certain number of trees—or grubs—there are only a certain number of woodpeckers.

If birds are *over*protected by giving them absurdly magnificent handouts of food or by eliminating their predators (such as snakes or sparrow hawks), the ecology is in trouble. As pointed out by Harold Mayfield, president of the American National Ornithologists Union, over five billion birds a year have to be lost in the United States to maintain a reasonable balance in the total avian population. The trouble is that our normal agricultural practices inevitably unbalance the nature of the bird population. There are no longer tens of thousands of whooping cranes, not because we shot them, but because their ancient breeding grounds are now growing wheat. This is an unfortunate but inevitable ecological happening. (The astronomically heavy use of DDT, on the other hand, affects most direly just those predator birds, such as eagles and falcons, that result in natural conservation and equilibrium.)

With birds that can all too easily become crowded on the ground, because they have little desire or aptitude for flying, such as domestic chickens, fatal heart disease may result from overcrowding. Excessive population density in that nervous bird the white stork results in the killing, sometimes the eating, of the chicks, usually by the father. This is especially true in stork families who are young and have lower status in the pecking order. It is a drastic expedient, but has been used in the history of ancient man.

In birds who become social during the mating season, some rather elaborate rituals are enforced, the net result of which is to assure not only a limit to reproduction but a sort of eugenics, involving considerable subsequent inbreeding. For example, among the sage grouse, a dominant male takes up his stand in a small area which may have been used for this purpose for many generations. Subordinate males form a ring around him at a respectful distance. If a strange male bird comes near, they drive him off. These little circles of guard cocks around a master cock will be seen during early spring just before dawn all over the mating ground. When the females arrive they are admitted into the circle but most of the mating is done by the master cock. The mating of subordinate males is strongly objected to by the master; thus the offspring are limited essentially by the amount of sperm the dominant cock can distribute, certainly not an indefinite number, while the apprentice cocks are limited to voyeurism. This technique is common throughout a large part of the animal kingdom.

Where birds do not rely on a profession which associates them with food near the ground, such as swallows, who catch insects on the wing, there is no "territorial imperative." Their nesting habits are casual and in some cases downright peculiar. The purple martin has come to rely on apartment houses built for him by men. Before the whites came to America, the Indians hung gourds on poles with crossarms, thus creating the colonial nesting conditions which the purple martins require when they come home from a hard day's chasing of mosquitoes.

Some birds have formed even more intimate associations with mammals. Magpies and mountain jays help the deer with his pests. They perch on his back or antlers, pecking very carefully. This is "cleaning symbiosis" and is quite common. Other partners in such behavior are the crocodile and the Egyptian plover, cattle and the egret, the rhinoceros and the tick bird. Even in the sea certain species of animals have come to specialize in cleaning parasites and rotten tissue from fishes that visit them. The cleaner is fed and the cleaned fish is the better for it. In the Bahamas Conrad Limbaugh has described the highly organized relationship between the Pederson shrimp and its numerous clients. It sets up shop in quiet water where fishes congregate, always for some reason in association with a sea anemone, who is simply a silent partner. When a fish approaches, the shrimp will whip its long antennae and sway back and forth, obviously inviting business. If the fish is interested, it will swim directly to the shrimp and stop one inch away. The fish usually presents its head or gill cover but if there is an injury near the tail, he presents the tail first. The shrimp swims or crawls forward, climbs aboard and walks rapidly over the fish, checking irregularities, tugging at parasites with its claws and cleansing injured areas. The fish even allows the shrimp to make minor incisions in order to get at the parasites under the skin. He is allowed to forage among the gills and even to enter and leave the fish's mouth. Fishes line up or crowd around for their turn in receiving this service.

In view of the enormous popularity of parasitism as a way of life, such cleaning arrangements are of crucial benefit. One might even go so far as to maintain that mutual cleaning or grooming between members of the same species is a valid reason for forming a social group. Known "cleaners" in the sea include twenty-six species of fish, six species of shrimp and Beebe's cleaning crab. Limbaugh tried the experiment of removing all known cleaning organisms from two small isolated reefs in the Bahamas where fish were unusually abundant. Within a few days the number of fish was drastically reduced. Within two weeks almost all except the territorial fishes had disappeared. Many of the fish remaining developed fuzzy white blotches, ulcerated sores and frayed fins. Fishes in an aquarium developed a stubborn bacterial infection. After Limbaugh put a cleaner shrimp in the aquarium it went to work and cleaned up the sick fish, possibly averting a fatal epidemic.

(We need to know more about such relationships. In some cases the parasite itself may be necessary to the existence of the animal. This seems to be the case of the marine iguana of the Galápagos, who relies on an intestinal worm to help him digest his diet of seaweed.)

Some aggregations of birds are based on an ancient predator-prey relationship that probably began with the evolution of the species themselves. The skua, for example, is not primarily a colonial nester but because skuas prey on penguins and penguins *are* colonial, the skuas (evil and nasty creatures) find it convenient to form bad-tempered colonies adjacent to the penguin cities. In Macedonia the great nests of imperial eagles often contain on their fringes nests of starlings or house sparrows who act as housekeepers for the eagles. The eagle may occasionally exact tribute from her serfs but she has learned that it is a waste of energy to try to catch the quickly darting smaller birds. Some birds, including the pigeon, have found that close association with man in crowded communities is a good way of life. The masked weaver of the Cameroons in Africa builds nests along the village streets with the heaviest traffic. In Europe the serin nests along congested streets in preference to quiet byways. Before he was destroyed by DDT it was not unusual to find a peregrine falcon nesting on the loftiest ledge of a New York skyscraper, this being the nearest thing he could find in the way of a tall cliff.

Sea birds are not polite to trees, with which they are usually not on familiar living terms. Cormorants and boobies sometimes nest in such dense treetop colonies that their guano kills the trees. Herons and other fish-eating birds of Tampa Bay used to be killed in order to save the fish supply. After twelve years of protection, however, their rookeries grew so large that they daily dropped fifty tons of guano in the bay and the mullet fishing, because of increasing plankton, became better than at any time in the last fifty years.

The beautiful studies by Lorenz of the graylag goose and the jackdaw illuminated a hitherto obscure and marvelous phase of bird sociality. Especially fascinating is the friendship bond formed via the mysterious "triumph ceremony" between two wild ganders. Although this may at times develop into homosexuality, the gander finds in another male in the long run a far better partner and companion than he would have found in a female—at least for the purposes of status seeking. Since aggression within the species is far stronger in ganders than in geese, the inclination to perform the triumph ceremony is also stronger and the two friends stimulate each other to acts of courage and of bullying. No pair of opposite sex can compete with them. Thus such gander pairs always attain the highest place in the ranking order of the colony. (In spite of Lorenz's rather mystical view of the "triumph ceremony," it can be viewed simply as a means of threatening or coercion. Thus the companionship of ganders is a double-barreled instrument for controlling the colony's population. It takes sperm out of circulation and intimidates the young and normal. It is as if a human society were run by a pair of formidable queers.)

Among jackdaws, a bird of exceptional innate intelligence, there is a pecking order, but it is of a strangely benevolent sort. Those of higher caste, especially the despot of the colony, are not aggressive towards the birds that stand far beneath them socially. It is only in relation to their immediate inferiors that they are irritable and picky. The fighting is between number one and number two. In fact, a high-caste jackdaw will take the side of the weaker in fights among the hoi polloi, thus ensuring active protection of the nests of the humbler members of the colony. Although this appears noble, it is in fact unnatural and counter-eugenic and it may explain why the jackdaw is, on the whole, a waning species. Since in jackdaws recognition of predatory animals is not innate but is learned by every young bird from the behavior of experienced old birds, veneration of the elders is a jackdaw trait and perhaps the most important one left favoring preservation of the species. It is only when an *old* jackdaw gives the alarm that all take flight.

Pecking status and consequent control of the reproduction of lesser birds are spectacularly demonstrated by A. J. Marshall's studies of the Australian satin bowerbird. When he becomes important in the colony the male turns blue, while the males who cannot make the grade remain a pusillanimous green. All the blue males of a satin clan constitute an elite class. They are the ones that build the exquisite bowers for mating with the females of their choice. The greens will do no better than collect a mess of sticks, to which no self-respecting hen would be seduced.

We see this theme of reproduction being confined to an elite repeated not only among various grazing mammals but among predators who form societies, such as wolves. Jerome H. Woolpy of the Brookfield Zoo, Chicago, has studied the habits of wolves, both in the wild and semiconfined in zoo areas.* The leader, or "alpha," male is the focal point of respect and solicitous attention from the rest of the pack, or "phalanx." (When the wolf becomes a dog, this same affection, tail wagging, nuzzling, etc., is transferred to a human master.) The wolves may gather around the leader and howl in ceremonial greeting. There is a pronounced pecking order among the females. The "alpha" female is not only boss over all other females but over most of the males. She exerts a puritanical control over the relationship of the rest of the females to the pack.

Successful intercourse among all canine species is complicated by the fact that the penis contains true bone and once inserted into the vagina the pair is "tied" for some twenty minutes. In fact, fertilization is never achieved without this period of tying. The pack as a group mind does not seem to approve of sex. Copulation actually is a rare occurrence. The more dominant males constantly watch the lower ones and frequently chase them away from receptive females. Among the bitches, control by the alpha females is like the ferocious watchfulness of lady chaperones among the polite society of Spain or of Victorian England. A dominant female will snarlingly attack any lower-caste female that allows or entices a male to mount her. Under the alpha's scowling scrutiny the poor bitches are so bullied that they quiver underneath the male to the extent that intromission is impossible.

Despite all these social restrictions, a number of successful ties occur in the pack every season *but mostly between the same two animals.* (Curiously the male leader is seldom involved. Although solicited by the alpha females and other bitches of high social status, he seems to be too busy or too haughty to accept their invitations.) When this habitual tying of the same happy pair occurs, the whole pack gets very excited and gathers around, often punishing one or even both of them with sharp nips. (The male involved in the successful union is often the "heir apparent"—he would be number one if the present "alpha" died or grew feeble.)

* *Natural History,* May 1968.

When the alpha female herself is tied, her intolerance is, if anything, increased, but the rest of the females have a few minutes during which they may hastily court preferred males. On one occasion this behavior so infuriated the alpha bitch that, even though tied, she dragged the male over to another courting pair and attacked them fiercely.

In the pack observed by Woolpy in the zoo, in five consecutive seasons, from 1960 through 1964, only one litter was born in the pack each year and was whelped by the same female and probably fathered by the same male. That similar restrictions on mating also exist in the wild is supported by observations of protected wolf packs on Isle Royale and near Mt. McKinley. By significant contrast, in parts of Southern Alaska, where the wolf social organization is constantly being destroyed by the indiscriminate killings by bounty hunters, the birth rate suddenly jumps up, becoming close to one litter per season per sexually mature female.

Among male wolves, unlike their degenerate cousins the dogs, "marking" by lifting the leg to urinate is allowed only to the dominant class. But where wolves are actively hunted down or when domesticated as wolf dogs, such social conventions go out the window along with mating restrictions.

Although it is not certain that wild wolves mate for life, one never observes an older wolf develop first preference for a younger one. There are no reciprocal preferences between wolves of different ages. Since preferences develop by the second mating season, an alien wolf would have great trouble in mating into an established pack. The hierarchy, the puritanism and the permanent sex preferences by age result not only in control of population but in increased inbreeding, with the result that gene drift could be expected in isolated packs to favor evolutionary changes in wolves. The very fact that wolves were easily domesticated by man probably depended upon an evolutionary process.

Unfortunately we now have a chance, because of the perverseness of twentieth-century man in the United States, to see the reverse process—the "wolfization" of dogs. Wild dogs running in packs are now estimated in the state of Georgia alone at 300,000.

Of the thirty million dogs in the country it is impossible to guess how many are wild, but the proportion is growing fast. An increasing number of city dwellers seem to be finding dogs impractical and are abandoning them to rural areas, where other dogs are being left by farmers moving to town. People in their increased selfish petulance get tired of a dog or there are unwanted puppies, so they are all taken out to the country and simply dumped. The dogs, once they realize they have been abandoned for good, band together to hunt for food. They are a fierce but sorry lot, since although the banding instinct is overwhelming, they do not observe the finely tuned population control devices of the wolves but, when overcrowded, they are quickly decimated by epizootics of distemper or rabies. (This practice of abandoning dogs or cats is the most abominable example of human cruelty that I know of and the fact that it is accelerating is proof positive that we need something better than the present kind of disturbed human being if the planet is ever going to amount to anything.)*

Because the order of rodents is such an immensely successful one, and because many rodent species compete with man for certain kinds of food, more is known about rodent societies, such as rat packs, than about any other social animal. In general the rat is regarded with more disgust than a mouse, but this may be unfair. Within the "family," which may include a huge number of individuals (grandparents, uncles, aunts, innumerable half brothers and half sisters, cousins of all degree of consanguinity), rats are gentle and even tender. Such rat communities even meet the strictest criterion of sociality. Rat mothers in the same family gang put their children in the same nest and may tend each other's offspring.

That the formation of such a "family" is actually a result of an instinct for population control is suggested by the experiments of E. Steiniger with the brown rat and of Otto Eibl-Eibesfeldt on the house mouse. Steiniger put brown rats from different localities into a large enclosure which approximated natural conditions and

---

* To illustrate what may be done in more civilized human societies, Israeli scientists have developed a practical contraceptive pill for cats, which works when given once a week. This is extensively used.

watched what happened. Society began, of course, with pair formation. If one pair was formed before the others had started, the
tyranny of the united forces of the two sexual partners at once increased the pressure on the unpaired co-tenants of the enclosure
so much that any further pair formation was prevented (a performance that reminds one of wolves and graylag geese). The
poor bachelors and spinsters were remorselessly pursued by the
married couple. Even in the 100-square-yard reservation it took
only two or three weeks for such a pair to kill all the other resi-
dents, ten to fifteen strong adult rats. Death was seldom caused
by deep wounds. Usually the persecuted animals died of exhaustion and nervous strain leading to (or resulting from) disturbance
of the adrenal glands. Population control by mental stress is perhaps peculiar to vertebrates because of the intimate interrelation-
ship of the brain, the pituitary and the adrenal system. The strange
pathology of overcrowding in Norway rats was the object of a
famous investigation by John B. Calhoun of the National Institute
of Mental Health.* He put the rats in an enclosure where they
were plentifully fed and free from predators and from disease.
Based on food availability and adult mortality rate, the colony
should have grown to about 5,000, but at the end of twenty-
seven months it had stabilized at 150 adults, most of them psychopathic by the usual rat standards. What had happened?

Overcrowding had resulted primarily in terrific infant mortality.
This in turn was caused by the loss of motherliness—the nervous
inability, for example, to build a nest or to carry the pregnancy to
full term. Among the males the behavior ranged from homosexuality to cannibalism and from frantic overactivity to a sulky withdrawal, from which certain rats would emerge to eat, drink and
move around only when the other rats were asleep. At the same
time, killing each other as they were by too much "togetherness,"
like the human population of Oran in Albert Camus' *The Plague,*
most of the rats idiotically insisted, as time went by, on more and

* *Scientific American,* February, 1962.

more togetherness. They would crowd together in only one of the four interconnecting pens. They would rarely eat except in the company of other silly rats. Extreme congestion naturally ensued in the pens adapted for eating. This lunatic insistence on swarming together disrupted the orderly sequence of a normal rat's life. It prevented courting, the building of nests, nursing and the care of the young. Among the most disoriented groups, infant mortality ran as high as 96 per cent.

This did not happen all at once. It took place in stages, the first being the normal attempt at population control by the struggle for status among the males. Shortly after the Norway rats reach maturity (about six months) they enter into a round robin of fights that establishes their position in the hierarchy. During the period when the male hierarchy was being fixed in Calhoun's pens, the subordinate rats in all pens got into the habit of arising early to eat and drink in peace. The subordinate male rats in the end pens were likely to feed in one of the middle pens. When they wanted to return, the boss male would be awake and would fight them as they started down the home-pen ramp, always awakening at a sign of male intrusion but not at the comings and goings of females. Thus he would build up a harem not by driving other males out but by preventing their return. Such harem masters would tolerate a growing class of phlegmatic male perverts. These curious creatures (as the result of psychopathic crowding in the middle pens) never attempted to flirt with the harem females, but when they encountered the harem master (which was rarely) they would try to mount him. The master superciliously tolerated these advances. In the middle pens there were more males than females and both sexes were half crazy. In the end pen, on the other hand, the harem females made good mothers and infant mortality was low.

As the population increased, however, the craziness spread through all pens. The mad urge to eat and drink in the presence of other rats was reinforced. Finally the rats would rarely eat *except* at hoppers already in use by others. Nest building was forgotten. The females lost the ability to carry their young to and from the spot where a nest should have been. The infants would die where they were dropped and finally were eaten by adults. The females in heat would be pursued fiercely by a pack of foaming young males (Calhoun calls them the "probers"), who, against all rules of rat etiquette, would even follow one into her burrow. There they would often find dead young and as a result developed a taste for cannibalism, a perversion that flourished toward the end of the colony's experimental existence. Even the dominant rats developed a tendency to biting other rats' tails—an unheard-of act of misbehavior among normal Norway rats.

Wild house mice tolerate each other at much higher population densities than rats if food is available. But they also reach a population density limit where their glands kick back at them and the population is drawn down by miscarriage or other maternal misadventures. The adrenal cortex swells, the thymus acts up and the increased secretions curtail reproductive activity in both sexes. Sexual mating is delayed and at very high population densities it is totally inhibited. Although the estrous ("in heat") cycles may be prolonged, the rate of ovulation and implantation of fertilized eggs in the uterus is diminished. (The females act, in other words, as if they were women on the pill or using the intrauterine device.) The mortality of fetuses greatly rises. Mothers produce too little milk or even none at all. At high population densities an epidemic may occur, in part because the resistance is lowered. (In rats this may show up as decreased resistance to the plague bacillus, so that a population explosion among rats is usually the prelude to bubonic or pneumonic plague among humans.)

The effect of social rank in a freely growing mouse population becomes exaggerated. A class of excessively submissive, thoroughly beaten-up, badly scarred mice develops which has very *low* concentrations of corticosterone (from the adrenal glands). The mice that sink to this level are so abject that the dominant animals no longer pay any attention at all to them, let alone bullying them. Because they no longer interact with other members of the population in any way whatsoever, they cease to be part of it.

They may as well be non-succulent insects. They are "non-mice."*

Deer mice have an exquisitely sensitive automatic control of population surges. When four males and four females are confined in a space not big enough for their liking, yet provided with excess water and food, at the most only two of the females will reproduce and then only for a limited time. More important, *about 35 per cent of the few offspring are born sterile*. A constant population can thus be achieved over a short period of time. This form of control is evidently triggered delicately through the senses of touch, smell, sight, hearing and taste, whereby the pituitary is prevented from the release of hormones. (How simple the human problem would be if women had such a socially responsive pituitary!)

Meadow mice, or voles, are subject to sudden population irruptions. In normally arid regions this happens after a wet spring and plenty of green vegetation, as in the Central Valley of California during 1941 and 1942. Years earlier in 1926–27, the meadow mice explosion made the state a disaster area. Both house mice and meadow mice in incredible numbers moved out of fields of milo and barley at Buena Vista Lake and completely devastated the surrounding ranchlands. The packs would often travel ten miles every night. They devoured everything—grass, corn, the roots of all plants. At one ranch more than two carloads of house mice were poisoned with strychnine. The skies were dark with immense flocks of gulls, owls, hawks, ravens, etc., attracted to the unprecedented mice population. Disease finally ended this plague of mice. Normally the predators of meadow mice are so numerous that a majority of the young never reach maturity. In America snakes of all kinds are perhaps more effective than any other population check (garter snakes, king snakes, bull snakes, milk snakes, pilot snakes, blue racers, copperheads, rattlers) but the unusual damp weather that lights the bomb of meadow mice population explosion is not to the liking of most native snakes.

---

* In all studies of rodent psychopathology caused by overcrowding, one notes the remarkable Kafkaesque resemblance to the human inhabitants of overcrowded cities.

Swings in lemming population usually follow the same course. On an upsurge the lemming females are producing not only more litters but larger litters than usual. The famous migrations of lemmings (which often lead them, good swimmers as they are, to enter the ocean, mistaking it for a large river or lake) are not started because of exhaustion of food but to get elbow room—to escape from a *future* famine. According to Sally Carrighar, who has studied lemmings at first hand perhaps more thoroughly than any other biologist, the lemming is a delightful little creature. They are more vocal than mice, more individual, more inventive in their play. They seem to get a lot of sparkle out of life. With crowding, however, they all begin to show irritability. Instead of friendly pushing contests, nose to nose, they stand on their hind feet and box, trying to reach each other's throat, with their tiny fangs bared. The collared lemming (*Dicrostonyx*) keeps right on breeding during winter under the snow. When the signal of excess population is sounded the population of the entire lemming city will start moving, mostly by night, in a straight course down the valleys, which in Scandinavia takes them to the sea, which is too big a lake for them to cross. They do not commit mass suicide; they merely make a mass mistake in geography. Muskrats in the United States sometimes make similar suicide-like migrations, drowning in great torrential rivers.

Chipmunks, according to Dana Schreider of the University of Massachusetts, have a stringent sense of population control, usually exercised by the females. The mother chipmunks go into Lysistrata moods, in which they refuse to mate. They also wean the young earlier and kick them out of the burrow, sometimes too early to survive. Even the young that are allowed by an indulgent mother to cling to her until maturity find it hard to buck the establishment. Older chipmunks drive them out of the area when there are too many adults around to start with.

That peculiarly American phenomenon, the prairie dog, is a classical example of organized society and rigorous number controls. Even in national parks, where the predators are often reduced below a natural level and shooting or poisoning is forbidden, there is no evidence of overcrowding. Their gigantic colonies are divided up into condominiums or "coteries," each inhabited by a male and several females. An orderly expansion of the city or the recolonization of empty territories is constantly taking place, leaving old burrows to the young. Only a limited number of animals are allowed in a given area—a rule enforced very violently, so that some observers imagine they are looking at territorial aggression and even warlike conquests. In effect the prairie dogs with the heavy police power of patrolling male burrow-owners create megalopolises without ghettos. Those who might become ghetto dwellers are eaten by snakes or owls. At one time those cities of underground dwellings stretched hundreds of miles across the shortgrass plains. Each home had guard rooms, bed chambers and toilets. Little circular dikes protected the doorways against floods. It is estimated that one city was 1,000 miles long and 250 miles wide and harbored a thriving population of over 400 million. (This is about the human population of India but it was much better regulated.) Of course, this was before the cattlemen virtually destroyed this great prairie dog culture, which was undeniably competing with beef stock for the shortgrass.

Rabbits try, but sometimes in vain, to keep their populations within reason. A typical social system in Australia has been described by Roman Mykytowycz. The rabbits there normally live in small groups of eight to ten, the group territory being strongly marked by the deposits of glandular secretions from the anal region and from under the chin. Each territory has a warren—a burrow with a number of entrances—as the center of group life. At the onset of the breeding season the males establish a hierarchy by fighting and so do the females. Thus a king and queen rule over each group or territory, which is fiercely defended by its occupants and recognized as a legal establishment by rabbits of other groups.

The high-ranking females give birth frequently and regularly, housing the young in a special breeding chamber dug as an extension of the burrow. These privileged youngsters have a much higher survival rate and growth rate than the young of low-ranking females. Some of the subordinate females in fact are chased away from the warren and forced to drop their litters in low burrows or "stops" some distance from the warren. The little exiles have small chance against foxes and crows. When they try to enter the central warren, the resident females and young fight them off. Some subordinate females, although physiologically fit and mated, never give birth. The embryos are absorbed in the uterus, presumably as the result of strain and hormone imbalance. (We see once again the theme of population control combined with a kind of enforced eugenics.)

The European hare, also widely distributed in Australia, is much less social-minded, correlating with the fact that, although they are four times as large as the rabbit, their anal and chin glands for marking territory are only one tenth of the size of the rabbit's. In North America the swamp rabbit, which is strongly territorial, "chins" much more frequently than the weakly social cottontail and both the anal and chin glands are quite large.

The populations of the snowshoe rabbit go through great pendulumlike swings which appear to correlate in some way with the eleven-year cycle of sunspots. During a population surge the rabbits commonly die of some stress disease connected with enlargement of the adrenal gland and frequently undergo fatal heart attacks. Rabbits and hares of all species under drastic crowding show the peculiar and convenient ability to dispose of their fetuses, not by miscarriage or some animal form of abortion, but by interruption of embryo development. The cells of the fetuses disintegrate and their substance is absorbed by the mother's body, just as if she had eaten them. This resorption process takes place very quickly, usually within two days. Overcrowding stress also causes embryo resorption in foxes and deer. When the Minnesota jack rabbit reaches a period of population excess, there is another, less smooth disease which kills off the adults. The liver undergoes fatty degeneration and atrophy with a striking decrease in liver glycogen. Extremely low sugar content of the blood (hypoglycemia) precedes death. The rabbit usually dies in sudden seizures in which he hops with one hind leg held out stiff, and will leap into the air to fall dead upon alighting. Such tantrums are typical of liver disease, high blood pressure with atherosclerosis and adrenal failure and are characteristic of the acute stress that results from overactivity of the pituitary-adrenal system in combined malfunction.

Deer show the same symptoms after crowding at a density of more than one deer per acre. In the Philadelphia Zoo it was found that in those animals who were crowded for exhibition purposes the incidence of atherosclerosis was ten times greater than normal.* When deer or elk in the wild increase too fast (as they often do if their predators, the wolf, for example, are shot down under an unwise bounty system), their reproduction powers decrease. Luckily this usually happens before actual famine conditions prevail. People who know little about them give them grain, which destroys the micro-organisms in the rumen, which they need to digest their normal diet of tree shoots and other cellulose-containing vegetation. This is a good way not to save a deer population in the wintertime but to destroy it forever.

Extreme arctic conditions impose the most rigorous population control. Thus the musk ox will often breed only once every other year.

In all animals controlled by evolutionary memory the instinct to control population is as basic as the instinct to preserve the species and perhaps is merely another form of that most primal of all urges. Traits which seem useless or even dangerous for individual survival permit the whole social group to adapt to the general problem of the survival of all. It is only in man and possibly the elephant that we find behavior definitely endangering the species. As we have seen, the territorial display and noises of birds do not mean the aggrandizement of the individual bird ego but quite the opposite. Singing and displaying his redness, as a male cardinal does, makes him a target for predators, but not only diverts predation from his family but keeps the population down. The alarm

---

* Indirect evidence indicates that the stress syndrome from overcrowding accounted for many deaths in wartime concentration camps. Perhaps crowding stress (constant exposure to telephones, transistor radios as well as excessive personal contacts) is primarily responsible, rather than diet, for the large amount of atherosclerosis in modern man.

signals of antelope may cause the alarm sounder to be the first to be attacked by a cougar, but it makes it difficult to surprise any other member of the group. The shrieks and dashes of parent robins may disturb a prowling cat as he lets the fledgling escape and takes after mamma and papa.*

A herd of dairy cows shows a butting order like the pecking order of barnyard hens. The butting cow gains nothing specifically of advantage with respect to access to food or bulls or shelter but that is because she is under the eye of man. In a wild society this habit undoubtedly would establish a hierarchy of breeding in which the most stubborn butting cow would mate more often than those butted.

In elephants there appears amazingly little hierarchism and consequently little control of population density. Since the elephant has no predator except man, in a game reserve in Africa he is on his own to adjust his numbers to the available food trees. This he fails to do and as a result we have elephant population explosions which have to be taken care of by the game warden's rifle. In so otherwise social and intelligent an animal, this lack of control is inexplicable and needs more study. It is possible that the elephant requires a revolution in social customs so that a herd will be led and supervised by old females rather than the strongest males. In sheep organized on a natural basis the old female with the largest number of descendants consistently leads the flock. In the wild herds of red deer of Scotland the older females similarly lead. We have seen that in wolf packs the rate of breeding of other females is under the severe scrutiny of the alpha bitch. This type of strongly regulated animal society seems natural if somewhat autocratic. I was approached most closely by humans perhaps in the Geneva of Calvin, who was psychically a sort of vicious old maid.

Among monkeys and apes social structure is the rule, the only

---

* One has difficulty in explaining in urban man the curiously accelerating habit of *non-involvement*. Whole crowds can let an old man be beaten up and robbed by ruffians or allow a girl to be raped without blinking an eye. Groups of people urge a neurotic on top of a building to jump. Perhaps this is a *disease* of overcrowding.

exceptions being the orangutan and the gibbon, both of whom prefer the one-family system. The orangutan is a species on the verge of extinction but the gibbon is mildly successful, a fact which can perhaps be attributed to his dazzling ability as an acrobat in the trees. When you can get about so skillfully in a special habitat you do not need a social organization. Perhaps connected with the strict one-family system is the fact that of all apes, they are the only ones who have incessantly practiced incest for millions of years. The device of control of population by hierarchism or by banding in mutually exclusive clans is used by practically all other apes and monkeys. Sometimes extraordinary male dominance can cause social trouble. C. R. Carpenter, in his superb studies of rhesus monkeys, noted that one single group was able to infringe on its neighbor groups and get away with it. Eventually he found that this apparently privileged group was led by a male of incredible forcefulness and vigor—a sort of Alexander the Great of monkeydom. The same phenomenon sometimes occurs among lions. A lion pride, as a tactical hunting unit, has a strong male who seldom kills but flushes the game and drives it within range of his lionesses. His dominance consists of size and sexual vigor, but sometimes one lion will be so overpowering in his roaring maleness that he acts as a magnet to effect a coalition of prides into super-prides. These are intrinsically unstable societies, depending as they do on one individual and, like all overweening autocracies, sooner or later break up into social confusion.

Associations between animals of different kinds still puzzle us. Although in the grooming relationship between shrimp and fish we found a perfect hygienic logic, it is not so easy to understand other strange tolerances and affections, especially when no mutual benefit is obvious. Consider the extraordinary hospitality of the kangaroo rat, who in his well-constructed burrow seems to get along with the following tenants, either singly or en masse: toads, horned toads, lizards, gophers, king snakes and rattlesnakes, centipedes, scorpions, black widow and other spiders, crickets, wingless locusts, cockroaches, dung and other beetles, ants, sow bugs and millipedes. There are certain limits to his tolerance, which

5. Man and the Loss of Population Control

Before we consider the human population problem, we must assert the crucial importance of what man is doing to the livability of a planet insofar as it concerns other animals, including future ones, superior to man, who may come after man's likely disappearance from the face of the earth. Man has an incalculable potential for upsetting or changing things. Let us record first, as an example, the effect that the slightest change in man's habits may have on a local ecological equation. We have mentioned the domino effect of some DDT in Borneo. Let us go backward in time to a more pleasant ecological adventure. Why in the early nineteenth century in England was there more clover in villages after the Industrial Revolution? Firstly, during the Industrial Revolution, the number of spinsters living in English villages increased. It was a popular custom among the spinsters to have cats as pets, so the number of cats increased too. The cats killed small animals such as dormice and moles, who had been consuming many earthworms and bumblebees. Thus as the feline predator increased, there was a larger population of earthworms and bumblebees. More earthworms enriched the soil by their way of life, while more bumblebees made the pollination of clover more certain, so that more clover grew in the fields of the villages where many spinsters lived.

We do not know whether primitive man had any instinctive urge to thin the population of his bands in accordance with the availability of food. Julian Huxley has made a political statement that, of all the animals on earth, modern man and the harvester ants are the only creatures that have carried on organized war (that is, fighting among the same species) and that the implements of primitive man were designed only for clubbing, stabbing, dressing or eating the bodies of other species, not for organized fighting among men themselves. Yet this depends perhaps on too limited a definition of the word "war." It is a matter of the density of the numbers involved and the concept of a "public." American pioneers, crossing for the first time the great, beautiful rivers of North America, had no compunctions about defecating in such rivers but this was not an act of public water pollution, because there was no public. (Thus the concept that any river purifies itself within ten miles, probably ecologically correct for the year 1770, has no bearing whatsoever on a 1970 river, yet it has survived as a mystical catchword to defend industrialists and river dwellers against the insistent attacks of hygienists and conservationists.)

We know that in the case of Peking man (*Sinanthropus*) every one of the skulls found bore the evidence of heavy clubbing. Moreover, the limb bones were all split open—something that only man could do in search of marrow. Perhaps this was not evidence of war in the sense of massed troops but simply the proof of cannibalism—a reasonably effective way of keeping the population down, perhaps in conjunction with a caste system in which only some people qualified as eaters of other people. Even in the primitive folk of historic times cannibalism has often attained not only respectability but the aura of religious obligation. There are human creatures that eat only friends, others that eat only enemies. There are cultures in which only old people are eaten and others in which infants are eaten. James Bonner, the distinguished Cal Tech molecular biologist, has suggested with only partial levity that as the vast gulf widens between the "have" and the "have-not" nations it may some day become conventional for the "haves" to eat the otherwise useless and helpless "have-nots" (as the Morlocks in H. G. Wells's perceptive extrapolation in *The Time Machine* eat the Eloi).

Among the primitive jungle people of the Yanomamö of Venezuela and Brazil a population contraction is occurring which is leading them to certain extinction—an example of a very drastic control technique which has been applied very often in patrilinear kinds of man. They commonly kill the first daughter in a family so that, for ritual reasons, a son may be the oldest child. Some villages now have a 35 per cent excess of males, most of them constantly feuding and killing each other for the available women. This culture also has certain taboos which decrease female fertility, such as a prohibition against sexual intimacy during pregnancy or while the mother is suckling. The chief himself may have four wives, many other men none. Much bickering is caused by such unfortunates as they chase after the wives of other men. This frequently leads to the splitting of larger groups into small, mutually hostile villages. Such villages must then establish military alliances with each other or undergo constant bullying on the part of the larger neighboring village. Is this "war"? Certainly it has all the diplomatic trappings—the jockeying for balance of power, and men dying in combat. "Treaties" are constantly being negotiated, a process involving many feasts between villages, in which grown men partake not of champagne but of a native hallucinatory drug, and women are exchanged, at least for the duration of the party.

It may, of course, be dangerous logic to equate the behavior of primitive tribes of the present day to our remote ancestors of the paleolithic past, even though in some Australian aborigines and some Surinam tribes the weapons and tools may still be the ones of over 50,000 years ago. The Wama in the southeast corner of Surinam, for example, use a stone axe and possess absolutely no agriculture. Yet they speak a Carib language common from the Antilles to the Mato Grosso, in most of which territorial agriculture has been practiced for 4,000 years. Were the degraded Wama a degenerate group of offcasts from an ancient race or are they the sole remnant of a time when the Carib-speakers knew no agriculture? As one used to describe the Caucasian "squaw man," a white who preferred the simplicity of the past to the infuriating complexities of the present, perhaps one can think of whole tribes or races of squaw men—people who simply refused to join the parade. At any rate, the important point is that all primitive societies that are limited to the food they can get by hunting or by gathering invariably restrict their numbers by tribal traditions and taboos, such as prohibiting sexual intercourse for nursing mothers, practicing compulsory abortion, infanticide, cannibalism and other such expedients as are no longer regarded as legal in polite modern society. Almost always the residual instinct of man as an animal to guard against future famine by present population control is disguised under a sheath of ritual or religion, since as soon as man learned to talk his actions became *symbolic* rather than explicit. A certain essential hypocrisy accompanying speech enters into all the dealings of mankind. With the gift of speech he gets as an inevitable companion the gift of the forked tongue and the ritualistic pretension.

It is quite possible that the nearly universal prohibition against human incest is a prime example of such ritualistic hypocrisy—the clothing of an instinct against population explosions and also a realization of a higher degree of sociality in the guise of a social taboo. In other primates who stick to a society of the family rather than the group or band (i.e., the gibbon) incest has been practiced with no noticeable physical deterioration for millions of years, but in men, who became social apparently from the start, it became taboo, partly because man's incorrigibly oversexed nature would result in almost continuous overcrowding and partly because in *groups* of people the only assured way of distributing property rights was for men or women to pair outside the immediate family.

In some cases the residual instinct to keep the numbers of the tribe within reason, especially when the habitat is rather thin in nourishing food, takes the form of puberty rites. Circumcision of young males and excision of the clitoris in females, although now confused with religious and even pseudo-hygienic justifications, probably were steps in this direction—to make sexual intercourse less pleasurable and thus less frequent. The ultimate grisliness in such surgery is practiced by the Australian Aranda: the ritual surgeon seizes the boy's penis, inserts a twig deep into the urethra and proceeds to slash at the organ with a sharp flint until the penis finally splits open like a boiled hot dog. (This is known as subincision.) The subincised youth has a hard time enjoying or even performing normal copulation and he has to squat to urinate. Some anthropologists assert rather dreamily that this operation is to make the ritualized young man more like a kangaroo, who has a bifid penis rather resembling that of the altered youth. The male kangaroo also has to squat to urinate but his virility is said to be much admired, since a single copulation lasts up to two hours. (The length of this activity probably is connected more with its difficulty than its pleasure.) It is noteworthy that such rites are the most severe in societies where survival is the most precarious. Australian aborigines who live along the coast, where things are less harsh, do not practice subincision. They submit the youth to the milder ordeal of having a tooth pounded out.

Certainly we must carefully distinguish between the social habits of early man before and after he became a farmer, and prehistorically this is difficult since, unlike the Industrial Revolution, the "agricultural revolution" which changed all of prehistory did not occur within a few years but took place over millennia. There seems little doubt that it happened independently in the Old and the New World. The last ice age was rich in great mammals, who were hunted by paleolithic man with the utmost courage and skill. This was indeed the time of man as a mighty hunter—especially in North America. The remains of the so-called Paleo-Indians (up to 7,000 years ago) are nearly always associated with the bones of extinct ice-age mammals. Although the ice age, in lowering the surface of the oceans by tying up so much water in the form of ice, made it easy for both men and animals to cross the Bering Strait at a date as early as 50,000 years ago, it has not been proved that the Paleo-Indians at that early period were technically equipped to hunt the mammoth and the paleo-bison. Their spears may not have been sharp and strong enough. It was about this time that in Europe and Western Asia the Cro-Magnons were clashing with the Neanderthals and already in Africa the great climatic extinction of large mammals had begun—precisely at a time when a human culture that specialized in hunting with large stone axes had spread over that continent.

Almost all the early sites of paleolithic man discovered in Alaska and northwestern Canada are located on the flanks of mountains. With no competition from new incoming men from Siberia and with abundant food, Alaska was probably the first great population center in North America. Yet toward the end of the last ice age the plains were crisscrossed with mighty fragrant rivers and dotted with lakes and marshes. Tall grasses grew that fed the enormous mammals—an abundance such as the world is never likely to see again. The hunters who thrived on this abundance of great game animals are now classified according to the designs of their spears. Sites where early "Plainview" man flourished show that the trick of stampeding bison over cliffs—a bad habit still used by the Plains Indians of the nineteenth century—was an early invention and, like man in all stages, the Plainview savage had no compunction in killing more animals than he could use. It is, in fact, a widely held and persuasive theory that early man was ultimately responsible for the extinction of all the thirty-five kinds of mammals of 15,000 years ago whose skeletons were preserved in the La Brea tar pits (including mammoths, horses, camels and the big horned bison). Nine thousand years later not one of them survived in North America. Undoubtedly the climatic change—the melting of the ice, the rise in average temperature, the loss of cloud cover, the increase in evaporation of water from the land made life more difficult for these great animals, who found it harder to make a living, but, just as we believe the early ratlike mammals erased the great reptiles by eating their eggs, so we similarly believe that it was early man's incessant hunting that finally obliterated this magnificent natural zoo of great, beautiful creatures. This caused a more sudden revolution in man's society than the much later discovery of agriculture. Man had to become a food collector, a trapper or catcher of small animals, insects and edible roots and seeds and berries. Thus the so-called *archaic* people (post ice age) of North America specialized in nothing at all. In South America the change was not so drastic, probably because the tribes were so thinly scattered.

In Europe toward the last of the ice age (about 8000 B.C.) a similar disappearance of the great mammals caused a decrease in the human population and a grievous restlessness. One of the great fundamental changes was the salting up of the Baltic Sea. Pine and hazel in Northern Europe gave way to mixed oak forests that were less favorable for the grazing of large animals. The aurochs and the red deer decreased. Sea hunting and fishing appeared as a new means of subsistence; thus the people tended to move towards the coast, and once finding a job as a fisherman or clam-digger, a man is likely to stay put. Wanderings cease. The scene is set for the acceptance of farming, which had been invented as long ago as 9000 B.C. in Southeast Asia but took another 2,000 years to result in stable farming villages even in that fertile area, still another 1,500 years to spread to the coastal plains of the Aegean and another millennium or so to become established, first in the Hungarian plains near the Danube, then gradually over all of Europe. (There is no proof at all for food production in Europe before the introduction of wheat and barley from Southeast Asia.) One of the reasons for the slowness of diffusion of this remarkable invention was that many parts of Europe had developed a "forest efficiency" —a food-gathering technique comparable to that of the Eastern archaic people of North America, who used 275 species of plants for medicine, 130 species for food, 31 as magical charms, 27 for smoking, 25 as dyes, 18 in beverages and flavoring and 52 others for various purposes (including abortion).

Long before the period of the great hunters in Europe there appeared Neanderthal man (about 100,000 years ago), often viewed as a sort of freak who actually provided no substantial proportion of genes for the present human race. Yet at the time of the discovery of the Neanderthal skulls, an eminent French scholar referred to one as that of a robust Celt resembling an Irishman with "typically low mental organization." Hans Mayer even suggested that the Neanderthal was a deserter from a Russian army that chased Napoleon across the Rhine in 1814—a low-grade Mongolian cossack who had crawled into a cave for refuge. Gustav Schwalbe was the only nineteenth-century anthropologist who regarded Neanderthal as an ancient man directly in the line of human evolution but probably extinguished in warfare with more modern Cro-Magnon man, vaguely from the East. Since 1931 remains have been found in Israel intermediate in nature between Neanderthal and "modern" paleolithic man and these so-called Neanderthaloids have been found in Morocco, Greece, Uzbekistan, China, Java and Africa. There seems no longer any valid reason to consider Neanderthals as isolated European phenomena or to disregard them as ancestors. There seems little doubt that they could mate fruitfully with the more photogenic Cro-Magnons. If a Neanderthal were to appear (shaven and clothed) in a modern crowd, he would seem short, stocky, large of jaw, but nothing more than that. One might take him for a member of Cosa Nostra or a Prussian of noble descent (some of his "reproductions" without the hairiness look remarkably like the late Erich Von Stroheim) but there would be no reason to shriek for the zoo-keeper.

It is quite remarkable that paleolithic art in Europe developed during the period of the last glaciation (between 30,000 and 10,000 B.C.) and disappeared until classical times, long after agriculture had become established. The overwhelming impression that one gets in standing before the great cave wall paintings of Lascaux in France and Altamira in Spain is of overall balance and mastery of the genre. They obviously were not scribbled on the spur of the moment. In what is now termed by experts as "Style IV" (about 12,000 B.C.) the animal pictures are handled with amazing uniformity from Spain to Central Europe, and with incomparable grace and fidelity. This suggests not only contacts between regional populations but a cosmopolitan artistic tradition. A strange hierarchy of *placement* appeared to be universal among the cave artists. For example, the middle panel or the most prominent chamber in the cave would consist, to the extent of 85 per cent, of pictures of bison, wild oxen and horses. The next most prominent would show pictures of deer, ibex and horses. Pictures of three other species—the rhino, the lion and the bear—would be in the deepest part of the cave.

This treatment in artistic or religious thought of animals as mystically important persons with hierarchic niches and godly perquisites is an inevitable process in hunting cultures. In many tribes one apologizes to the animal before killing it, and in totemistic communities one animal or another is regarded as having a sacred affinity for a human clan. (Perhaps the ultimate in animal worship is among a Hottentot tribe which regards the praying mantis as God.)

Closely associated with the art of hunting cultures is the shaman. (The word originated from the Tungus people of Siberia, among whom it meant "excited and restless.") Shamans are found in all surviving hunting peoples, from the Eskimos to Tierra del Fuego, the Kalahari desert and in Australia. Essentially the shaman is a weak paranoiac—who "transfers" his delusions to the whole tribe, always in a wild mythology involving animals. Apparently his function is to help dissolve the terrible anxieties of a small, lonely band in a world not obviously dominated by the will of man. (A wise old Eskimo, a one-time shaman himself, once said, "What do we believe? We don't believe. We only fear.") The shaman is supposed to divert attention from—not actually to prevent—such catastrophes as the lack (or excess) of female fertility, the disappearance of game, the decimation by strange fevers. It is thought that some of the enigmas of the paleolithic cave art and its placement are related to the abnormal intensity of the artist's state of mind—he might have been regarded as a shaman.

In Australia today (as related by Andreas Lommel) some of the old shaman mythology is becoming popular again due to the airplane. Lommel was given a dramatic account by a native of the killing and resuscitation of a man. An aborigine in the field hospital had undergone an operation, which several others had watched. The man had lain dead. The white doctor had killed him; then he took out his entrails, washed them and replaced them. The dead man came back to life. He could not remember anything. In northwestern Australia the white doctor appears in an airplane and throughout the primitive tribes of the Pacific the airplane is obviously a shamanistic device. In Australia shamanism is not connected apparently with psychedelic drugs but elsewhere this is a common association in hunting societies—and even in mixed modern societies we have, all too evidently, shamans. A shaman may even be a clown. Indeed, the whole complex of "taking things with a sense of humor" (an explosive psychological method of diverting the mind from catastrophe or danger) may be regarded as a modern form of shamanism. "The rich get richer and the poor get—children" is perhaps the most poignant shamanistic utterance of urban society.

Cities could not evolve until agriculture had reached a certain stage of sophistication in which not only could crops be raised over and above the needs of the farmer and his family but the transport of grain or flour for the use of city dwellers and soldiers could be managed with some degree of rapidity. And it is only when soldiers can be well fed that organized war is feasible. There seems to be no doubt that war and famine or disease caused by war were the chief means that early agricultural man found instinctively to check the great population surges that resulted from the growth of ancient cities. War in organized form was only possible when the political device of the chiefdom or kingdom came into existence, since a war without a military chief is merely a riot. In barest essentials, war as a profession only becomes possible when there is some central authority responsible for feeding a group of men (soldiers) who are incapable of feeding themselves without looting. Even when looting is a way of military life, the chieftains must direct the distribution of the loot.

While the wars of the Old World consisted either of interminable battles between city-states or of the periodic invasions of city-states by nomadic wanderers grouped together in looting and massacring *systems,* the wars of the New World took two quite distinct modes. Agriculture in the Americas was of a peculiar kind, compared with the wheat and barley cultures of Asia and Europe. In Europe and Southeast Asia development was relatively fast, agriculture multiplying the population over a hundredfold in 8,000 years. Whereas the wheat plant grew wild and domestication was quite straightforward, the maize plant (which ultimately supported the great American seats of population) needed to be bred from a trivial weed into an unnatural form, in which it became virtually incapable of pollination without man's help. This took a long time. Prehistorically there came into existence the maize-bean-squash complex of farming which spread through all the Americas from Mexico—a fortunate combination since nutritionally corn by itself does not contain all the essential amino acids. In some of the early North American Indian cultures we see war and agriculture inextricably interwoven, with agriculture on trial, so to speak, in competition with food gathering from the seemingly inexhaustible eastern forests. Agriculture made the wars of the Iroquois possible but this warfare kept the population down to the point where more agriculture was not needed. These people and their confederates had finally, under the clever politicking of Hiawatha and other diplomats, reached an uneasy stability before being crashed into by the white man. An equilibrium of a more terrible kind had been attained in Mexico, where the Aztecs, subduing gentler cultures such as the Mixtecs and Olmecs, had arrived at a theatrical means of keeping the population density of the region at a bearable but by no means comfortable level. This was human sacrifice on a grand scale. It has been estimated that at the apex of the Aztec empire as many as 50,000 people were being disposed of by this means every year. (The superstition involved in this case was that the Aztecs were protectors of the Sun and the Sun demanded a steady stream of bloody bodies.) Most of the victims were prisoners of war and, in fact, the Aztecs waged war deliberately in order to obtain sacrificial victims. They did not need more population to feed, since corn products had already made Mexico City about five times as large as Elizabethan London and as poorly nourished as present-day Calcutta. War conducted for the purpose of taking live prisoners can be very inefficient, however, as it proved against the Spanish of Cortés, a tough lot of *hombres* with the incessant violence of the wars against the Moors bred into their minds and muscles.

There has arisen a school of demographers who insist that war has little influence on the growth of populations, but this opinion seems to be based on the results of World Wars I and II, where, although the carnage seemed great at the time, it actually did not compare in percentage killed with such earlier bloodbaths as the Thirty Years' War and its accompanying famines.

One must admit that even today demography is a disconcertingly inexact science. The population of China is not known within 300 million people. It may be 700 million; it may be less than 400 million. And exact information on the population trends of the past are handicapped by the fact that the taking of a census is a remarkably new invention, made necessary only when taxation began to involve unhandy numbers. Even now the analysis of population in terms of the changes that occur from one calendar year or decade to another (obtained via periodic census taking) is not very helpful. It must be supplemented by so-called "cohort" analysis, in which one takes all the people born in one year or married in one year and follows them through their lives. The adoption of cohort analysis has allowed some significant discoveries in demography.

Let us see, for example, what has happened in Ireland. Reasonably good early records are available because the English rulers were determined that the Irish should be kept under suspicious scrutiny, like animals in a zoo. The great Irish famine similarly had a lot of accounting work done on it since, albeit ungraciously, the English had the ultimate responsibility of trying to feed the starving (at a cost of over a billion pounds sterling) and check the epidemics of typhus. How and where the potato got to Ireland is still a historical mystery but when it became established, within a hundred years a whole country became completely dependent on an entirely new crop. The potato fitted neatly into the region, where the previous cattle and grain economy had been disrupted by wars, revolutions and the continuous unrest caused by English adventurers. (No economy is as frail as one based on cattle, since they are so easily stolen. The Karimojong of Africa find it necessary to associate themselves so intimately with their cattle that the herdsmen live entirely on milk and on blood obtained by temporarily piercing the neck artery of the animal.) As a result of the potato the population of Ireland probably grew faster than any before in history. It increased from about two million in 1687 to 8,175,000 in 1841. All that was needed to support a family of five was one acre of land. A sod hut could be built for thirty shillings. Children were of help in the simple chores of tending a potato patch and life was easy—one might say, lazy. The men had time to tell wonderful stories and get drunk on poteen. Early marriage was universal and human fertility was amazing.

Then came the potato blight in 1845 and a worse one in 1846. Over one million people died and many more emigrated. The population of the Republic plus Northern Ireland is now about 4,300,000 (about one half of the pre-famine days) and has remained almost static at this figure for the last fifty years. Through catastrophe Ireland has achieved true birth control, and not merely by the mechanisms of famine and disease but through a complex change of habits of life. Ireland now has the lowest marriage rate in Europe. In 1941, 64 per cent of all the women in Ireland between the ages of twenty-five and twenty-nine were unmarried (compared with 2 per cent in India). Since the Catholic inhabitants of the Irish Republic are noted for their moral propriety (fornication, for instance, being almost nonexistent), Ireland remains as a sort of model for the possible success of one kind of birth control: don't get married or at least don't get married until it is too late to have a lot of children. Although Americans and Europeans are not likely to regard Ireland as a model to be imitated, the fact remains that through a combination of religious scruples and fear of the repetition of a dreadful experience, the Irish have made themselves over. Perhaps they have indeed undergone some sort of genetic shift.

That within the vast species of *Homo sapiens* it is possible for

genetic changes, especially in an inbreeding society, to effect both
the reproduction rate and the *age of reproduction* is shown by a
comparison of two utterly dissimilar communities—the Melanesians
and the Hutterite communities of South Dakota. As we have seen,
the unmarried adolescent girls of the Trobriand Islands are completely licentious and promiscuous, yet they almost never produce
bastards. Evidently inbreeding has produced a type of human
which, without birth control techniques of any type, is capable of
interminable copulation without pregnancy up to close to the age
of twenty.* The Hutterites, a communistic Anabaptist sect, completely cut off socially (although not technologically) from the
neighboring "gentiles," have long practiced inbreeding. Here a new
kind of genetic woman has evidently evolved who bears more children in the years from forty to forty-four than the average American or European woman in the peak childbearing years of twenty
to twenty-four. With an annual increase of about 4 per cent the
Hutterites may be the fastest-growing population on earth. This
results from a combination of superfertility at all ages (the average
Hutterite woman bears 10.4 live children) with a low death rate.
Some practices, such as midwifery, remain old-fashioned, but in
general the Hutterites have adopted modern facilities. Although
anti-intellectuals, like their cousins the Amish of Pennsylvania,
they send members to the Mayo Clinic and may be spending more
per capita on drugs than most Americans. Certainly they spend
nothing on contraceptive drugs, since all methods of birth control,
including the rhythm method, are prohibited. The only restraint on
an unparalleled explosion of these inbred people is the relatively
late age of marriage and the prohibition of premarital intercourse.
While this works as effective birth control with the Irish, it has
little restraining power on the Hutterites, who go to work in a
hurry. The fertility rate** (425/1,000) for Hutterite women in
the thirty-five to thirty-nine age bracket far exceeds that for women
in any other culture on record, past or present.

As we shall see later, control of family size seems to appear

* This is found also to be true generally of native American Indian girls.
** Defined as births per year per thousand women.

automatically when there is some, as yet dimly understood, social incentive for it. But the Hutterites are unaffected by the society surrounding them. Contractual matters and the control of funds of the sect are communal. Cooking is done in a communal kitchen and eating in a communal dining hall. The fact that a Hutterite family has no responsibility of maintaining its individual household and facilities eliminated the motive of "keeping up with the Joneses." Radio, television and movies—those great stimuli for improving one's lot—are strictly forbidden. The low education costs, the early age at which youth enters the colony's agricultural enterprises, all keep the incidental costs of childbearing very low.

The Hutterites are cunning farmers and buy all the new tools. In this respect they are more enduring than the Anabaptist Amish, who have begun to fall behind for the simple reason that they have stuck to the agricultural tools of the nineteenth century. They not only refuse to accept buttons but also bulldozers. It is a rather frightening possibility that the South Dakota Hutterites, a 20,000-person enclave of unprecedented procreation and communism of the complete know-nothing type, could at their wild present rate of multiplication literally bore from within and become a worm that occupies the whole apple. The chances are, however, that the apple, as we shall show, will destroy itself without help from the worm.

6. Incentives against Fertility

The most perspicacious of modern demographers, such as Kingsley Davis of the University of California (Berkeley), emphasize that we do not understand what we assuredly must understand: why do certain cultures decide en masse to reduce average family size? Direct financial bribes, based on the notion that people will do anything for money, have failed in the positive direction but we do not know about the negative. Although bellowing for more *Lebensraum,* both Hitler and Mussolini were desperately trying to increase their respective populations with the idea of thus creating *less Lebensraum* and more justification for war. All that Hitler's bribes accomplished in prewar Germany was to crowd an unusually large number of first births into one year, and Mussolini had even less luck. Had their policies succeeded, the flood of births would have made their chances of winning the war even less. The "pro-natalism" policies of the fascist nations did not actually interfere with their war effort, because they did not succeed. There is little or no evidence that bribes to get families to have *fewer* children will succeed either, but the system has not really been tried.

Nevertheless a great spontaneous trend to lower growth rates *did* occur, especially in Northeast Europe. Part of the problem of overcrowding was solved by emigration. Between 1846 and 1932 it is estimated that twenty-seven million people emigrated from Europe's ten most advanced countries. The three Scandinavian countries alone sent out 2.4 million, so in 1915 the combined population was 11.1 million instead of the 14.2 million it would otherwise have been. At the same time the age of marriage rose. Childless marriages became frequent. By the 1930's most of the industrial European countries had fertility rates so low that, if these rates had continued, the population would have ceased to replace itself. (Those that have lived through the Great Depression will recall that, far from worrying about population explosions, the popular fear was "race suicide.") However, the idea that numerical limitation comes from the threat of poverty (as in the birds, it is an instinctual dread of *tomorrow's* starvation) can be shown to be false. In every one of the industrializing countries of Europe, economic growth far outpaced population growth, even allowing for the economic stutter of the Depression years. Davis believes the stimulus to lower childbearing arose from the clash between new opportunities on the one hand and larger families on the other hand. In some way *personal aspirations* almost overnight became more important than a swarm of offspring.

Yet it is difficult to pin this concept down, mainly because in our own country, comparatively prosperous from the beginning to the present, unusual surges and dips in fertility have occurred. The most massive factor in population growth in the world has, of course, been the decrease in death rate—especially in infants. Two thousand years ago the average baby in Rome had a life expectancy of twenty years. Among their less crowded contemporaries in Roman Africa at that time life expectancy was, however, between forty-five and fifty. At the beginning of the twentieth century it was about the same as this in Europe and North America.* Startlingly effective hygienic developments, such as the pasteurization of milk in the early 1900's, vastly increased the chances of a

---

* In fact it is believed by anthropologists that human life expectancy, averaged over the whole planet, changed very little from the time of the Neandertals to the twentieth century.

baby surviving beyond the age of five, since the terrible afflictions of diarrhea and enteritis (the chief killers of the very young) were nearly abolished. About 100 years ago over 50 per cent of the population of the United States was less than twenty years old. During the past fifty years, persons less than twenty years old decreased to about 34 per cent. The median age of the U.S. population in 1900 was twenty-three. It is now close to thirty. It is no coincidence that 100 years ago the age distribution of population in the U.S. and the rest of the Western World was the same as it is in the Far East today. Thus the undeveloped countries of Asia and South America now have 80 per cent of the world's children but only 69 per cent of the earth's adults.

Throughout the world there is still an enormous difference in life expectancy caused by local circumstances, varying from over seventy-six years for girls in Iceland to thirty-one years for girls in Upper Volta and twenty-five years for boys in Gabon.

In the United States of Revolutionary War days the birth rate was somewhat higher than it is in the undeveloped Asiatic and South American countries today but the population growth was incomparably less because of dolorously high infant mortality. In the 1920's and 1930's (thus starting *before* the Depression) a decline in birth rate began, paralleling similar declines in Europe and in Japan. Couples with better education and higher incomes married late and had few children. This tendency at the depths of the Depression caught up with everybody, educated or not, and in 1936 the national reproduction rate was about 25 per cent below that needed for replacing the dead.

A tremendous and still poorly understood reversal occurred in the 1940's and 1950's. Many theories concerned with the concept of "war babies" (a supposed instinct of women to have more babies in times of war, wartime laxity in sexual morals, the increased abundance of material things following the *end* of war, etc.) have been propounded by professional and amateur demographers but the truth seems to be that we simply don't know the reason for the American and European explosion of fertility during these decades. If we knew, we would perhaps have a handle on a method for preventing such a future disaster. We do know that it was in couples of relatively high social and economic status that the explosion was most evident. The sudden rocketing of fertility was caused by a preference for more children among those who *planned* their families (although even among such married couples it is estimated that about 12 per cent of pregnancies were "accidental"). The number of children born per North American woman was as high in 1957 as it was in 1900. In fact the birth rate was as high in 1957 as in India. People married younger, started raising children in a hurry and seldom stopped with two.

We can trace part of this exuberance to a growing faddishness and togetherness of young married couples. New housing developments, where all the people were the young and married, perpetuated the idea that having three and four children was an "in" thing to do. Abundant children became fashionable along with shopping at large supermarkets and having two cars in the family. It is edifying to reread the textbooks of the 1930's which predicted that the then low birth rate would continue and that the population of America would *never* surpass 150 million. In 1945 it was universally predicted that the rate would rise after the war (when more young men were home) but then it would decline in a few years to the 1936 level. Instead, the boisterously high fertility continued for a full fifteen years. Then suddenly it began to decline again. By 1965 it had dropped to the 1940 level. (It is obvious that demography is a frighteningly imprecise science.)

Today's average American woman has babies earlier in marriage than ever *but she also stops earlier.* The low birth rate of the 1960's, furthermore, is perhaps more a function of age distribution than of female fertility. The American mother in the 1960's has still a statistical average of 2.66 children. Although the national birth rate is now about the same as in the Depression days, the fertility rate is higher (this being defined as the number of children born per year to women between the ages of fifteen and forty-four). In 1968 the fertility rate was eighty-eight babies per 1,000 women of childbearing age, whereas a generation ago it was seventy-six. The reason for the paradox (of lower birth rate plus higher fertility) is that a generation ago women of fruitful age comprised one quarter of the population while in the late 1960's they comprised only one fifth. Thus in the 1960's relatively fewer women were bearing more children than in the Depression days (but not nearly so many as in the population-explosion days of the 1950's). The decrease in fertility between the 1950's and 1960's is therefore a real phenomenon and still remains to be explained. The drop in fertility has not been confined to any one class or even to one race. Between 1959 and 1966, for example, fertility rates for whites decreased by 27.5 points while for non-whites the decrease was 30.1 points.

The question now is whether, as the "war babies" become of home-owner age (thus increasing the percentage of young married couples in the society), they will continue at a high or at a low rate of fertility. In 1972 the number of children in the first grade of all U.S. schools will be 5 per cent smaller than now. This is a projection of fact, for all the babies have been born and counted. The question is how many first graders there will be in 2000. Obviously one needs to know about the incentives for and against having more than two babies throughout the world.

7. From Infanticide to Pop Bottles

It is a grave mistake to assume that contraception or "family planning" has ever depended or ever will depend on the availability of novel scientific devices. When people have decided not to raise children they have done it very effectively throughout history. In ancient times the children were simply murdered—especially the girls—and even in primitive Southeastern Asian societies today it is not uncommon to leave an unwanted newborn girl for the water buffalo to stomp to death. In the more refined classes of Mediterranean antiquity coitus interruptus obtained a good deal of momentum (a practice which Saint Augustine chose specifically to damn), and this technique was especially popular among slave owners who kept concubines in addition to legal wives. The reason for this that in most slave-owning societies, the offspring of master and slave automatically attained the legal status of a freeman, including the right to inherit property from the father.

Abortion, however, has been and still is by far the most effective and popular method of birth control. Up until historical times (judging by the practices of today's primitives) a stick or a twig (or in today's slums a wire coat hanger) was simply inserted into the cervix. This crude expedient persists among illegal lay abortionists today in the United States, although it is usually a rubber tube which brings on abnormal contractions of the womb, bleeding and eventual expulsion of the fetus. Part of the placenta may remain in the uterus, so bleeding persists and, if she wants to avoid dangerous infection, the woman must go to a physician or have the placental fragment scraped out (curetted). With the advent of kings and philosophers, more exotic techniques were recommended. The chronicles of the Emperor Shen Nung 4,600 years ago contain recipes for abortion by the use of mercury. Hippocrates recommended violent exercise. Both Aristotle and Plato advocated abortion (of an unstipulated kind) to limit the population, especially of the hoi polloi. After the Renaissance abortion was not regarded in English common law as a punishable offense unless practiced after "quickening" (the feeling of life in the womb). Abortion in fact did not become a statutory crime in England until 1803, and in the United States until 1830.

When practiced by experienced and ethical physicians, abortion has for many decades involved the technique known as dilation and curettage (D and C). A series of metal dilators, successively larger, are inserted into the cervical canal to stretch it and when the passage is opened wide enough the contents of the uterus are scraped out with a curette. (The whole operation takes only a few minutes.) This classical technique has recently been rendered obsolete by the suction method, developed in Eastern Europe. After dilation of the cervix, a tube with side openings near the end is inserted into the uterus and moved about to dislodge the embryo from the wall of the womb. Fetal and placental fragments are then drawn out by a vacuum pump. This method is even quicker and causes less shock and trauma than D and C.

Abortion is very seldom used on a fetus over twelve weeks old and, if it is, the embryo is either removed by Caesarian surgery or the practitioner injects into the uterus highly concentrated solutions of salt or soap, which ends development and causes expulsion within a few days. The countries with the longest uninterrupted experience with legal abortion are Sweden and Denmark, which began to liberalize the laws in the 1930's. The new British law, a pattern for some states in America, authorizes the operation after certification by two doctors that continued pregnancy would risk the physical or mental health of the mother, even if the risk is very slight. This practically lets the woman home free since the "risk" need only be greater than the risk of abortion, which, when properly performed, is less dangerous than childbearing or even the state of continued pregnancy. The British law also permits abortion if the prospective birth could be construed to endanger the physical or mental health of existing children. This practically blankets the field and the additional stipulation that abortion is allowed if there is any substantial risk that the child could be defective becomes hardly necessary.

(There is every reason for Great Britain to be peculiarly conscious of the danger of a multiplying population, since through two world wars the island has been close to famine on account of submarine blockades.)

In Eastern Europe abortions for "medical reasons" (actually merely on request) are performed routinely in hospitals and without charge. *In Hungary the number of legal abortions now exceeds the number of births.* Recently Romania put at least a temporary stop to abortions-on-request when the rate skyrocketed to 24.7/1,000 of population (a rate indicating at least that fecundity was still high) and the government began to realize that the country was skidding far below the rate of live births necessary to avoid a sharp population decrease.

Japan has had a recent history of efficient and government-promoted abortion. The number of legal abortions rose from 246,000 in 1949, the year after passage of the permissive law, to 1,170,000 in 1955. However, Japan being an exceedingly prosperous country, it has lately become the habit of many Japanese physicians, in order to cut down on their income tax, to forget to report all the abortions they perform. Thus the number of *reported* abortions has declined, instead of rising when the birth rate dropped sharply again in 1966, the very boomish "Year of the Fiery Horse."

In both Japan and Eastern Europe the mortality from legal abortions has been close to zero. (For example, in 1964 Czechoslovakia reported no deaths in 140,000 legal abortions.) Not so with the Scandinavian countries, the chief reason being that, while Japan and Eastern Europe prohibit the operation after the third month of pregnancy, except for urgent medical reasons, Sweden permits it up to the fifth month and Denmark up to the fourth month. Because of bureaucratic delays, babies are often aborted even later in Sweden and may cry for hours before they die. Because of such a tragic mess, many Swedish women travel to Eastern Europe to abort their children.

Illegal abortion is most prevalent in Latin America, especially among the poor of the cities. In Chile, where the abortion laws are similar to those of the United States, R. Armijo and T. Monreal of the University of Chile estimate that in one recent year there were over 20,000 illegal abortions compared with 77,440 births in Santiago. The same situation holds in Seoul, Korea, this country maintaining restrictive abortion laws similar to those in most of our states.

Throughout the world there are at present about twenty-five million *legal* abortions compared with about 120 million live births. If one estimated the illegal abortions, the number of aborted children throughout the world probably approaches the number of live births. It is a tragic fact that *without* illegal abortion the world would doubtless today be in the condition of stifling overpopulation now predicted for the year 2000.

The Roman Catholic Church is responsible, but not wholly so, for the prejudice against abortion. Pope Sixtus V (1585–90) ruled that abortion was an excommunicable sin at any stage of development of the fetus, but this edict was reversed by Gregory XIV, who approved excommunication only after the fetus was at least forty days old. In 1869 Pius IX returned to the Sixtus theory, which claims that "ensoulment" begins at conception. In 1930 Pius XI made it clear that abortion is absolutely forbidden, even to save the mother's life at any stage of pregnancy. The state of New Hampshire embodied this horrible concept in its state laws. Some Islamic countries, in spite of the fact that the Koran does not forbid specifically abortion or contraception, are also very strict. In Pakistan the penalty for abortion is officially death although there seem to have been actually few executions for this crime in recent years. In the game of population numbers, Islam controls the largest religious group in the undeveloped world (about 400 million) and the "over-birth" of Egypt and Mohammedan Java is as bad or worse than in Catholic South America. It can in fact be argued that Catholic rules on marriage and reproduction are given much less attention in Catholic Latin America than in the Catholic (especially Irish Catholic) parts of North America. For example, among seventeen Latin American countries where statistics are available, in nine of them over one half the births are illegitimate.

It is curious that two religions relying in such matters on the Old Testament for advice have come up with such diverse theological opinions in regard to abortion and other modes of birth control. The Jews do not consider abortion as homicide. According to Judaism the soul that God implants into the fetus is pure, untouched by original sin, so when the fetus is killed the soul goes to heaven. This is really the crux of the matter. The story of Onan, which is interpreted by Christians as a dire warning against coitus interruptus and (by extension) against masturbation, is typically regarded by the Jews as a tragedy of an individual who proved to be a poor family man. God killed Onan because he and his wife—his dead brother's childless widow—failed in their obligation to continue his brother's bloodline. (The spilling of semen was a mere detail.) Although the Jews, as a harassed people, faced the challenge to survival for the tribes of Israel, and the indignation of the Old Testament prophets against the fertility rites of the pagans was directed against their licentiousness rather than the concept of fertility, modern Judaism is quite consistent with population control. In post-canonical Judaism, having only two children is thought to meet the requirements of the *mitzvah*. Modern American rabbis, such as Eugene Mihaly, emphasize that Eve was created to be a helpmate to Adam (since "it is not good for man to be alone") and only later were they commanded "to be fruitful and multiply."

Aside from the ancient expedients of infanticide, abortion, and coitus interruptus, the nineteenth century saw the development of the condom, the vaginal diaphragm and the spermicidal lotion and douche, while in the twentieth century came the disastrous "rhythm method," the intrauterine coil and the "pill," vasectomy and tubectomy.

The condom is probably the most popular of relatively modern devices, although it interferes to some extent with the physical pleasures of intercourse, especially for the male, as does the vaginal diaphragm for the female. In Japan, where sexual engineering has always been an ingenious specialty,* a new kind of soluble condom has been introduced. It contains a spermicidal composition and is kept in aluminum foil to prevent drying. It is placed on the penis before intercourse but disappears, so to speak, in the course of the action.

(There have been numerous amateur switches. Douches in the course of teen-age orgies have, for example, consisted simply of applying a shaken-up bottle of warm Coca Cola to the vagina.)

There are very roughly estimated to be fifteen million women in the world who use the contraceptive pill, although the figures are subject to large swings because of the high proportion of "dropouts." Even in literate groups in the United States, only 39 per cent of women who go to private doctors use the pill for two years or more.

In effect the pill is a hormone combination that falsely tells the woman's body that it is already pregnant and therefore cannot conceive. Progesterone is secreted after ovulation mainly by the corpus luteum, which is freshly formed from the wall of the follicle, or sac, from which the ovum is discharged. After ovulation, progesterone prevents the brain-pituitary complex from secreting more of those hormones that would cause an ovary to discharge another fertilizable egg. It was largely due to the studies of Gregory Pincus and John Rock that mixtures of progesteronelike substances combined with an estrogen were found to be practical ovulation suppressants. From more than 200 substances chemi-

---

* The Japanese developed special devices for autoeroticism—"masturbation machines"—for males, and for women they discovered that a specially shaped, weighted and textured ball or weighted plastic pebble, when placed in the vulva, would enable the female to undergo prolonged clitoral orgasm while swinging in a hammock, rocking in a chair or swimming.

cally related to progesterone which had been screened by Pincus and his co-workers, three turned out to be the most promising. These are so-called steroid compounds (progestins) derived from the roots of a wild Mexican yam. Although they vary only slightly from natural progesterone in molecular constituents, they are many times more potent than this hormone and thus effective in much smaller dosages. Since this discovery Mexican firms specializing in the preparation of progestin concentrates have made a lot of money and nearly every pharmaceutical firm in the Western World has introduced synthetic variations on the same theme.

There has grown up a great controversy as to the side effects of the pill. For example, it has been claimed that the effects of the steroids on the liver can be serious when the nutritional level is low and where there is parasitic infection (worms, etc.), as in poor countries. (This has effectively blocked the use of the pill in India.) In the well-fed, the death rate from clotting diseases and strokes is reported to have increased among American and British women since the mass introduction of the pill in 1962. Drug firms, such as G. D. Searle and Co., have indignantly challenged especially the British reports. They introduce data to show that the incidence of blood clots among pill users is actually lower than among women in general and report only one case of thrombophlebitis per two thousand women per year using the pill. This is definitely less than the incidence of this clotting disease in pregnant women. Women have, in general, not been impressed by fears of strokes and the like, but they have taken seriously a sort of girlish gossip campaign against the pill which claims it causes gain in weight and loss of sexual drive. The very fact that a woman must have a prescription to get the pill in the Western world makes it difficult to propagandize mass use of oral contraceptives in the poor countries.

There is extreme activity in trying to develop better pills or substitutes for pills, including hormone-secreting capsules inserted under the skin. One approach is the "morning after" pill. This does not prevent the maturing of the female's eggs by convincing her body it is already pregnant but it allows the egg, even if already fertilized, to pass out of the body without development. Successful experiments have been carried out on rats, rabbits and monkeys by the Upjohn Company and human tests have been under way at the Karolinska Institute in Stockholm. Sheldon Segal of the Population Council in New York has favored low dose progestin ("mini-pills") taken every day rather than the usual estrogen-progestin combination. The main effect of the mini-pills seems to be the thickening up of the mucus covering the cervix, preventing sperm from getting by and acting as a sort of chemical condom. (Normally the cervix acts as a preserver and reservoir of sperm and many childless women have been made fertile by treatment to increase the rate of cervical mucus flow.) Segal and Howard Tatum of Rockefeller University have also tested a permanent contraceptive plastic capsule on animals which releases slowly and continuously a very small amount of progestin. This is inserted hypodermically. It has the advantage of maintaining the normal hormone balance in the body and, in countries or circumstances where women are absent-minded, the problem of forgetting to take the pill would be eliminated.

(Assuming this capsule to be perfected, William Shockley, the inventor of the transistor, who also busies himself with sociological matters, has proposed a pseudodemocratic road to population control, which has a distinctly utopian flavor. The public would vote on what rate of population growth it wants. The Census Bureau would determine how many children each couple would be allowed to have. Certification on this basis would be issued to all married couples. Previously all girls would have been temporarily sterilized by Segal's time capsule. When the married couple wanted a child, the capsule would be removed and they would turn in a certificate. After birth of the child the capsule would be reimplanted. Couples not wanting any children or as many as the law allowed could sell their certificates on the open market. Thus only people who wanted and could afford children would have them.)

Techniques of controlling male fertility, such as the implanting of progesterone or testosterone, have been examined. So far the researchers have yet to find a compound that does not cause *permanent* infertility in the male when it is given in dosages large enough to suppress sperm production temporarily. New compounds have recently been found by Upjohn's researchers, however, which when injected into the male do not prevent production of sperm or kill them but simply, in some mysterious way, render them incapable of fertilizing an egg. The sperm look and act normal under the microscope but, as far as the egg is concerned, they might as well be little alien animals, and the egg shuts the door in their face. This important advance, which would transfer the responsibilities for deliberate infertility from the female to the male, has worked well on rats, guinea pigs and monkeys. At the time of writing, it has not yet been proved out on men.

Vasectomy, a simple operation on the male in which the vas deferens, a canal which carries the sperm during ejaculation, is excised, is becoming unexpectedly popular in poor countries and among the poor in America. Although it renders a man permanently infertile, it does not detract from his enjoyment of the sexual act. The analogous operation on women, tubectomy, is also fairly popular—especially if it is accompanied by an award from a government agency.

The intrauterine devices (IUD's), or plastic coils placed in the uterus, have met with a mixed reception. They are greatly preferred to any other method in Taiwan, for example, but for reasons that we shall examine later, they are not well accepted in India. Perhaps seven million women throughout the world use the IUD in one form or another. The discovery of this remarkably simple gadget is usually attributed to the German physicist Ernst Gräfenberg about 1930. His device was a ring made of silver but it invariably caused bleeding. Israel, Japan and the U.S. revived the study but in the form of plastic bows, spirals and double-S loops. There is no agreement on how IUD's work. They definitely do not block the uterus. Apparently they encourage peristalsis of the fallopian tubes, so that the ovum makes its journey from the ovary to the womb in much less than the usual seventy-two hours. Thus even if the egg is fertilized, it is immature and the wall of the uterus is unprepared for its implantation. The device costs only a few cents and can easily be removed. An improvement is the use of Silastic material, which can be soaked with a progestin. In rats and rabbits this has been found to be better retained in the uterus and to cause less bleeding. This is important when we consider the dilemma of India.

As to the "rhythm" method, which is the only technique of birth control accepted by the Catholic Church, it got off to a very poor start because of incorrect physiology and continues in ill repute because of the danger of deformed children.* The estimate of the period of ovulation in women was about 100 per cent wrong in the nineteenth century because of the assumption that human beings behave like dogs. Theodor Bischoff in 1853 noted eggs in the genital tracts of bitches in heat with bloody vaginal discharge. This set the science of gynecology back three quarters of a century since it confused the estrous bleeding of dogs with the menstrual bleeding of primates—two diametrically opposite phases of the sexual cycle. Like all bad ideas, this association held on tenaciously. (At about this time the vaginal diaphragm was invented and its sudden popularity evoked the Catholic Church's thundering condemnation of any mode of control except abstinence or rhythm.) In the next phase of this tragic farce, Carl Capellman proclaimed that women are most apt to be fruitful during the first fourteen days after menstruation begins and the three to four days before the next period. This fantastically screwball analysis greatly

* In mongoloid idiot children the twenty-first set of chromosomes is a triple. James German of Cornell University shows that the greatly increased incidence of mongolism in the children of mothers over thirty-five years of age is probably caused by the decreased frequency of sexual intercourse. Gene defects, such as the tripling, are more likely to occur when the egg is, so to speak, stale. Since the sperm retains its potency for forty-eight hours after entering the womb, any woman having intercourse at least once every two days will have a constant supply of sperm, while a delay in fertilization may more often result in the pairing of a fresh sperm with an "old" egg. This is one reason why Catholics who practice the "rhythm method" may be running a grave risk of having a mongoloid offspring or a baby otherwise mentally retarded or physically deformed. When, by miscalculation of the period of ovulation (usually determined, but by no means infallibly, by rectal thermometers), the sexual intercourse takes place at the very end of the period of ovulation, the result is the same as that of infrequent intercourse during the whole ovulation period. A "stale" egg is likely to be fertilized, with the consequent increased possibility of chromosome abnormality.

influenced Catholic moralists of the pre-World War I era and persisted even in the 1923 edition of Capellman's book. Since it directed "safe" intercourse on the fourteenth day of the cycle, which is now known most commonly to mark the *peak* of fertility, it helped bring the rhythm method under ridicule and inspired many people to suspect the whole business of constituting a popish conspiracy.

In 1931 Kyusaka Ogino of Japan and Hermann Knaus of Austria concluded correctly that ovulation usually occurs fourteen days before the onset of the next menstruation. This basic finding has been amply proved by subsequent studies, the most notable confirmation being the discovery that the process of ovulation causes an appreciable increase in basal body temperature. Yet, even with the most sophisticated couples, quite hep to rectal thermometry, the failures in rhythm contraception continued to be at least three times more frequent in the world than with couples using any other method (even including douches with warm pop bottles).

The irremediable flaw in the rhythm concept is that ovulation in many women is *not* rhythmic. A complete cycle between ovulations may take twenty-five days on one round and thirty-two days on the next. Even among women whose menstrual cycles approach calendar regularity, many obscure facts may cause ovulation to take place five or six days off schedule. Luteinizing hormone (LH) is the substance that appears actually to trigger ovulation. But the pituitary gland does not discharge its periodic supply of LH into the bloodstream all at once. The secretion increases steadily over a period of *about* fourteen days, sometimes less, sometimes very much more. There then occurs a sharp rise followed in only a few hours by the release of an ovum. In other words, when the concentration of LH reaches an extremely critical level in the blood, ovulation abruptly results. But it is dangerously tricky to follow this build-up and thus to predict the crucial day. (As far as I know, it is only *astrologists* of the most expensive kind, versed in mystical mathematics beyond the ken of us poor working scientists, who can claim infallibility in these matters.)

through its eyes, since its literacy gave it a monopoly on the recording of history.

After the establishing of the People's Republic, the marriage law of 1950 did nothing very positive, as did the Japanese, in the way of reducing the rate of population increase, but it did cut away a number of ancient perquisites and habits of the gentry. It abolished bigamy, concubinage, child betrothal and the exaction of marriage gifts. Widows were encouraged to remarry. Marriage became voluntary (no parental dictation, theoretically). The minimum ages of marriage were raised to twenty for men and to eighteen for women. As a communist country, China, like Russia, had established no doctrine against excessive childbearing and, in fact, the doctrinaire Communist, following Marxian historical analysis, vaguely considered that the more children the poor people of the world had, the more likely they were to rise and throw off their chains. However, the Chinese census of 1954, a rather sloppy one which showed a population of some 600 million, jolted many Communists in positions of power. Propaganda leaflets now assure their readers that it is best to wait until the age of at least twenty-five to get married. Emphasis is on the supposed fact that labor pains are hardest to bear at earlier ages.

We know much more about India. Here the problem has been immensely complicated by religious differences and by some peculiarities of the Indian women. Hinduism typically absorbed a fertility cult in the worship of Shiva, who, among other things, was the god of reproduction. Hinduism, in fact, is not so much a specific religion as a conglomeration of superstitions and folkways. The Hindu pantheon, like the Greek, contains many deities who act like anything but well-behaved ladies and gentlemen. The "seed and soil" concept of procreation along with the *ahimsa,* or non-injury, doctrine might show a prejudice against birth control. Yet there is a strong ascetic element in Hinduism. In the *yoga* ideal (diluted in the Bhagavad-Gita edited for the layman) the dedicated Hindu is encouraged to place more emphasis on spiritual attitudes than on rules of behavior. Child marriage is a special Hindu curse, but intercourse shortly after puberty is not only dangerous to female health but to fecundity, so the overall effect may be neutral. Also the Hindu ban on the remarriage of widows may have had some checking effect. (In postwar Germany there has been a sort of de facto prohibition on the remarriage of women widowed during World War II, because of the extremely comfortable pensions they have received but which they must forfeit upon marriage. The surplus of about three million women in West Germany has made this "merry widow" group a source of some anxiety on the part of married women. There are a good deal of men called "uncles" by fatherless children. These are men who came to dinner—and stayed to enjoy without matrimony a share in the widow's bounty.)

Perhaps of some importance is the fact that Gandhi himself strongly opposed birth control aside from complete abstinence. He regarded contraception as the moral equivalent of prostitution and even included "rhythm" in the same category.*

Buddhism theoretically has quite a different slant. There is very little doctrine of parenthood and on the whole it seems calculated to discourage fertility. Moreover, there is a good deal of sexual equality in Buddhism, which generally in the undeveloped lands goes along with family limitation. Under Buddhism the married man is definitely a second-class citizen. In the tale of Kali, reference is made to the use of an abortifacient given by the barren wife to the pregnant wife, but the moral point is the evil of hatred rather than the immorality of abortion. There is no evidence that in Buddhism the "seed" or the fertilized egg is regarded as a living creature. It must, however, be admitted that Buddhism has few rules. Rather than a detailed ethics, it provides a certain spiritual tone to the culture that accepts it.

In Islam the fetus is not considered a human being until it has reached a distinctly human form; hence abortion is theoretically allowed. But as we have previously indicated there is no trend to control the population in Moslem lands by this or any other means.

---

* Incredible as it may seem, Thomas Malthus, the author of the population dilemma, did not advocate the physiological control of conception. As a clergyman, he in fact called such devices "improper arts" and classified them as a form of vice.

India, as a vast arena for competing religions (including Christianity), feels the unwholesome brunt of the spiritual collisions. One of Hinduism's top holy men, Jagatguru Shankaracharya of Puri, has told his people to ignore family planning and launch a "baby race" with the Moslem minority. Sripati Chandrusephar, the Indian minister of state for family planning, has been quoted in 1968 as horrified by Paul VI's encyclical *Humanae Vitae*. He points to the fact that India was probably the only nation that even tried the rhythm method officially (between 1951 and 1957). "It was a complete failure," he said. He hoped that India's seven million Catholics would think of the nation's interest first. He feared that if the Catholics follow the Pope's admonitions, other religious groups will be afraid that the ratios between the sects will be unpleasantly altered and that a general baby derby will ensue.

One can be skeptical about the fundamental significance of such religious rat races, except in a sense probably older than formal religion itself—the desire for sons. For example, in Hinduism a man or his wife cannot die properly without a son, since it is improper for a female to arrange for the funeral of her parents. A son must take their bodies to the ghat to be burned. Then he must be shaven. Without this ceremony the parents cannot be reincarnated. Besides this ritualistic necessity (which happily can now be obviated by adopting a son), to ask a poor farmer in India to limit his offspring (especially his sons) is like asking an American to burn his insurance policies and to tear up his Social Security card. Let the other guy do it. It is impossible for this poor man to assimilate the idea that when everybody has too many children, the one with the most children is the *least* likely to bring them up to provide him with grandchildren.

Watered with money from the Ford Foundation and other private or public international agencies, an immense propaganda campaign has been carried out by the Indian Government, symbolized by the "red triangle." A man and a woman represent one vertex, a boy and a girl the other two, with the message "one daughter and one son—the Happy Family." Elephants with red triangles on their sides march on trips designed to cover every

Indian village. On the twelfth anniversary of India's independence, a parade in Delhi included more than a million people, each of whom had been given a brown paper eyeshade with the red triangle and four faces and the "Happy Family" legend. There has been a little progress—almost microscopic but visible. In three states—Marashtoa, Mysore and Kerala—during the years from 1962 to 1969 the birth rate declined from the horrible to the merely intolerable (respectively, from 41.2/1000 to 32.8; from 41.6/1000 to 33.8; and from 38.9/1000 to 34.5). India's population of about 525 million is still growing by over 30,000 per day.

The pill is hardly used, nor, in spite of its brilliant reception in Taiwan, is the intrauterine device. Indian women are almost morbidly prim and will not submit to gynecological examination by male doctors. There are only 10,000 women doctors in all India and only 1,000 of these are engaged in birth control work. Furthermore, in India the IUD *always* results in serious bleeding, while in other countries there is less than 50 per cent bleeding, most of it trivial. As Ved Mehta has said, "Our women bleed because they are anemic, and they are anemic because they have nothing to eat and they have nothing to eat because they have too many children." This is almost too pat a vicious circle but, in addition to the bleeding, the superstition has somehow raced through village after village that, if the woman's womb contains such a contraption, her husband in attempting intercourse with her will receive a fatal shock.

Vasectomy has been perhaps the most popular method of control, although from 1956, when this surgical sterilization was first introduced, through 1967, only about 3.5 million Indians had had the operation—a pitiful few in comparison with the statistic that in the United States, with no such pressing population problem, about two million American men have undergone this operation. Dr. Chandrusephar has concentrated his propaganda for vasectomy among fathers who already have three or more children. His government's stated objective is to cut the present overall birth rate of forty-one per thousand to twenty-five per thousand, which is still too much, but even this reduction requires that half the couples of childbearing ages, or about forty-five million *couples,* practice birth control of some effective sort. Yet instead of 50 per cent, only 5 per cent do so today (1969).

There is no charge for vasectomy and the men in some Indian states are paid twenty rupees ($2.50, enough to feed a family for two weeks). Women can be paid fifteen rupees for a tubectomy. Again the male doctor phobia is a handicap and in fact it is the shortage of all doctors capable of carrying out either operation that makes the whole project dubious. There are not enough hospitals. It has been proposed that "camps" of men volunteers for vasectomy be set up with a sort of assembly-line technique for surgery, bandaging and recovery, but as in India generally there is much more rhetoric than action. Nirad Chaudhuri, the old philosophic realist, explains that in India there is a conspiracy against reason even in the supposedly educated classes. Most Indian institutions, he says, are basically authoritarian and hostile to the life of reason. Working strongly against the Indian intellectual he lists Gandhism, the climate, the diet, the family, living conditions, the income, almost anyone for whom he is likely to work—and the Indian universities.

In Puerto Rico there is a kind of large-scale laboratory of population dynamics, perhaps representative in some respects of all of Latin America (at least up to the time that American industry and tourism practically took over the island). By 1959 the population density already exceeded that of any European nation. Its industrial exuberance depended upon the remarkable efficiency of the conversion of sugar cane into an easily transported and marketed foodstuff. An acre of sugar cane over the years can outproduce an acre devoted to any other crop— with the possible exception of potatoes. In 1959 the death rate dropped to below that of the United States and infant mortality was about the same as that of America's rural areas. In the 1950's the emigration to the mainland was so high that, in spite of a live birth rate of over thirty per thousand people, the growth of population had virtually ceased. The hills and mountainsides became much greener and less eroded, for the country people, being able to afford kerosene for cooking, had stopped collecting faggots for making charcoal.

Judging from first-hand experience in Puerto Rico, it is now the belief of most demographers that the concept of *machismo* (male-ness—a *macho* is any male animal) has been exaggerated as a reason for large families. According to this idea, a Latin American man needs children, and quickly, to prove he is *un hombre completo* and his pride as a *macho* is enhanced by a large family. Large families occurred almost invariably where the wife had less than three years of schooling or the husband was an unskilled laborer. Given a choice of contraceptives (and a willingness to limit the size of the family) Puerto Ricans in the cities preferred the diaphragm or the spermicidal jelly, while the foamed powder douche was better liked in the countryside. There was an unexpected and even enthusiastic acceptance of tubectomy, especially if performed at the time the last child was born.

Experimentation with the pill was actually aided in Puerto Rico by the noisy objections of the Catholic hierarchy, since contraception thereby got more publicity.

2. The Tragic Farce of "Family Planning"

In 1967 thirty members of the United Nations, interested in population control, came up with the following statement agreed upon after numerous deliberations:

The Universal Declaration of Family Rights describes the family as the natural and fundamental unit of society. It follows that any choice and decision with regard to size of family must irrevocably rest with the family itself and cannot be made by anyone else.

All international and national efforts, including that of the Agency of International Development, the Population Council, most especially and significantly the governments of all such dangerously reproducing countries as India, have been based on this romantic notion: if individual parents can be told how advantageous small families are and can be taught how to limit their families, the problem of overpopulation will be solved. As reported by such discerning experts as Kingsley Davis, Roger Revelle, Garrett Hardin, Paul Ehrlich, Richard Holm and others, this notion has proved to be as dangerous as any fallacy ever proposed for humanity. It is part of a more general fallacy included in what Hardin calls "the tragedy of the commons," in which, for example, it is mistakenly assumed that people or corporations can be persuaded by rhetoric rather than by law to stop polluting the water or the air.

Faced with obvious failure, the actual "family planning" programs, moreover, have adopted goals which are almost meaningless in terms of substantial population control. Pakistan aimed in 1966 to reduce the birth rate from fifty to forty per thousand by 1970. The Indian plan was to accomplish the reduction from forty to twenty-five per thousand "as soon as possible" (a phrase which turns out to have about the same pragmatic meaning as the Supreme Court's "with all deliberate speed"). South Korea aims to cut population growth from 2.9 per cent to 1.2 per cent by 1980. But under conditions of modern hygiene (even the hygiene of undeveloped countries) a birth rate of twenty-five to thirty per thousand people will represent such a buglike swarming as to make the term population control idiotic. A rate of increase of 1.2 per cent per year would allow South Korea's already dense population to double in less than sixty years. Even in the developed countries extremes run from Hungary's average gross reproduction rate of 0.91 to New Zealand's 1.99.

The clean and clear answer of absolutely zero population growth is apparently unacceptable to most nations and to most religious and ethnic communities, yet it is the rational answer. In the long run it can be the *only* answer.

For fast, emergency reduction of population, induced medical abortion is the only route suited to the threshold stage—the crash stage—of a population control program. It was the chief factor in the declines of birth rate of Eastern European satellite countries after legalization in the early 1950's; it suddenly halved the Japanese birth rate at a time of desperation and it has unquestionably been used significantly in reducing the fertility of industrializing nations from 1870 to the 1930's. Abortion is the foremost method of birth control in Latin America. Yet this method is rejected in nearly all national and international population control programs. American foreign aid is actually being used to *stop* abortion. The United Nations excludes abortion from family planning and in fact justifies the latter by presenting it sanctimoniously as a means of *combating* abortion. A lot of time is wasted by biologists turned theologians in hair-splitting arguments over whether or not some contraceptive agent (for example, the intrauterine device) is really an abortifacient or not.

As Davis has cogently pointed out, by sanctifying the notion that each woman should have the number of children she wants and by assuming that if she has only that number, it will automatically curb population growth, the leaders of the family planning policies escape the burning necessity of asking why women desire so many children. The fact is overlooked completely that a desire for contraception is compatible with very high fertility. What happens is simply that the woman has four or five children, then decides she's had enough. That's when she becomes interested in the contraceptive. But as far as the community or the planet is concerned, she has already done the damage. This is the type of problem that the family planning people seldom discuss. In rural Punjab, for example, females start to seek advice only at the fag end of a reproduction period, with eight *living* children.

Favorable results (much bragged about in the family planning circles) have been obtained by propagandizing the well-tolerated IUD among the women of *urban* Taiwan. The campaign began in 1963 and could have affected only the end of an inherent trend. The population decline thus represents a response to modernization of the culture similar to that in most countries that have become industrialized. By 1964 two thirds of Taiwan was urban, with a density of 870 persons per square mile, which is greater than that of Belgium. Actually the Taiwan campaign was not designed to provide population control and shows no sign of doing so. It is a thoroughly dishonest showpiece. More value has been obtained by questionnaires showing the distribution between different districts of the number of children wanted. In 1957 the average was 3.75 for women between the ages of fifteen and twenty-nine in Taipei, Taiwan's largest city. In the satellite towns this increased to 3.93, in the fishing villages to 4.90 and in the farming villages to 5.07. With an overall average of 4.5 births per woman and a modern-type life expectancy of seventy, the rate of natural increase of population in Taiwan was close to 3 per cent per year—suicidally large.

(In the United States in 1966 an average of 3.5 children was considered ideal by white women over twenty-one.)

A survey in Tunisia showed 69 per cent of married couples willing to use birth control but the average number of children they wanted was 4.3. Faced with dismaying results over the past two decades, the leaders of present birth control policy, instead of asking themselves the right questions, tend merely to redouble their efforts to find a perfect contraceptive that will appeal to the most illiterate peasant. They forget that it is precisely this peasant that wants a good-sized family.

Davis and others have challenged the simpering semantics used by family planning leaders, who refuse to admit that their "fertility control" is useful only to the individual couple, not to the community. The word "compulsory" is avoided like the plague since it guarantees frenzied and noisy opposition (just as *compulsory* gun control or *compulsory* gun registration raised such a ruckus in its time, although compulsory registration of automobiles, since it concerned a less ancient companion of man, was readily tolerated).

It can be argued that the family-plannists are not only *not* helping reduce the population explosion but are preventing the organization of means for doing so. Although smoothly spoken of as a "first step," family planning is obviously not that, since no country has ever taken the "next step." The industrialized countries have had family planning for fifty years without acquiring control over either birth rate or population increase. Further and more dangerous, the financial support of research on population control, other than family planning, is nearly zero: it consists mostly of speculation and anecdotes. There is some reason to believe, for example, that poor peasant families in India, if they had transistor radios or bicycles, would have fewer children. Peasant families who even have *visited* a big city apparently tend to have fewer children. And actually in the vast, almost interminable bureaucracy of India—urban dwellers with miniscule incomes but with some smattering of education—the average number of children satisfies the Red Triangle's maximum of two.

The average age of marriage and the degree of preoccupation with marriage are doubtless important but we don't know how important. The swings in rates of population growth in this country have usually corresponded with swings to early or to late marriage. In industrial societies, late marriage is generally caused by housing shortages, unemployment, military service overseas, the high costs of education and the inadequacy of consumer services. (How many young women would rush into marriage and childbirth if they knew how many diapers they might have to wash themselves without automatic washing machines or diaper service companies or disposable diapers? The answer is we do not know and are not trying to find out.) What if the whole basis of taxing were turned upside down so that it became the working spinster and bachelor who received the exemptions, marriage licenses were made extremely expensive, enormous luxury taxes were levied on baby food, diapers, baby oil, etc? Would substantial rewards for sterilization help? What if abortions were not only legal but free? We do not know. We know only that efforts to *increase* birth rates by precisely the opposite systems of taxes and awards have failed to work. There is no reason to suppose that the symmetry is complete, however, and that women (or couples) could not be bribed into mass birth control.

If women were paid as workers as well as men and given equal educational and occupational opportunities, and *if social life were organized around the place of work,* rather than around the home or neighborhood, many women would develop interests that would compete with family interests. We are not guessing in this case, for approximately this policy is followed in several communist countries and even the less developed of these populations now have very low birth rates. International power and exuberance pass to the nations whose populations are adjusted to their resources. India would have a much better chance to be one of the great powers if it had 200 million fewer citizens. Also lacking in deserved power because of excessive population are Egypt, Japan, China, Pakistan and Mexico. The high birth rate which Russia had during all her wars, and which was one of the factors making her a weaker nation than her total population entitled her to be, has now receded sharply. In the Soviet Union during the 1960's the demographers have taken to worrying about too low a birth rate as did their American counterparts during the 1930's. Net growth in the U.S.S.R. fell from eighteen per 1,000 people in 1960 to less than 11/1,000 in 1968. This points to a static population in the 1970's, a potential source actually of military strength rather than weakness. Some mistaken Muscovite alarmists have now advocated state-provided houses with the first or second child instead of with the fourth, as is done now, in order to encourage procreation.

Roger Revelle has argued that better nutrition in the undeveloped countries would automatically lower the birth rate, since it would still further lower the rate of infant mortality and thus reduce the desperate incentive of poor people to have at least four children in order to wind up with one living son. In the Middle Ages in Northern Europe the population increased very fast around the ninth and tenth centuries due to the invention of the heavy plow, the horseshoe and the horse collar. This made possible a "three-field system"—one field fallow, one spring crop of beans or peas, one winter crop of oats, wheat or barley. The spring beans and the winter cereal provided the combination of amino acids that people and animals needed. There is no such substantial balance in the undeveloped countries today.

The "green revolution" is supposed to feed India and other crowded lands. But when you talk to ecologists about this green revolution, you get scowls and shudders, since the introduction of the new strains of rice and wheat and maize are inevitably associated with an immense use of pesticides of the general DDT type. The result of temporary increase in food production by this vast planting and spraying could be an ultimate reduction in the number of people the earth can support for the long term. In fact Paul Ehrlich of Stanford University insists that the most important thing to be done, now that it is too late to prevent eventual world famine and the reduction of population by a rise in the death rate, *is to*

*alert people to the dangers of constantly trying to increase food
production.*

Perhaps it is too late even for this. Garrett Hardin of the University of California (Santa Barbara) in his great essay *The Tragedy of the Commons** has pointed out that the failure of population control represents one of those "no solution" problems like "How can I win in the game of tick-tack-toe?" It is well known that I cannot win if my opponent understands the game as well as I do. The "population problem" is one of this class of problems, which includes the dilemma of increasing military power and decreasing national security. The tragedy of the commons derives essentially from the fallaciousness of Jeremy Bentham's goal of "the greatest good for the greatest number"—an intrinsically impossible situation both sociologically and mathematically. It is not possible to maximize two or more variables at the same time, as has been shown explicitly by John Von Neumann and was understood even in the early theory of partial differential equations by d'Alembert (1717–83). Even if we are given an infinite source of energy, continued population growth still presents an inescapable dilemma in which the problem of acquisition of energy is replaced by the problem of its dissipation (the "hot earth" situation which we described at the beginning of this part of the book). Bentham's goal is inherently unachievable. And yet what constitutes an *optimum* population is not understood either.

Hardin emphasizes that we can make little progress in defining an optimum or working toward it until we burn Adam Smith's book *The Wealth of Nations* and exorcise his spirit. The perniciousness of Smith's doctrine was the idea that an individual who "intends only his own gain" is "led by an *invisible hand* to promote the public interest."

The first harsh rebuttal to the invisible hand in population control was sketched in 1838 by an amateur mathematician, William Lloyd. Lloyd pictures a pasture—"the commons"—open to all. Each herdsman is expected to try to keep as many cattle as possible on

* *Science,* December 13, 1968.

the commons. What is the utility (Adam Smith's "gain") to an individual of adding one more animal to his herd? In the positive sense the utility is +1. In the negative sense it is some function of the additional overgrazing created by adding one more animal. But since this negative effect is shared by *all* the herdsmen, the negative utility is only a fraction of −1. Left to his own accountancy, therefore, each herdsman will continue to add cattle to the commons. There is no invisible hand except the one that can count up to one. Freedom of access to the commons thus brings ultimate ruin to all.* Similarly Adam Smith's "rational man," with only his gain in mind, finds that his share of the intangible total costs of polluting a common river is less than the cost of purifying the water that he discharges into it. Since this is true for everyone, we become locked in a system of fouling our own nests as long as we follow the Adam Smith theory of social morality. Adam Smithism could work only under early frontier conditions, because there was no public—only a few scattered hunters and trappers.

Now, if Adam Smithism were continued without commas and parentheses—in a completely dog-eat-dog society—the overfertile poor would disappear ultimately because they could not keep their children from dying of disease or hunger. The people who bred too richly on too little income would actually have fewer descendants. But our society—and the world as a whole represented by such agencies as the United Nations—is profoundly committed to the welfare state. We are still trying to make Bentham's sick doctrine work. Although we lecture the poor peasant on having a dozen children, we do our best to doctor and feed them. The result is that the population growth today of the undeveloped nations exceeds any growth in history—even when the Irish were at their fattest and sexually liveliest in the late eighteenth century.

To make such appeals as we are making to the *conscience* of these people is to set up a selective mechanism by which con-

---

* A modern analogue is that even today cattlemen leasing the national land on American western ranges constantly pressure the federal authorities to increase the head count to the point where overgrazing produces erosion and weed dominance.

science is eliminated from the species. Desperately we are in need of working ethnologists and anthropologists to guide our every move.

Let me give one example. It has been dinned into us that poor people of the less prosperous countries frantically desire a living son. Is this also true in the black ghettos of industrialized nations? Probably not, since it is usually a daughter that winds up by providing support for her aged mother, the husband and sons having long taken flight in miscellaneous and unspecified directions. But if we can verify the urge of South Americans and Hindus and Pakistanis for having a son as *incorrigibly basic*, first of all, it then explains the rough arithmetic of reproduction. Since one son may die, it is fundamental insurance practice to have two sons. This means on the average four children—the two daughters, from the standpoint of population growth, being more important than the sons, because it is girls rather than boys who determine the future population.

If we are then agreed upon the fundamental nature of the desire for sons among the unprivileged of the undeveloped countries who have already produced 80 per cent of the world's population of children, why not concentrate on the problem of having a superfluity of male offspring? This involves, from what we know at the present, a combination of artificial insemination and spermatozoa fractionation.

This is not so difficult as it might seem. The applied science of animal husbandry has already been able to breed 80 per cent to the desired sex (usually female) by artificial insemination with semen filtered through special diaphragms. The success of the method depends on the double fact that it is the sperm that determines the sex of the fertilized egg and that there is a minute external difference in male-producing and female-producing sperm. If the sociological anecdotes are true and a Pakistani farmer, for instance, holding two to ten acres of land would be willing to pay fifty dollars (a veritable Pakistani fortune) or more for the guarantee of a son, one would expect that he and his wife would also be willing to trade off normal fertilization for artificial insemination with processed sperm from the father. Let them have their son. Let them even have two sons. Then let them submit to sterilization or to foolproof contraceptive methods, having completed their unnatural Red Triangle.

This approach provides so brutally simple an answer that it offends the moralists, who fear the social consequences of large ratios of boys and men to girls and women in a future society. Would we not be plagued with prostitution and homosexuality? But America was so plagued in its frontier days and yet managed to survive. Most of the raffish heroes of the nineteenth century— Billy the Kid, for example—were blatantly homosexual. Between the tenuous menace of homosexuality, which among the ancient Greeks was a glamorous and respected way of life, and the fearful sordid immensity of the population explosion, who but a fundamentalist or a nit-picker would hesitate to make the choice? If the research which lags in this matter of sex determination were stepped up by a few orders of magnitude, we might still be able to save the planet. But among the research projects which would have to be included is a verification of the son bias and the acceptability of artificial insemination combined with non-fertilizing sexual intercourse.

In the long run it might prove possible to combine the two, using cervical diaphragms, for example, which would reject the female-producing sperm. Or hormonal drugs might be developed which prejudice the female-producing egg from development or even change it by chromosomal agents to a male-producing egg. The mere act of artificial insemination, in spite of Hindu primness, may be acceptable, because the people in many parts of the world now feel it a privilege to be struck somewhere in the body with an instrument resembling a hypodermic needle.

It is extremely doubtful, however, that this approach will be perfected or, if so, adopted in time to do any good.

Let us summarize the conclusions of this latter part of the book.

First, nearly all animals have an instinct, based on evolutionary memory, to limit the population density of the species.

Unfortunately this instinct has been lost in man. Because man's evolution, since the invention of speech, has been social rather than biological, one can only hope to reverse the continued dangerously high birth rates by social acceptance or social authority.

It appears that Adam Smith's notion of an "invisible hand" that automatically causes what is good for the individual or for the family to be good for the society is disastrous nonsense. Furthermore, the individual or the family cannot really recognize what is, in the long run, good for *it*. Someone has to tell the individual or the family what to do.

In the end the problem must become one of leadership. But we then are faced with the phantasmal problem of who is fit to make the necessary decisions, bearing in mind that nearly all the decisions by governments or collections of governments, in regard to population control, have so far been entirely fatuous?

The tragedy is complete in the Whitehead sense. Tragedy resides not in unhappiness but in the "remorseless working of things". But in a still more profound sense the tragedy is not complete at all. The more destructive the inevitable famines, diseases and wars that arise from the overpopulation of the planet, the more obvious will be the necessity of giving the governing of the shattered world to people who are willing to accept its enormous challenges.

Bibliography

Since this book is not intended as a scientific treatise, I have not tried to attach a learned reference to every name and statement given in the text. In the case of especially crucial references, where a periodical rather than a book is involved, I have used footnotes.

In addition to the books listed later, my reliance has been upon the following sources:

SCIENTIFIC AND TECHNICAL PERIODICALS

American Anthropologist, American Journal of Physical Anthropology, American Journal of Physiology, American Journal of Sociology, American Naturalist, Annals New York Academy of Science, Anthropologica, Auk, Behavior, Behavioral Science, Biological Review, Birth Control Review, British Birds, British Journal of Psychology, Chemical and Engineering News, Condor, Current Anthropology, Daedalus, Ecology, Emu, Ethnology, Eugenics Quarterly, Extrait de Mammalia, Fertility and Sterility, Folio Primatologica, Genetics, Ibis, International Anthropological and Linguistic Review, Journal of the American Medical Association, Journal of Biological Chemistry, Journal of Comparative Psychology, Journal of Home Economics, Journal of Mammalogy, Journal of Personality, Journal of Psychology, Journal of Washington Academy of Science, Mankind Quarterly, Natural History, Nature, New England Journal of Medicine, Physiological Zoology, Practical Anthropology, Proceedings National Academy of Sciences (U.S.),

Proceedings Zoological Society of London, Psychologica, Psychological Review, Quarterly Review of Biology, Science, Scientific American, Soviet Anthropology and Archaeology, Zoologica.

POPULAR JOURNALS AND NEWS SERVICES

Associated Press, *Business Week, Chemical Week, Congressional Record, Fortune,* Los Angeles *Times* News Service, *National Geographic, National Wildlife,* Newspaper Enterprise Association Service, *New Yorker,* New York *Times* News Service, Science Service, *Times* United Press International, *Wall Street Journal,* Washington *Post* News Service.

BOOKS

ANSHEN, RUTH NANDA, editor. *The Family: Its Function and Destiny.* New York: Harper and Row, 1959.

ARCHER, J. C. *The Faiths Men Live By.* New York: Nelson, 1934.

ARDREY, ROBERT. *African Genesis.* New York: Atheneum, 1961; London: Collins, 1961.

———. *The Territorial Imperative.* New York: Atheneum, 1966; London: Collins, 1966.

BASSLER, RAY S., RESSER, CHARLES E., SCHMITT, WALDO S., and BARKSCH, PAUL. *Shelled Invertebrates of the Past and Present.* Vol. 10 of Smithsonian Series, Washington, D.C.: Smithsonian Institution, 1938.

BATES, MARSTON. *The Forest and the Sea.* New York: Random House, 1960.

———. *The Prevalence of People.* New York: Scribner's, 1955.

———. *Gluttons and Libertines.* New York: Random House, 1967.

BEACH, FRANK A. and FORD, C. S. *Patterns of Sexual Behavior.* New York: Harper and Brothers and Paul Schoeber, Inc., 1951; London: Eyre & Spottiswoode, 1965.

BERGER, M., ABEL, T., and PAGE, C. M., editors. *Freedom and Control in Modern Society.* New York: Van Nostrand Co., 1954.

BÖLSCHE, WILHELM. *Love Life in Nature: The Story of the Evolution of Love.* London: J. Cape, 1931.

BROWN, HARRISON. *The Challenge of Man's Future.* New York: The Viking Press, 1954.

BUDDENBROCK, WOLFGANG VON. *The Love Life of Animals.* New York: Crowell, 1958.

BURTON, MAURICE. *Infancy in Animals.* New York: Roy Publishers, 1956.

CALAHANE, VICTOR R. *Mammals of North America.* New York: The Macmillan Co., 1961.

CALDER, RITCHIE. *Common Sense About A Starving World.* New York: The Macmillan Co., 1962.

CARR, ARCHIE. *So Excellent a Fishe, A Natural History of Turtles.* Garden City, N.Y.: Natural History Press, 1967; published also as *The Turtle,* London: Cassell, 1968.

CARR, DONALD E. *The Eternal Return.* Garden City, N.Y.: Doubleday and Co., 1968.

CARRIGHAR, SALLY. *Wild Heritage.* Boston: Houghtoh Mifflin Co., 1965; London: Hamish Hamilton, 1965.

CARR-SAUNDERS, A. M. *World Population.* Oxford: Clarendon Press, 1936.

CARSON, RACHEL L. *The Sea Around Us.* New York: Oxford University Press, 1961; London: Panther Books, 1969.

CHANG, CHUNG-LI. *The Chinese Gentry.* Seattle: University of Washington Press, 1955.

CHEN, WEN-HUI. *The Family Revolution in Communist China.* Maxwell Air Force Base, Alabama: Human Resources Research Institute Memorandum No. 35, 1955.

CHURCHILL, WAINWRIGHT. *Homosexual Behavior Among Males.* New York: Hawthorn Books, Inc., 1967.

CLARK, COLIN. *Population Growth and Land Use.* London: Macmillan & Co., 1967.

COCHRAN, DORIS MABEL. *Living Amphibians of the World.* Garden City, N,Y.: Doubleday and Co., 1961.

COMFORT, ALEX. *The Anxiety Makers.* Camden. N.Y., and London: Thomas Nelson and Sons, 1967.

CONNELL, K. H. *The Population of Ireland, 1750–1845.* Oxford: Clarendon Press, 1950.

COOK, ROBERT C. *Human Fertility: The Modern Dilemma.* New York: William Sloane Associates, 1951.

DARLING, FRANK FRASER. *A Herd of Red Deer: A Study in Animal Behaviour.* London: Oxford University Press, 1937.

DARWIN, CHARLES GALTON. *The Next Million Years.* Garden City, N.Y.: Doubleday and Co., 1952.

DARWIN, CHARLES ROBERT. *The Descent of Man in Relation to Sex.* New York: D. Appleton and Co., 1930; London: C. A. Watts, 1930.

DAY, LINCOLN H., and TAYLOR, ALICE. *Too Many Americans.* Boston: Houghton Mifflin Co., 1964.

DE CASTRO, JOSUE. *The Geography of Hunger.* Boston: Little, Brown and Co., 1952.

DECKERT, KURT, and GÜNTHER, KLAUS. *Creatures of the Deep Sea.* New York: Scribner's, 1956.

EHRLICH, PAUL. *The Population Bomb.* New York: Ballantine Books, 1968.

FABRE, JEAN HENRI CASIMIR. *Book of Insects.* New York: Dodd, Mead and Co., 1921.

——. *The Hunting Wasps.* New York: Dodd, Mead and Co., 1915.

——. *The Life of the Fly.* New York: Dodd, Mead and Co., 1913.

——. *The Life of the Grasshopper.* New York: Dodd, Mead and Co., 1917.

——. *The Life of the Scorpion.* New York: Dodd, Mead and Co., 1923.

——. *The Life of the Spider.* New York: Dodd, Mead and Co., 1913.

——. *The Sacred Beetle and Others.* New York: Dodd, Mead and Co., 1918.

——. *Insect Adventures.* New York: World Book Co., 1918.

——. *Social Life in the Insect World.* London: T. F. Unwin, 1922.

FAGLEY, RICHARD M. *The Population Explosion and Christian Responsibility.* London: Oxford University Press, 1960.

FARB, PETER. *Man's Rise to Civilization as Shown by the Indians of North America from Primeval Times to the Coming of the Industrial State.* New York: E. P. Dutton and Co., 1968.

FIELD, JAMES ALFRED. *Essays on Population.* Chicago: University of Chicago Press, 1931; London: Bailey Brothers, 1967.

FRAZER, SIR JAMES. *The Golden Bough.* New York and London: Macmillan & Co., 1936.

FREEDMAN, RONALD, editor. *Population: The Vital Revolution.* Garden City, N.Y.: Doubleday and Co., 1965.

FREUD, SIGMUND. *Totem and Taboo.* London: Routledge and Kegan Paul, 1960.

——. *Three Contributions to the Theory of Sex.* New York and Washington: Nervous and Mental Disease Publishing Co., 1930; London: Hogarth Press, 1962.

FRIELING, HEINRICH. *Liebes- und Brutleben der Tiere.* Stuttgart: Kosmosgesellschaft der Naturfreunde, 1940.

GERTSCH, WILLIS J. *American Spiders.* Princeton, N.J.: Van Nostrand Co., 1949.

GILLIARD, E. THOMAS. *Living Birds of the World.* Garden City, N.Y.: Doubleday and Co., 1958; London: Hamish Hamilton, 1958.

GUTHRIE, MARY J., and ANDERSON, JOHN M. *General Zoology.* New York: John Wiley and Sons, 1961.

GUTTMACHER, A. F. *The Complete Book of Birth Control.* New York: Ballantine Books, 1961.

HARTMAN, C. G. *Time of Ovulation in Women.* Baltimore: Williams and Wilkins, 1936.

HATT, P. *Backgrounds to Human Fertility in Puerto Rico.* Princeton, N.J.: Princeton University Press, 1952.

HAUSER, PHILIP. *Population Perspectives.* New Brunswick, N.J.: Rutgers University Press, 1960.

——, editor. *The Population Dilemma.* Englewood Cliffs, N.J.: Prentice-Hall, 1963.

——. *Population and World Politics,* Glencoe, Ill.: The Free Press, 1958.

HECK, LUDWIG. *Tiere wie sie wirklich sind.* Berlin: P. Parey, 1934.

HEINROTH, OSKAR and KATHARINA. *The Birds.* Ann Arbor: University of Michigan Press, 1958.

HIMES, NORMAN E. *Medical History of Contraception.* Baltimore: William Wood, 1936.

HOBHOUSE, L. T. *Morals in Evolution.* New York: Holt, 1915.

HORNEY, KAREN. *Feminine Psychology.* New York: W. W. Norton and Co., 1967; London: Routledge & Kegan Paul, 1967.

HULSE, FREDERICK S. *The Human Species.* New York: Random House, 1953.

HUTCHINS, ROSS E. *Insects.* Englewood Cliffs, N.J.: Prentice-Hall, 1966.

HUXLEY, JULIAN. 'Knowledge, Morality and Destiny', from *New Bottles for New Wine.* London: Chatto and Windus, 1957.

KAMMERER, PAUL. *Geschlecht, Fortpflanzung und Fruchtbarkeit: eine Biologie der Zeugung.* Munich: Dreimasken Verlag, 1927.

KEYS, ANCEL, BROZEK, J., HENSCHEL, H., MICHELSEN, O., and TAYLOR, M. L. *The Biology of Human Starvation.* Minneapolis: University of Minnesota Press, 1950; London: Oxford University Press, 1950.

KINSEY, ALFRED CHARLES et al. *Sexual Behaviour in the Human Male,* London and Philadelphia: W. B. Saunders Co., 1948.

——. *Sexual Behaviour in the Human Female.* London and Philadelphia: W. B. Saunders Co., 1953.

KROEBER, A. L. *Cultural and Natural Areas of Native North America.* Berkeley: University of California Press, 1950.

LA BARRE, WESTON. *The Human Animal.* Chicago: University of Chicago Press, 1954; London: Phoenix Books, 1954.

LANDERS, RICHARD R. *Man's Place in the Dybosphere.* Englewood Cliffs, N.J.; Prentice-Hall, 1966.

LATIL, PIERRE DE. *The Underwater Naturalist.* Boston: Houghton Mifflin Co., 1958.

LESTAPIS, STANISLAS DE. *La Limitation des Naissances.* Paris: SPES, 1959; Also published as *Family Planning and Modern Problems.* London: Burns, Oates, 1961.

LEVI-STRAUSS, CLAUDE. *The Savage Mind.* Chicago: University of Chicago Press, 1966.

LILLY, JOHN CUNNINGHAM. *The Mind of the Dolphin*. Garden City. N.J.: Doubleday and Co., 1967.

LORENZ, KONRAD. *King Solomon's Ring*. New York: Crowell, 1952; London: Methuen, 1952.

——. *On Aggression*. New York: Harcourt, Brace and World, 1966; London: Methuen, 1966.

MALINOWSKY, BRONISLAW. *The Sexual Life of Savages*. New York: Harcourt, Brace and World, 1929; London: Routledge, 1932.

MALTHUS, THOMAS R. *Essay on the Principle of Population*. London: J. M. Dent and Sons, 1816 (seventh edition).

MARAIS, EUGÈNE. *My Friends the Baboons*. London: Methuen, 1939.

——. *The Soul of the White Ant*. London: Methuen, 1939.

MARX, KARL. *Capital*. Chicago: Charles H. Kerr and Co., translated from the third German edition by Samuel Moore and Edward Aveling, and edited by Frederick Engels, 1906. London: Allen & Unwin, 1946.

MEAD, MARGARET. *Coming of Age in Samoa*. New York: Dell Publishing Co., 1968; London: Penguin Books, 1928.

——. *Sex and Temperament in Three Primitive Societies*. New York: William Morrow and Co., 1935.

——. *Male and Female*. New York: William Morrow and Co., 1949; London: Penguin Books, 1964.

MEDAWAR, P. B. *The Future of Man*. New York: Basic Books, 1960; London: Methuen, 1960.

MEIER, RICHARD L. *Modern Science and the Fertility Problem*. New York: John Wiley and Sons, 1959.

MICHELMORE, SUSAN. *Sexual Reproduction*. Garden City, N.Y.: Doubleday and Co., 1964.

MOMENT, GARDNER. *General Zoology*. Boston: Houghton Mifflin Co., 1967.

MOORE, GEORGE FOOT. *History of Religions*. New York: Scribner's, 1932; Edinburgh: T. & T. Clark.

MYRDAL, ALVA. *Nation and Family: The Swedish Experiment in Democratic Family and Population Policy*. New York: Harper and Brothers, 1941.

ORGANSKI, A. F. K. and KATHERINE. *Population and World Power*. New York: Alfred A. Knopf, 1958.

ORR, JOHN BOYD, and LUBBOCK, DAVID. *The White Man's Dilemma*. London: Allen & Unwin Ltd.; New York: Barnes and Noble, 1953.

ORTEGA Y GASSET, JOSÉ. *The Revolt of the Masses*. New York: W. W. Norton and Co., 1960 (from *La Rebelion de las Masas*, 1930); London: Allen & Unwin, 1951.

OSBORN, FAIRFIELD, editor. *Our Crowded Planet*. Garden City, N.Y.: Doubleday and Co., 1960; London: Allen & Unwin, 1963.

OSBORN, FREDERICK. *On Population: Three Essays*. Princeton, N.J.: Princeton University Press, 1958.

——. *Preface to Eugenics*. New York: Harper and Brothers, 1940.

PARSONS, TALCOT. *Essays in Sociological Theory Pure and Applied*. Glencoe, Ill.: The Free Press, 1949.

PEARL, RAYMOND. *The Natural History of Population*. London: Oxford University Press, 1939.

POPE, CLIFFORD H. *The Reptile World*. New York: Alfred A. Knopf, 1960; London: Routledge, 1956.

PORTMANN, ADOLF. *Animals as Social Beings*. New York: Viking Press, 1961; London: Hutchinson, 1961.

RASMUSSEN, KNUD JOHAN VICTOR. *Intellectual Culture of the Copper Eskimos*. Copenhagen: Glydendal, 1932.

REMANE, ADOLF. *Das soziale Leben der Tiere*. Hamburg: Rowohlt, 1960.

ROCK, JOHN. *The Time Has Come*. New York: Alfred A. Knopf, 1963.

RUSSELL, FRANKLIN. *Watchers at the Pond*. New York: Alfred A. Knopf, 1961; London: Hodder, 1962.

SALAMAN, R. N. *The History and Social Influence of the Potato*. Cambridge: Cambridge University Press, 1949.

SANGER, MARGARET. *My Fight for Birth Control*. New York: Farrar and Rinehart, 1935.

SAX, KARL. *Standing Room Only: The World's Population Explosion*. Boston: The Beacon Press, 1960.

SCHALLER, GEORGE B. *The Year of the Gorilla*. Chicago: University of Chicago Press, 1964; London: Collins, 1965.

—— *The Deer and the Tiger*. Chicago and London: University of Chicago Press, 1967.

SCOTT, JOHN PAUL. *Animal Behavior*. Chicago: University of Chicago Press, 1958.

SEIDENBERG, RODERICK. *Post-Historic Man*. Durham, N.C.: University of North Carolina Press, 1950.

STEARN, E. W. and A. E. *The Effect of Smallpox on the Destiny of the Amerindian*. Boston: Humphries, 1945.

TEMBROCK, GÜNTER. *Verhaltensforschung*. Jena: G. Fischer, 1961.

TINBERGEN, NIKOLAAS. *Social Behavior in Animals with Special Reference to Vertebrates*. New York: Wiley, 1953; London: Methuen, 1965.

VOGT, WILLIAM. *Road to Survival*. New York: William Morrow and Co., 1966.

WELLS, H. G., HUXLEY, JULIAN and WELLS, G. P. *The Science of Life.* Garden City, N.Y.: Doubleday and Co.; London: Cassell and Co., 1934.

WELTY, JOEL CARL. *The Life of Birds.* New York: Alfred A. Knopf, 1963; London: W. B. Saunders Ltd., 1962.

WENDT, HERBERT. *The Sex Life of the Animals.* New York: Simon and Schuster, 1965.

WYNNE-EDWARDS, V. C. *Animal Dispersion in Relation to Social Behaviour.* New York: Hafner, 1962; London: Oliver & Boyd, 1962.

YERKES, ROBERT M. and ADA. *The Great Apes.* New Haven: Yale University Press, 1929.

YOUNG, LOUISE B., editor. *Population in Perspective.* New York, London and Toronto: Oxford University Press, 1968.

ZIMMERMANN, RUDOLF. *Das Liebesleben der Vögel.* Dresden: E. Reissner, 1922.

ZINSSER, HANS. *Lice and History.* Boston: Little, Brown and Co., 1935.

ZUCKERMAN, S. L. *The Social Life of Monkeys and Apes.* London: Kegan Paul, Trench, Trubner and Co., 1932.

Index